DIAGNOSTIC
MENTORING

HOW TO TRANSFORM
THE WAY WE MANAGE

LUKAS MICHEL

ADVANCE PRAISE

"Despite the wealth of papers, presentations and books available on agile, managers are hesitant about the transformation of their organizations. Too often, projects are abandoned early, and organizations fall back to traditional ways of doing things. Like no other book, with *Diagnostic Mentoring*, Lukas Michel offers the diagnostic tools that help managers bridge theory and practice with a proven three-step process. At its core is the fresh perspective on managing people. Readers benefit from the abundance of thought pieces and practical guidance for their agile transformations."

Michael Tröscher, CEO, NewTec GmbH, Freiburg, Germany

"In his new book, *Diagnostic Mentoring*, Lukas Michel convincingly features the 'people' side of management and organizations, and how to make it work the agile way. Complex and dynamic challenges require differentiated approaches without superficial buzzwords. *Diagnostic Mentoring* offers a deep dive into better management with ample practical guidance to make it work."

Michael Kühner, CEO, Strametz & Associates GmbH, Hansestadt Warburg, Germany

"Better management is every manager's primary job. If you want to know how to make it work for yourself, then Lukas Michel's new book, *Diagnostic Mentoring*, will get you there. Lukas' managerial application of the Inner Game is impressive, consequent and transparent. The idea is simple. Its application is not easy, but a rewarding path to follow to experience its (magic) breakthrough."

Dr Roberto Buner, CEO, PotenzialEntwicklungCoaching GmbH (flowstate.ch), Speicher, Switzerland

Published by
LID Publishing
An imprint of LID Business Media Ltd.
The Record Hall, Studio 304,
16-16a Baldwins Gardens,
London EC1N 7RJ, UK

info@lidpublishing.com
www.lidpublishing.com

A member of:

businesspublishersroundtable.com

Printed by Severn, Gloucester

ISBN: 978-1-911671-65-7
ISBN: 978-1-911671-66-4 (ebook)

Cover and page design: Caroline Li

DIAGNOSTIC MENTORING

HOW TO TRANSFORM THE WAY WE MANAGE

LUKAS MICHEL

MADRID | MEXICO CITY | LONDON
NEW YORK | BUENOS AIRES
BOGOTA | SHANGHAI | NEW DELHI

CONTENTS

To my wife Charleen and her support.

ACKNOWLEDGMENTS

Diagnostic Mentoring marks an important milestone on our journey to better management. It guides executives on the three essential features of 21st century management: people-centric management, agile organization and dynamic operating systems. Diagnostic Mentoring is the response to outdated traditional management that fails to support executives coping with the challenges of a dynamic market context. It supports executives becoming more aware, acting on insights and learning fast, rather than blindly following consultants' general advice, simple tips, latest tricks or outdated 'best practices.' Diagnostic Mentoring follows the same principles as better management: it creates awareness, offers choice, trusts executives to do it themselves and focuses their attention on what matters most.

Diagnostic Mentoring is what the members of the AGILITY-INSIGHTS network — a global community of certified mentors, professionals and practitioners — have been doing successfully for nearly 20 years. They have evolved the methodology that emerged from practical work with executives. This new book documents that practice and provides insights from our research. In that sense, my thanks go to all members of the network who have used *Diagnostic Mentoring* with their clients, worldwide. It is your book. The research team, with Prof Herb Nold and Prof Johanna Anzengruber, has extensively published on our model and the diagnostics. Without their groundwork, we would not be where we are today, offering a timely managerial and consultative approach for managers in 21st century organizations.

We are thankful to all clients who have trusted us, our diagnostics and the mentoring we've offered. With the publication of *Diagnostic Mentoring*, we have made our approach to 21st century management consulting fully transparent.

We have reached an important milestone, not the destination. There is more in our pipeline, and we remain committed to improving the world through better management. To that end, I look to all of you for your continued support.

Lukas Michel
May 2021
St. Moritz, Switzerland

FOREWORD

Here we are, back in 2002. We have returned to the Engadine Valley, Switzerland, where I am to conduct yet another *Inner Game of Skiing* coaching session. On the way there, we just passed St. Moritz and, on the left, the famous Corviglia ski area. We turn right into the snow-covered Bernina Pass road that leads us to our destination, the Lagalb ski area — one of the few remaining freeride skiing areas. The slopes are steeper, more challenging, some deliberately unprepared. We have just arrived at the peak — they call it the top of the world — and with a quick glance toward the Valtellina Valley in Italy, our focus shifts to our slopes. They are filled with powder snow, with plenty of bumps for us to play on. We truly enjoy our skiing experience, and the higher knowledge we have gained in such a playful manner. After that intense day, we are back in the parking lot, hugging each other. Happy, with glazed eyes. Truly fulfilled. We drive back to our hotel, relaxed, and in the evening sit together around the fireplace, enjoying a good glass of wine and reflecting on our experiences, and the insights of the day, as we did every day in that skiing master class.

What has happened? Why am I writing here — in the Foreword of a book on management and leadership tools — about skiing experiences? First, Lukas, the author, was part of that expert skier class. Second, it's hard to get to the real essence of Lukas' new book without that experience. But, how to get to these insights without that experience? If you, the proud owner of Lukas' book, had the opportunity to participate in the master class, you would have come away with your own, personal, specific experiences — your own process for getting into that magical flow state, where performance is at its peak, where capabilities are perfectly balanced with challenges, where everything comes together. For me, personally, it's the concrete experience that unites mind and body, connects my feet to the skis,

3

my hands with the ski poles, and makes me feel the snow and the whole environment as one.

It all starts with a big challenge. This is when the inner game unfolds its true power. As in business, it's not the easy things that bring forth the challenge. It's the complex, uncertain and volatile contexts and occurrences that demand extra agility, speed and resilience, where all skills are needed to cope with the challenge.

Back onto the ski slope. The inner game is not for the machine-prepared easy slope, where any imbalance can be overcome immediately, where easy swings get you down anyhow, where fun comes easily. To be clear, I have nothing against traditional, mass-audience skiing, with its party atmosphere. It has its place and is undeniably fun. But, the real joy comes when challenges arise. The latter is the domain of Diagnostic Mentoring. The story makes you aware of what the Diagnostic Mentoring theory and methodology can do for you as a leader and manager.

Why am I writing all of this? Simply because Lukas has helped me apply my inner-game sports coaching (be it skiing, tennis or golf) to business. Leadership and management are what Diagnostic Mentoring is all about. Lukas and I have evolved our approaches based on Timothy Gallwey's inner game theory and coaching methodology, which he has documented in many books, including *The Inner Game of Work*. There is a difference: while Tim's original focus was sports, Lukas brings his leadership and managerial experience to the game. I am pleased to see that thoughtful application of the inner game to the theory and practice of leadership and management.

Lukas' inspiration for *Diagnostic Mentoring* began that day on the slopes of Lagalb. While he had studied the inner game for years, he only 'crossed the Rubicon' through his own experiences, be they on skies, playing golf or managing people and organizations. People gain these profound insights only through experience — by doing it. Lukas has done it. Perhaps you have had your own flow experiences and my story sounds familiar. By reading *Diagnostic Mentoring*, you will take a deep dive into new management and leadership theory and discover how it feels to learn and perform through awareness, trust, choice and 'letting it flow,' all applied to business. *Diagnostic Mentoring* initiates the inner game by establishing awareness through diagnosis, the essential tool for any transformation to better management. That establishes the right focus of attention. Trust and choice follow. Flow is the goal.

Chances are high that you will get into the flow by reading *Diagnostic Mentoring* and eventually practising its methodologies. The book will open your eyes to the ways of better management and humane performance.

I am grateful to have known Lukas, and continue to enjoy our collaboration and ongoing, mutual inspiration. While I am the coaching practitioner, with a focus on helping individuals perform in their specific contexts, Lukas has put it into writing and works with leaders on management. With his inspiration — and invitation to write this Foreword — writing on my laptop is my inner-game experience today. With my fingers on the keyboard, I get into the flow, translating my experiences and knowledge about the inner-game approach into words once again. Thank you, Lukas, for pushing me to do that.

And to all readers: I wish you a joyful experience in reading this book and eventually applying the knowledge it contains in your daily leadership work.

All the best, and keep in mind: just trust yourself and 'let it flow!'

Dr Roberto Buner
Owner and CEO,
PotenzialEntwicklungCoaching GmbH (flowstate.ch)
April 2021
Speicher, Switzerland

PREFACE

It's another opportunity to finally get it right: better management. We are living in uncertain, volatile times, and have grown uneasy with traditional management. Risks have emerged that weren't on our radar, closer to home than we have ever seen, to an extent we've never experienced, with a deadly pandemic forcing business lockdowns around the world. The volatility, uncertainty, complexity and ambiguity (VUCA) phenomenon has suddenly become everyone's personal experience. The management of Covid-19 is an everyday conversation. Crisis management has taken over normal management, which seems insufficient in dynamic contexts. Traditional ways of managing — 'the way we've always done it' — seem to have reached their limits.

But, that's only part of the story. In the headline of a recent article, INSEAD business professor Gianpiero Petriglieri asks us, 'Are Our Management Theories Outdated?' (*Harvard Business Review*, 2020). He blames management for the harm of ultra-capitalism, "...the unquestioned practice of a dehumanized view of how management works and should work. It's an instrumental view that casts it as a technology of sorts, a means to an end, a tool to maximize efficiency, alignment, and performance — even when seemingly acting with concern and care for people." Theories and tools seem to help with instrumental managerial questions, but they seem of little help when we're confronted with existential challenges, like the disruption of Covid.

Petriglieri likens it to a human midlife crisis: "Trying to change the world without wanting to change our world is a classic sign of midlife and common defence when our worldviews collapse." To change management, he suggests, we need to change our concept of management. We need to replace it with truly *human* management that makes room for our bodies and sprits alongside our intellect and skills; an approach that cares for what work does and feels like and means to us, not just for what we can do at work, and how. This is management that abjures the relentless pursuit of efficiency and alignment. Petriglieri concludes that management as we know it has to die. "There is no other way," he insists. "Because, in truth, it does not have a problem. It *is* the problem." While I agree with management being the problem, replacing old with new management is not the solution. However, adding a people-centric perspective certainly makes a lot of sense. I will explain and expand on this.

The time has come for better management. However, this is not merely about adding new labels to the current ways of doing things. It is much broader than efficiency and alignment. It's what is embedded in the much broader perspective of culture, as management expert Edgar Schein explains in *Organizational Culture and Leadership* (2010). He describes how "...a set of basic assumptions defines what to pay attention to, what things mean, how to react emotionally to what is going on, and what actions to take in various kinds of situations." Better management is a different way of thinking about work. Some of it is very much the opposite of what we are used to.

There are many ways to look at what 'new' means. The challenge with this is that comparisons shift our attention. We look at the features and attributes of other companies and get distracted by the infinite number of differences. But, as psychologist Barry Schwartz, author of *The Paradox of Choice: Why More is Less* (2004), explains in his 2005 TED Talk,[1] when we have many options our choice is limited, as it is difficult to make that choice.

But, what does better management look like? If I knew that, the task would be easy, and this would be the end of this book. Myriad new business books focus on one specific thing to improve — it would seem to be what a successful business book needed to do. *Diagnostic Mentoring* has gone the opposite route, which isn't an easy proposition, but one that can yield powerful results. This is especially the case in that publishing scene where the *agile or lean* recipe for success promises to 'save the world' with solutions for everything in management. In fact, the theory of better management is not yet written. Many popular, widely-cited examples of so called

21st century management are driven by heroic leaders, or are touted for reasons other than better management. It is clear that the new theory needs to be inclusive, integrative and coordinative, rather than offering up a single best practice.

As a client of services myself, a number of things have caught my attention. Perhaps, I've thought, diving into innovation and exploration-type business models is not what's needed the most. Postal services that do everything but deliver mail, printer cartridges that burst on the first use, car batteries that quickly die, otherwise-timely books that take months to go on sale through online shops — these are all examples of missing quality, lack of efficiency and distorted effectiveness. Management that would allow such things simply needs fixing. Nobody needs businesses that don't deliver on expectations. As I've often put it, nobody goes to a restaurant where the tablecloth is not clean. These problems will continue to spiral ever downward ... unless, before things get to that point, we first take care of the basics.

With the basics in mind, I have added yet another 'from old to new' list, in Appendix 1. I purposely positioned it in an appendix, as it serves as a summary of the quest for better management, rather than a to-do list. Problems with 20th century management cannot be resolved with the Cartesian mindset, with its logical analysis and mechanical interpretation. That created the problem in the first place. Better management is all about open-ended learning.

I keep reading the same story over and over on social media, from established leaders and consultants: 'Simply put talent, team collaboration and culture in place, and magic will happen, without a ton of management, rules and guidelines.' I have stopped reacting to any of this. Nobody can honestly disagree with obvious common sense. Common sense emerges from the same pattern, and is dependent on the same context and the same specific situation, none of which can be taken for granted. It's the hard work and the details of management — its design and application — that shape common sense. The key is better management, not shortcuts.

Dumbing down management through tips, tricks and the obvious is everywhere: simple steps, three solutions, graphic illustrations, 30-day programmes and more. More pragmatically, I equate better management with people-centric, agile and dynamic capabilities.

And better management comes through Diagnostic Mentoring that creates awareness, offers insights and facilitates rapid learning.

Diagnostic Mentoring is for management experts who facilitate conversations on management with managers and their teams. We call these experts *diagnostic mentors*. This book serves as guiding documentation for the master class that certifies management experts in Diagnostic Mentoring.

Diagnostic Mentoring, the book, comes in four parts. Part I outlines the why, how and what of better management as people-centric management. Part II introduces Diagnostic Mentoring Step 1: Raise Awareness, to identify the elements of an agile organization. Part III explains Step 2: Act on Insights, to establish a dynamic operating system. Finally, Part IV outlines Step 3: Learn Fast, to make people-centric management work.

Diagnostic Mentoring builds on my previous books. *The Performance Triangle* (Michel, 2013) articulated the agile model in response to a dynamic environment, identifying the elements that make up an agile organization. It now serves as the source for definitions, with examples and practices, for Diagnostic Mentoring. *Management Design* (Michel, 2017) offered the methodology and process for developing agile managerial capabilities. It illustrated the practice of Diagnostic Mentoring. *People-Centric Management* (Michel, 2020) outlined the application of key people-oriented elements for effective leadership. And, *Agile by Choice* (Michel, 2021) provided helpful nudges to guide agile development.

Diagnostic Mentoring offers a deep dive into better management. However, not every executive will want to go all the way, and not every management context requires the full depth. Level 1 includes Chapters 1-10, with the Performance Triangle, the Leadership Scorecard and the operating model. They offer guidance on agile capabilities in line with *Agile by Choice* and people-centric capabilities that flow from *People-Centric Management*. Level 2, covered in Chapters 11 and 12, offers insights on the alignment of strategy, the business model and the management model for organizations that want to refine the operating system. Level 3, detailed in Chapters 13 and 14, guides executives in the design of the Leadership Toolbox and the operating system, with the sorts of dynamic capabilities required in a fast-moving environment. Readers who don't need the depth of that content can simply skip these chapters.

The Diagnostic Mentoring approach is grounded in solid management research and 20 years of application in professional settings. It offers a learning journey based on executive experience.

Stories are important. With the data generated from the diagnostics, readers will be able to develop their own stories. The nice thing about Diagnostic Mentoring is that stories can always be traced back to data.

Diagnostic Mentoring follows management guru Peter Drucker's advice on consulting. He suggested that self-responsible people don't need smart advice. Rather, they search for guidance while they work on better management. Diagnostic Mentoring creates the necessary awareness, offers choice and trusts executives to do it themselves.

PART I

BETTER MANAGEMENT

Part I outlines the fundamentals of better management. It starts with *why* better management is every manager's primary job. It then introduces Diagnostic Mentoring as the methodology that outlines *how* to get there, and suggests the enabling operating environment that defines *what* better management looks like.

CHAPTER 1

EVERY MANAGER'S PRIMARY JOB

Chapter 1 explains *why* every manager's primary job is better management: changing the way they lead people and how they organize work in the new business context. We discuss the role of the operating system in accomplishing that, and clarify managerial priorities and goals. This sets the stage for Diagnostic Mentoring — the methodology that enables the transformation of the way we manage.

THE NEW BUSINESS CONTEXT

Before diving into the *what* and the *how* of Diagnostic Mentoring, it is essential to understand *why* we need better management. It's because businesses today operate in a context that is dramatically different from the past. Identifying valuable business opportunities and extracting value from them is more demanding than ever.

In this context, managers face challenges and opportunities that fundamentally alter the context in which they operate.[2] Competitive advantage has always been the ultimate goal of organizations. At their core is the need to perform and deliver value for their stakeholders. Transaction costs have been the drivers for competitive advantage, with the underlying assumption that business can control information in a stable environment. In such a context, traditional control-based management delivers the expected outcomes. However, unlike in previous centuries, information costs have decreased dramatically, enabling loosely connected networks of professionals to function remotely and create value.

Traditional organizations and management are barriers to achieving competitive advantage in a dynamic environment. Since many organizations today face a higher degree of VUCA (as defined in the Preface), an operating model is needed that can deliver the expected outcomes amid ever-changing conditions. Traditional organizations were built for stability, efficiency and control. With the dynamic context, the focus has shifted to faster learning and innovation. No company can control all the resources needed for innovation. Therefore, organizations increasingly need collaborative approaches, often with resources from outside the firm. As a consequence, they need to adapt their operating modes to the course, speed and conditions of the external environment.

Two trends — digitalization and the reduction of information costs — fundamentally change the nature of work, how we organize and how we lead people.

Digitalization lowers information costs and enables new forms of interaction. Today, information is readily available, large amounts of data can be processed quickly, and communication technologies enable remote work. With readily available information, organizations can gain new insights, capture opportunities early and promptly mitigate risks. The dramatic reduction of information costs shifts work from being purely material and physical to something much more knowledge-oriented. Information search, knowledge creation and learning call for engaging the know-how and skills of remotely-situated people who are driven by self-determination and self-organization.

Such decentralized, collaborative and self-organized management styles are in sharp contrast with traditional approaches dominated by micro-managers. When work requires the knowledge of employees, teams and communities, people-centric management dominates. In such modern contexts, formal 'control' approaches lose their function. Today's ease of communication permits management styles rooted in free choice, sharing, transparency and the absence of rigid structures.

That's why every manager needs to care about business context.

OPERATING MODES

Operating modes help managers succeed in different business contexts. Dynamic systems in a fast-moving, volatile and uncertain environment differ greatly from those in a stable context, where control dominates. When knowledge is important, an operating mode that enables people to effectively apply their knowledge is fundamentally different from one where work is highly standardized, and managers can take control. Human beings are really good at most complex, collaborative and creative work. They are much better at this than machines. The VUCA part is hard for machines. This is the context where teams and organizations of people, working together toward a common goal, can create immense value.

FIGURE 1: FOUR OPERATING MODES

Figure 1 introduces leadership and systems in their contextual setting: traditional, dynamic and people-centric operating modes. The combination of means (systems) and ends (people, leadership) leads to four operating modes: control, engagement, change and enabling.

- **Control**: In a stable environment where knowledge is concentrated at the top, traditional management and institutional control dominate. The thinking and doing are separated, which justifies traditional, bureaucratic control. Traditional management applies direct control through narrow targets. Interactions focus on disseminating strategy and overseeing performance. Decisions are made by leaders, and narrow targets maintain the focus to keep people on track.
- **Engagement**: In a knowledge-driven environment with little change, the engagement mode dominates. People (the ends) are tightly controlled by traditional means. People-centric leadership supports self-responsible people guided by broad direction. Management aligns individual interests through visions, beliefs, boundaries and values. As Harvard Business School Professor Robert Simons (1995) put it, "In the absence of management action, self-interested behaviour at the expense of organizational goals is inevitable." Self-responsibility and broad direction are balanced with hierarchical power and institutional bureaucracy.
- **Change**: In a dynamic market environment with centralized decision-making, direct intervention through change dominates. Dynamic systems (the means) meet traditional ways to lead people (the ends). Change modes operate through a market-control setting where managers alter the resource base, align interests through incentives, and restructure accountability and responsibilities in response to market changes.
- **Enabling**: In a dynamic context, with knowledge distributed throughout the organization, the enabling mode dominates. People-centric leadership (the ends) and dynamic systems (the means) match. Traditional rules-based management approaches are not effective. Under these conditions, enabling modes support fast decision-making and proactive, flexible action, which together lead to robust outcomes.

The ability to create a work environment where people can contribute to breaking down bureaucracy and hierarchy, no matter who they are and what they do, allows for self-organization, enabling organizations to explore new values and grow.

With this, it becomes obvious that the new enabling business context differs from traditional management. It requires an operating system with a design that enables people to operate in a dynamic environment.

As noted, *Diagnostic Mentoring* builds on my previous book, *People-Centric Management*, to suggest the enabling mode for better management.

THE OPERATING SYSTEM

In any organization, management operates on a system (Figure 2) that enables people to get work done. Such a managerial operating system facilitates interactions and creates a shared way of doing things. Think of the operating system in a computer: it makes the hardware work, enabling users to perform their tasks. In that sense, the managerial operating system does the same with organizations and people, through control, enabling, governance and support.

Operations encompasses business transactions, how work is carried out through core competencies, processes, workflow and output. The business model determines the nature of processes and work. Change in the business model means change in operations, the core processes and how we operate our business.

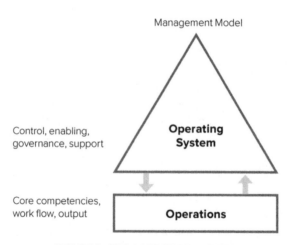

Management Model

Control, enabling,
governance, support

**Operating
System**

Core competencies,
work flow, output

Operations

FIGURE 2: THE OPERATING SYSTEM

The operating system — the system of how we manage — is deeper and less visible. It is governed by the management model that determines how we manage, lead, organize and operate through culture, leadership and systems. The operating system determines how we measure success, create strategy, implement plans, reward performance and govern the decision-making.

The Performance Triangle (Figure 3) represents the managerial operating system (with rules, routines and tools) to facilitate leadership and support people (with interaction skills). It also helps establish a shared culture (mindsets), be it for one's own firm, organization, unit or team, or as part of a farther-flung network, community, larger firm, organization, unit or team.

FIGURE 3: THE PERFORMANCE TRIANGLE

The triangle establishes performance through operations that facilitate learning as an opportunity, a capability and a state of readiness. The systems scientist Peter Senge (1990) put it as follows: "In a learning organization, leaders are designers, stewards and teachers. They are responsible for building organizations where people continually expand their capabilities to understand complexity, clarify vision, and improve shared mental models — that is, they are responsible for learning."

An organization's operating system needs to establish the opportunity to learn. It's the responsibility of the organization to offer the learning opportunity. An employee's skills are the prerequisite for the ability to learn. The role of leadership is to unlock the talent; the goal is to engage the capability to perform. It's a shared responsibility between the organization and the individual.

The mindset is a prerequisite for the ability to act. It enables learning and the application of skills. Culture creates the context for readiness. But, it's every individual's responsibility to learn and engage, and to remain in a state of readiness.

Operating systems have been increasingly challenged. Trust in systems is breaking down. And, this is not unique to business — it's happening everywhere. More often than not, current discussions in politics and business challenge systems. We see political campaigns in modern democracies where candidates propose that public administration systems be torn down, claiming they aren't effective, are too expensive, have too many rules, limit freedom, etc.

Thousands of books are written every year that claim to add yet another attribute to leadership. They promise to provide 'the key to success,' 'the five recipes,' 'the ultimate goal,' and so on. Leadership without systems does not work. Systems without leadership are meaningless. And systems without the right design by their managers don't effectively support leadership and people. The Catholic priest and management author Peter Scholtes (1998) put it this way: "Changing the system will change what people do. Changing what people do will not change the system. Yet because we don't understand systems, we act as though human errors were the primary cause of our problems."

Culture matters. It embodies the set of formal and informal social norms in an organization. It is in the organization's interest to establish these norms in ways that enable people to cooperate in support of the overall performance goals. Culture provides what systems naturally cannot: the invisible, cooperative glue where targets, incentives, imperfect monitoring and sanctions are based on the negative assumptions of people; and a solution to the 'free-ride' problem. One should not be surprised that cultures quickly turn sour and become infected by viruses (fear, control and power).

We often see new CEOs demanding radical culture change, in hope of better performance and improved client service. This means there's a need for a new and different system to scale and govern decision-making, actions and behaviours throughout an organization. A collaborative culture starts with positive assumptions about people, dynamic systems built in support of people, and people-centric management.

Every organization needs its operating system to ensure effective business conduct. The general critique that questions the need of systems per se is inadequate and misses the point. If a car does not perform to expectation, nobody would challenge the essence of cars in general. We know from our research that most culture issues, faulty leadership or sub-par performance originates from an erroneous operating system. If something produces errors, it needs to be fixed or exchanged. The critique, properly addressed, may demand a reset, an update, a change, or wholesale replacement of an organization's operating system.

The operating system for the new enabling business context needs a design that enables better management. *Diagnostic Mentoring* is the guide for better management and its operating system. We'll examine why that's the case.

MANAGEMENT

Does better management matter? This is more than a rhetorical question. Does it make a difference when it comes to success, results, performance and flow? The immediate response is yes — otherwise, why would we engage in developing better management practices? Yet, although there are lots of good anecdotal examples, it is hard to find substantial evidence of a direct management impact on outcomes. That said, there is significant literature that explains specific aspects of leadership and its contributions. The following formula shows a simple overview of the relevant factors. The purpose of this overview is to make the case that leadership, systems and culture — the three parts of the Performance Triangle (see Michel, 2013) — explain the things that can be managed and influenced to develop better management.

Success = f (leadership, systems, culture, opportunities and risks, serendipity)

Leadership, systems and culture are discretionary factors that require management decisions. They can be managed and therefore can make a difference. Opportunities and risks depend on endogenous factors, but also require decisions. They are the challenges that you accept. Certain factors depend on the quality of leadership. This leaves us with serendipity, which is outside our control.

The use of appropriate interaction mechanisms determines how decisions are made. They depend on the leader's skills and the quality of the supporting systems. The design of systems as tools, routines and rules provides choice about strategy, structure and capabilities to represent the operating constraints that explain important aspects of success. All these elements represent distinct executive decisions. It is important to note that investors can diversify this unsystematic risk: the promises, innovation, reputation, talent and (missed) opportunities.

Therefore, I conclude that managers can make a difference through actively shaping their management dimensions and elements: leadership, systems and culture. It's the work *on* your organization's operating system.

Current reality shows that control, change and engagement have taken over management. Managers think that their job is to control work, manage change or engage people. There are three failures of management that are apparent: traditional control, the change fallacy and employee engagement. They all fail in the new business context.

Traditional control, with a focus on efficiency, has lost sight of people. Erroneous systems and faulty leadership are the cause. To overcome the challenges, well-intended managers compensate for the lack of leadership or work-around systems through their own 'pragmatic' solutions. I call this 'working outside the system.' Systems and leadership that are replaced by ad hoc interventions will lead to a virus-infected culture.

Change replaces management through sophisticated change processes and methodologies. The argument is that management systems and practices are not helpful for change, and that's why another process or methodology is needed. I call this 'working with another system.' Replacing management through change is not helpful. In fact, most change processes fail. Change management has failed.

Employee engagement cannot cope with a dynamic environment. While such initiatives search for better ways of working, they're merely what I would call good 'working with a better system.' If so, then why not simply update management with people-centric principles, rather than to compensate for the apparent lack of good leadership?

The problem is not with managers. It is with the systems of control, change and engagement. Control fails to work with knowledge workers. Change has long circled around management to bring about a different way of getting things done. Employee engagement has tried to change how we lead and work. None of that has worked well. The evidence is clear, and I have reported on this many times:[3] If the fault is with management, then that needs fixing.

Distinguishing between operations (what managers want) and the operating systems (what most have not thought about) helps us emphasize where the true competitive advantage lies: the opportunity for real managers to think about how they lead, organize and manage. That's work *on* the system.

Real managers know that the task is to change the way we lead people, how we organize ourselves and how we get work done. It's the primary responsibility of managers to establish an operating system that suits the people, the purpose of the organization and the context of their business.

The shift to the enabling mode means better management — beyond what traditional control, change and engagement can deliver in a fast-changing market context. In most organizations, the shift means a transformation of the operating system.

Diagnostic Mentoring offers the methodology for the transformation journey and serves as a guide for how to move beyond control, change and engagement to better management.

PRIORITIES

The shift to better management starts by setting priorities right. The Performance Triangle helps you establish people-centric, agile, client-focused and dynamic capabilities at scale, with the right priorities in mind (Figure 4). The hierarchy becomes: people first (they are in the centre); agile organization second (the work environment); clients third (your job to be done); and dynamic operations fourth (your responsibility as a manager).

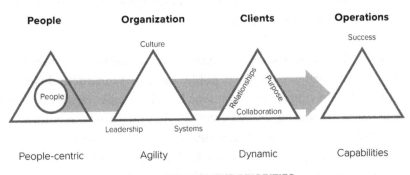

FIGURE 4: MANAGEMENT PRIORITIES

People-centric managers establish an environment aligned with four priorities, so keep this in mind while you work *on* the system, which is your primary responsibility:

1. **People are the centre of your attention.** People-centric demands an individualized environment where people can unlock their talent and perform at their peak. It's people who deliver value to clients. They should be able to experience flow, the state where challenges and capabilities meet to create a positive experience. That's the ultimate goal of people-centric management. As a leader, it is your task (and your obligation) to create that kind of work environment.

2. **Your organization sets the context.** Agile capabilities enable people-centric management. Systems, leadership and culture establish the operating environment for people to apply their talent and perform. Hence, it is important to be clear about the potential and interference in your own organization.

3. **It's people who work that care about clients.** People-centric principles enable you as a leader to demand self-responsibility, delegate work, facilitate self-organization and lead with broad directives. This means that the people in your organization can take charge and take care of clients. Client-focus is all about your people making sure that valuable clients are satisfied, come back and want more.

4. **Success is what appeals to owners.** They look for growth and return on their investment. Growth comes from clients who come back. Operational returns come from capabilities, efficiency gains and innovations. Long-term value creation must be the goal of the business.

Getting these priorities right balances the interests of all stakeholders in your business. It creates public value (Meynhardt and Gomez, 2013). People-centric management based on agile capabilities and a dynamic operating system creates value for society, regardless of whether you operate in a traditional or a dynamic mode.

Better management assumes that you put people first. As you will see in Chapter 2, the Diagnostic Mentoring methodology is well aligned with people-centric management.

RESULTS

While operational issues are not the focus of Diagnostic Mentoring, it is important to note that the sole purpose of better management with an operating system that fits is operations that deliver results.

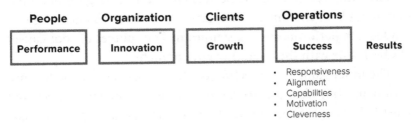

FIGURE 5: OPERATING RESULTS

Figure 5 identifies performance, innovation, growth and five success factors as the operations elements that indicate whether management and the operating system deliver results.

Diagnostic Mentoring uses questions to assess capabilities and results. The diagnostics initiate a mentoring relationship that supports managers, raising their awareness and moving from opinions to meaning, acting on insights by separating symptoms from root causes, and speeding up learning by translating ideas into action. Starting with the performance element, Diagnostic Mentoring offers guidance for both the mentors and managers. Mentors and managers capture the insights from their conversations about the diagnostic results on the canvas reporting tool with coloured Post-it notes marking assumptions, principles, potential, gaps and key issues. Chapter 4 — *Raise Awareness* — offers the details on the diagnostic and the canvas.

PERFORMANCE

Performance assesses the ability of people to apply their skills and knowledge, access resources and release their full potential with peak performance in mind. The performance metric offers an early indication of the amount of interference that keeps people from exploiting their potential.

The interpretation of the performance metric (Figure 6) immediately leads to the inner game, learning and the balance of goals. Inadequate performance is a symptom. The sources of root causes always reside with the operating environment.

The inner game is the technique that translates knowledge into action and transfers control to the learner. Awareness, choice and trust help people focus on what counts. The result is flow (Csikszentmihalyi, 1990) — the state in which learning, performance and joy collide to deliver superior results.

Question. The assessment statement for this element:
At work, I can unfold my full potential, and freely use and apply all my knowledge, capabilities and creativity.
Evaluation. The answer is scored as follows:
0 = Strongly disagree, 25 Disagree, 50 Neutral, 75 Agree, 100 Strongly agree.
Meaning. The score indicates the following known symptoms:
• **Top.** A high score means people have the means to perform at their peak • **Mediocre.** A medium score means interferences prevent people from using their full potential. Performance likely suffers • **Missing or blocked.** A low score means people don't use their potential. They are bored, stressed or work in an infected environment
Interpretation. Linkages to other elements offer insights and root causes:
• **People:** Awareness, choice, trust and focus • **Operating Modes:** Control vs. enabling mode • **Leadership Scorecard:** Success, motivation
Sources
• **Model.** *The Performance Triangle*, page 139 (on flow) • **Process.** *Management Design* (2nd Ed. 2017), page 45 • **Exercise.** *Agile by Choice*, page 111 (on flow)
Facilitation. Use Post-it notes and the canvas for the answers:
What are the assumptions and principles? Where is the potential? Use green Post-its. What are the instances of interference? Use red Post-its.

FIGURE 6: PERFORMANCE INSIGHTS

INNOVATION

Innovation is a measure of the organization's ability to excite clients with new products and services. The innovation metric signals agile and people-centric capabilities.

Innovation and agility are strongly correlated. We know that innovative organizations have agile capabilities, and agile capabilities lead to superior innovations. It's the classic chicken-and-egg problem — which came first? What matters is that agile capabilities lead to superior innovation. In an environment where people can unlock their creativity and create new knowledge, innovation is the outcome.

The interpretation of the innovation metric (Figure 7) starts with people, their ability to apply their creativity and agility, the systems, culture and leadership that enable superior innovation. Innovation is also the choice for an exploration-type business model. Missing innovation may be a choice or a symptom of the lack of an appropriate environment and management model.

Question. The assessment statement for this element:
Our organization is renowned for innovation. We turn ideas into reality and add value to our clients' projects.
Evaluation. The answer is scored as follows:
0 = Strongly disagree, 25 Disagree, 50 Neutral, 75 Agree, 100 Strongly agree.
Meaning. The score indicates the following known symptoms:
• **Productive.** A high score means a prospering organization where ideas turn into action. The task is to build on the current management approach • **Limited.** A medium score indicates an organization where the status quo prevails. New ideas take time to translate into action. Work on the system is needed • **Missing or wasted:** A low score indicates a hesitant organization. It draws from the past with nothing new coming forward. The task is to fundamentally work on the system
Interpretation. Linkages to other elements offer insights and root causes:
• **Organization:** Leadership, systems and culture • **Operating Modes:** Control vs. enabling mode • **Business Model:** Exploration
Sources
• **Process.** *Management Design* (2nd Ed. 2017), page 65
Facilitation. Use Post-it notes and the canvas for the answers:
What are the assumptions and principles? Where is the potential? Use green Post-its. What are the instances of interference? Use red Post-its.

FIGURE 7: INNOVATION INSIGHTS

GROWTH

Growth marks the organization's ability to develop from within. The growth metric offers early insights into the capacity for renewal and resilience. It indicates the degree to which the organization captures relevant business opportunities and turns them into stakeholder value.

By using purposeful, cooperative and knowledge-creating strategies, companies can reinvent themselves with new business models while they preserve their core. The way we set goals and how we deal with stakeholders determine much of the internal growth capacity of a company.

The interpretation of the growth metric (Figure 8) leads to the work environment where people have to contribute to value creation, the purpose they find in what they do, the ability to collaborate, and connectedness with others within and outside the organization.

Question. The assessment statement for this element:
Our organization captures relevant opportunities and grows steadily.
Evaluation. The answer is scored as follows:
0 = Strongly disagree, 25 Disagree, 50 Neutral, 75 Agree, 100 Strongly agree.
Meaning. The score indicates the following known symptoms:
• **Superior.** A high score means that the organization captures relevant opportunities. The task is to build on current capabilities • **Maintaining.** A medium score indicates an organization that hardly moves. The task is to move out of the middle ground by reviewing capabilities • **Missing.** A low score indicates an organization that loses market presence. The task is to review capabilities in order to change the current situation
Interpretation. Linkages to other elements offer insights and root causes:
• **Work:** Purpose, collaboration, relationships • **Operating Modes:** Control vs. enabling mode
Sources
• **Process.** *Management Design* (2nd Ed. 2017), page 79
Facilitation. Use Post-it notes and the canvas for the answers:
What are the assumptions and principles? Where is the potential? Use green Post-its. What are the instances of interference? Use red Post-its.

FIGURE 8: GROWTH INSIGHTS

SUCCESS

Success stands at the top of the Performance Triangle, representing the ultimate goal of management. Successful firms meet or exceed expectations by making performance visible, in the form of socially accepted outcomes.

In the Performance Triangle model, five attributes determine success: responsiveness, the ability to sense opportunities and react to them; alignment of the organization with strategy, a prerequisite to creating value; organizational core competencies, the foundation for sustainable competitive advantage; motivation of the team to get things done; and the wisdom of how the organization defines and uses its boundaries.

The five attributes define the primary, intangible value-creating elements of an organization, which drive success:

1. **Responsiveness,** to know with clarity. The promise to clients.
2. **Alignment,** to move in one direction. The attractiveness of the strategy.
3. **Capabilities,** to mobilize the energy. The core capabilities and competitive advantage.
4. **Motivation,** to maintain the focus. The aspirations of the entire team.
5. **Cleverness,** to remain in focus. The boundaries of entrepreneurship.

Responsiveness. Is the organization flexible and able to react to changes in the environment?

Alignment. Is the direction of the organization clear? Does the structure fit the strategy? Is it shared broadly, and are employees aligned to support the strategies?

Capabilities. Does the organization have the competencies and skills needed to deliver on promises?

Motivation. Are employees throughout the organization inspired to perform above and beyond expectations?

Cleverness. Are employees empowered to be creative, and to use their creativity to meet expectations or demands from customers within boundaries that do not stifle creativity?

If the answer to these questions is yes, these are signs of success and value creation.

Question. The assessment statement for this element:
We deliver on what we promise to our clients, with an attractive strategy and the right capabilities.
Evaluation. The answer is scored as follows:
0 = Strongly disagree, 25 Disagree, 50 Neutral, 75 Agree, 100 Strongly agree.
Meaning. The score indicates the following known symptoms:
• **Sustainable.** A high score means the organization has well-developed capabilities in place that enable superior outcomes • **Mediocre.** A medium score means the organization has limited capabilities in place, which may prevent superior outcomes • **Missing.** A low score means the organization has no (or the wrong) capabilities in place, which most likely prevents acceptable outcomes
Interpretation. Linkages to other elements offer insights and root causes:
• **Leadership Scorecard:** Systems -> leadership -> culture -> success
Sources
• **Model.** *The Performance Triangle*, pages 62-76 • **Application.** *People-Centric Management*, page 148
Facilitation. Use Post-it notes and the canvas for the answers:
What are the assumptions and principles? Where is the potential? Use green Post-its. What are the instances of interference? Use red Post-its.

FIGURE 9: SUCCESS

GOALS

Better management sets the right goals to impact value creation and results. Both institutions and individuals have three goals. For lasting, superior results, these goals need the right balance. Institutional and individual goals must match.

Performance, innovation and growth are three goals for businesses. Every business' primary purpose is to create and retain a customer. Excited customers contribute to growth. In return, that requires that businesses create new products and services, so that clients come back. As such, performance, growth and innovation are in balance.

Institutions		Individuals	
Performance	Excite clients	**Performance**	Do meaningful things
Innovation	Explore new opportunities	**Learning**	Unfold the potential
Growth	Capture new challenges	**Enjoyment**	Master greater challenges

FIGURE 10: GOALS

Learning, enjoyment and performance are three interrelated components of people's goals. When the learning part of goals increases, it certainly impacts enjoyment and performance. Likewise, if enjoyment is decreased, this negatively impacts learning and performance.

In most corporate cultures, performance is the dominant goal component. However, it's obvious to most people that solely emphasizing performance does not lead to better results. The three component goals work together as part of our goal system. When one is ignored, the others suffer.

In the knowledge era, learning is a significant component of work. When people strongly like their jobs, it increases their ability to learn. Just getting the job done without increasing knowledge is not an option for people whose jobs relate to knowledge. Both performance and learning contribute to the overall results of the organization.

The enjoyment component is the least acknowledged of the three, as there is a widespread perception that work is not supposed to be enjoyable. But, the belief that people should enjoy their work — for example, that they should find purpose in it — is slowly gaining acceptance. Enjoyment is likely the dominant component in an era when talent is scarce.

Peak performance for both the institution and the individual requires that goals naturally align. Better management starts by acknowledging the need for balance and alignment.

There is a desperate need for better management. In this chapter, we've made the case that this is every manager's primary job. Better management means enabling management with people-centric, agile and dynamic features at its core. We have learned from our research with 250 organizations worldwide that people-centric management, an agile organization and dynamic operating systems are the key to better management.

For success in a dynamic market context, traditional management needs a real transformation — perhaps a fundamental system reset. Diagnostic Mentoring helps you to do just that.

Now, it is up to your facilitation. Namely:

- What are your assumptions about the current operating context?
- What are the current managerial principles?

Document observations on your conversations with the team on Post-it notes. You will need them later, with what we'll call 'the canvas,' in Chapter 4 and beyond.

FIFTEEN BUSINESS CASES

Fifteen business cases illustrate various aspects of Diagnostic Mentoring throughout this book.

#1: Insurance Industry. The first business case presents an entire industry rather than a single company. The insurance industry case includes 25 companies in Central Europe. It offers a closer look at the alignment of the business model and the operations mode in an industry that is focused on efficiency but is starved for innovation. But, there is hope.

#2: City Mobility. The second case presents the public transportation system of a large city in Switzerland, with 250 employees. The CEO faced the challenge of the business' transformation from a government-run organization to one that suddenly faced private-sector competition.

#3: Logistics. The third case presents a global logistics company headquartered in Switzerland, with 4,500 employees worldwide. The new CEO needed immediate clarity on the key issues that required attention. There was no time to waste.

#4: Specialty Foods. The fourth case study is about a highly successful and fast-growing business in Italy, with 300 employees worldwide. The founder and current CEO turned 75 and asked himself what it would take to turn the helm over to an executive team.

#5: City Administration. The fifth case concerns the administration of a medium-size city in the US, with 2,500 municipal employees. The tasks were to identify the root causes of faulty behaviour and to raise awareness of why this was unacceptable.

#6: Energy. The sixth case is about the CEO of a regional Swiss energy supplier who felt he was not sufficiently supported by his office to get his work done.

#7: Music. The seventh study involves a German-based world market leader in musical instruments that faced a long-term substitution trend in its core product. Rather than playing music, children were now playing *mobile phone.* The challenge was to return to innovation mode, and fast.

#8: Mining. The eighth case is about a world-leading UK mining company with 50,000 employees in 150 divisions, and a new CEO in need of an agenda for the future.

#9: Pharma. The ninth case is about the research division of a US-headquartered global pharmaceutical company. The challenges included a thin product line, with research that was anything but agile.

#10: Insurance. This is the case of a Swiss-based global insurance company with 30,000 employees, known for exemplary knowledge-type workplaces, that had become slow, bureaucratic and risk averse. This was the opposite of what the new CEO had in mind. The task was to change the culture and return to a spirit of entrepreneurship.

#11: Cosmetics. This case is about a Swiss cosmetics company with 1,200 employees where leadership went beyond what systems were able to deliver. Management-by-objectives had become a barrier to innovation.

#12: Fast Food. The twelfth case concerns a large fast-food restaurant chain in Australia. The decision was to become more agile and faster in adapting to changing consumer demand.

#13: Sugar Manufacturing. The visionary founder of this Egyptian start-up asked himself what it would take to scale his business fast. The diagnostic offered his initial toolbox.

#14: Food Production. The fourteenth case is a South African company with 150 employees in frozen poultry production. While efficiency and quality were essential, it needed to cultivate a new leadership style to prepare for the future.

#15: Executive Search. The EMEA part of a global executive search company in London restructured its satellite offices in a way that created centres of excellence for hiring CEOs, CFOs, CROs and other functional leaders, while maintaining their highly effective local agents. The question was how to manage that tension between vertical and horizontal.

INSURANCE INDUSTRY – ON THE SEARCH FOR INNOVATION

The following snapshot of 25 companies in Europe presents the case of an industry that is stuck in exploitation mode, with an operating model where control dominates. The 2020 data is part of a long-term industry study on innovation capabilities.

The industry's diagnostic results (Figure 11) indicate medium to low scores on outcomes. The industry reports being halfway to success. For our purposes, success is the measure of whether their core competencies translate into a competitive advantage or not. In the insurance space, innovation and growth are at the low end of comparable industries.

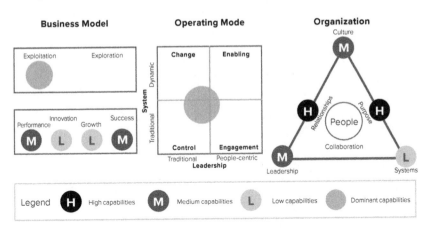

FIGURE 11: INSURANCE INDUSTRY

People performance is at a medium level. Control dominates, which means that employees are unable to apply their full talent and deliver peak performance. The control mode is also one of the causes of missing innovation.

Erroneous systems and partially effective leadership prevent people from getting work done, despite high scores on relationships and purpose. It seems that the companies depend on relationships as the way for people to get things done. Erroneous systems are not only a major cause of the lack of success and performance, but they're not a good fit for supporting the exploitation mode. This is the kind of situation where innovation is far out of reach.

Fixing systems — in particular, performance management — is the key to better results. Only then can the industry expect to successfully make the transition to innovation mode. We continue to monitor the insurance industry's progress.

The insights from our research[6] support organizations, companies and industries in finding new ways to superior performance and developing businesses with a distinct competitive advantage.

EVERY MANAGER'S PRIMARY JOB

As we said earlier, there is a desperate need for better management. Real managers know that the task is to change the way they lead people, how they organize themselves and how they get work done.

KEY CHAPTER IDEAS

- Control, change and engagement have failed in today's dynamic context
- The problem is not with managers, it's with *management*
- The operating system can bring that change
- Set balanced and aligned priorities and goals
- The focus must be on fixing management — on engineering a system reset

ACTION AGENDA

Focus every manager on better management as his or her primary job. Challenge current assumptions and principles.

FURTHER READING

Michel, L (2020). *People-Centric Management: How Managers Use Four Levers to Bring Out the Greatness of Others.* London: LID Publishing.

CHAPTER 2

DIAGNOSTIC MENTORING

Chapter 2 introduces Diagnostic Mentoring as the transformative pivot to working *on* the system, and the approach for managers to change the operating system of their organization. Diagnostic Mentoring is *how* you get to better management.

A DIAGNOSTIC TRANSFORMATION APPROACH

For most organizations, introducing people-centric, agile and dynamic capabilities means undergoing a transformation. In the 21st century, the idea of transformation has become quite popular. However, the word is overused, often empty and little understood. We should not use 'transformation' lightly. A transformation is not just another change. It is a change of energy in form, appearance and structure that fundamentally alters decision-making, behaviours and actions. Transformation means creating something new that has not existed before, and that cannot be determined in advance. Transformation is learning, and applied new knowledge, and requires experience.

The first step is transformation of the individual. It comes about through awareness, insights and learning about the system that determines how we, and organizations, function and operate. Self-responsibility, motivation and initiative are necessary to stretch beyond the normal. The inner game offers the structure required for the necessary mental process and paradigm shift in learning and performance.

The transformation of an organization requires the courage to lead a journey into the unknown. While agile management offers essential principles, their application is new for most people and organizations. We can expect different outcomes in different organizations. The transformation itself involves the continuous creation of awareness, insights and learning opportunities on the theories of people-centric management, agile organization and dynamic operating systems. The theories are highly individual; they will become your own way of doing things. There is no general theory to apply. Your organization's theory will become your management model.

Beliefs, patterns, habits and paradigms dominate management theories and how they are implemented. Our assumptions determine how we structure accountability, how we interact, and the rules, routines and tools of our systems (Figure 12). As a result, different organizations' structures, leadership processes and systems result in different decisions, actions and behaviours. Transformation challenges our assumptions.

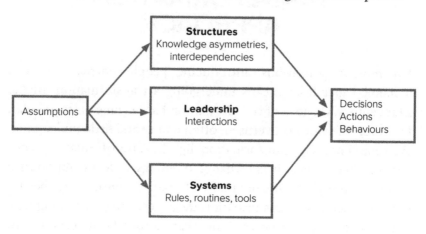

FIGURE 12: A TRANSFORMATION

The diagnostic transformation approach is how executives sit back, reflect and challenge current assumptions about their management.

THREE STEPS

Diagnostic Mentoring creates the learning experience you need to successfully master your transformation journey. Awareness, insights and learning guide your journey (Figure 13) with techniques, tools and frameworks to engage your team.

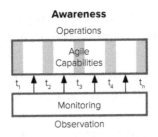

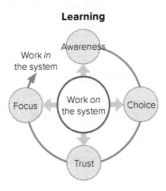

FIGURE 13: AWARENESS, INSIGHTS AND LEARNING

The journey to better management is a transformation where no one has the answers on the specific tools and practices that make up people-centric management, an agile organization and a dynamic operating system. It's a process that requires individual design, to fit it to the specific needs of the organization and its stakeholders. As such, the shift to better management is a transformation that follows design thinking in three steps: collectively raise awareness, act on insights and learn fast.

1. **Raise awareness.** Diagnose current capabilities, create awareness.
2. **Act on insights.** Identify the desired capability insights for decisions.
3. **Learn fast.** Enable better, people-centric management through agile capabilities and dynamic systems.

If you look at steps as part of a stairway, you can walk up and down these stairs. If you look at steps as a sequence of stages or things, you can go forward but also backwards. You can take a step back. The three-step transformation works like that. It's not a prescription for a start, and then one step, then two, then three, and you're finished. The three steps represent three mandatory parts that logically follow each other. But, more often than not, one goes back to 'step one' for a fresh look. The steps are circular in how they're applied.

Mentoring (Figure 14) applies the inner game to design. The self-mentoring process is central to the principles outlined in my book, *Agile by Choice*. It is the same approach that my organization's agile experts use when they work with their executive clients. As such, mentoring follows the same principles that establish the foundation of agile leadership, organization and management: awareness, insights and learning.

Awareness (Focus)	Insights (Choice)	Learning (Trust)
Sensing, diagnostics, observation points	Knowing, dimensions and models, shared language, intervention points	Transforming, expertise, leverage points

FIGURE 14: THREE STEPS

The three steps combine individual, team and organizational perspectives into a coherent approach. This establishes an institutional framework for a reflective opening of perspectives through authentic dissent, as a tool to learn about people-centric, agile and dynamic capabilities. The exchange and dissent on observations is what creates new insights and knowledge. Interaction and discourse are based on common language that establishes a shared language.

Figure 15 looks at capabilities that can be observed, modelled and transformed. In a systems view, monitoring and 'dynamization' can be treated as two separate functions (Luhmann, 1995). The science of cybernetics calls this *second-order observing systems* (von Foerster, 1992). The way we do things becomes a subject of reflection, and is opened up to alternatives. Through observation, capabilities become revisable.

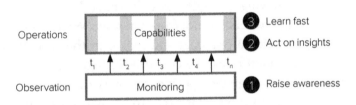

FIGURE 15: CAPABILITY MONITORING

Raise awareness: The diagnostic establishes observation points. Monitoring is a discipline that can be used to observe and alter design. By observing (scanning) capabilities, potential faults and malfunctions can be spotted at an early stage. By becoming aware of critical signals, potential design requirements can be identified. In this way, leaders can decide whether or not to address certain issues. As such, monitoring initiates design changes relating to capabilities.

Diagnostics are the sensing tools that help you see the invisible: your potential, and the interference that keeps you from delivering your expected outcomes. Observation points help you identify the systemic relationships between the critical elements of your organization, to help distil your dominant assumptions, principles and patterns. Awareness turns opinions into meaning, to create purpose.

Act on insights: The Performance Triangle (see Figure 3) distils the elements of agile. The use of agile capabilities and design is selective. The decision to employ a specific design excludes other alternatives. The design process is about the selection of managerial tools, routines and rules that make organizations agile. Design requires reflection and interactions. It is not free from politics. The setting of these conversations determines much about the design's quality.

The five dimensions — people, organization, work, operations and management — create a shared language for the transformation. With the help of Diagnostic Mentors, you can identify the critical intervention points and articulate your ideal design, with gaps and key issues. Your design choices will take you from symptoms to root causes, with clarity on where to interfere.

Learn fast: The inner game (see Chapter 5) offers the techniques involved in following the agile way of learning. Monitoring assumes that the design is reversible, not frozen in place. While deeply embedded in organizational practices and rooted in the past, managerial design and capabilities can be changed through interventions. The people-centric shift guides specific capability development projects in line with decisions on what needs to be changed. In this way, the idea of permanent change is replaced by the notion of combining learning and doing. It is an iterative process.

Expertise will help you transform your management and organization, and develop people-centric, agile and dynamic capabilities at scale. Trust yourself to identify the initiatives that will offer the most leverage on how to switch from idea to action. Establish a road map for how you and your team can collaborate, using your management skills to create superior value.

The three-step Diagnostic Mentoring process is how executives develop better management with their teams.

GUIDED REFLECTION
AND INTERFERENCE

Diagnostic Mentoring (Figure 16) guides the transformation from data to action, in line with Harvard academic Chris Argyris' *Ladder of Inference* (Argyris, 1990; Senge, 1990). Diagnostics establish the observation points on operations. The Performance Triangle (see Figure 3) connects the elements in a model that creates meaning. People-centric levers (Chapter 9) facilitate the questioning of assumptions. Four operating modes (see Chapter 1) offer choice on what management model best fits the business model. Awareness and insights (see Chapter 4 and 10) create inferences that can inform your choice of, and shift to, people-centricity. Learning is reflection. It creates new knowledge, and new knowledge leads to new experiences.

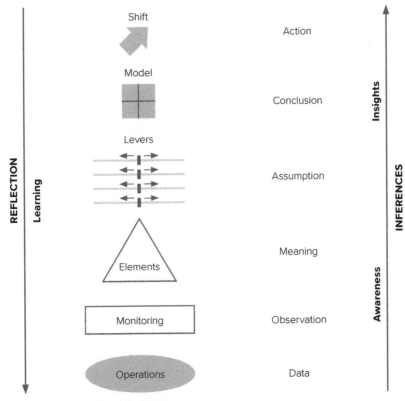

FIGURE 16: REFLECTION AND INTERFERENCE

With the same routines, tomorrow is always the same. To break out of that rut, successful leaders change their condition, their thinking and their feeling. Only if you are in a powerful place beyond space and time, where matter emerges (see Chapter 4), can you initiate real change. Figure 16 summarizes the Diagnostic Mentoring steps and activities you and your executives can take to activate experiential learning with the tools and dimensions contained in this book.

Diagnostic Mentoring is a transformation that *interferes*, to offer guided reflection about management and organization for the new era.

A TEAM EFFORT

The decision to undertake a transformation with an unknown outcome invariably comes with a bit of fear. It takes courage and clear intent: awareness, to know with clarity. But, leadership would be a safe and predictable place if all answers were already known. Transformation is a team effort, and the choice to move in one direction. Practice has shown that any successful transformation requires architects, translators and doers (Figure 17) who trust their talents and are able to mobilize their energy.

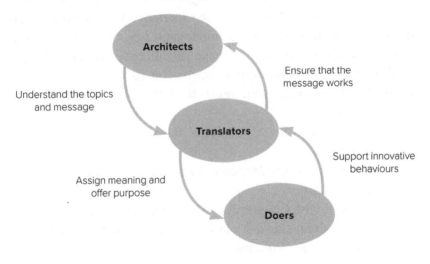

FIGURE 17: A TEAM EFFORT

Architects are the experts on the design of management, organizations and transformations. They can help you create the agile systems that will best work for your organization. Translators are experts in communications. They can turn your agile message into interactions — events, training and experiences — that support the transformation effort. Doers are executives with accountability for parts of the organization, and they lead the transformation in their units. Their task is to maintain the focus that stimulates further learning.

It is my hypothesis that most managers don't have a theory of management with a distinct management model they intend to create.

As their title implies, all managers use some form of management. In the absence of a theory, there is central command-and-control based on luck. Because management in practice and theory is invisible, but deeply rooted in any organization's culture, there is the accepted attitude that we should 'let sleeping dogs lie' and just get on with things. The transformation to better management is a paradigm shift in line with the four people-centric levers (self-organization, delegation, self-responsibility and focus of attention). It ensures clarity on the intended management theory, follows a deliberate management model, and includes emergent practices through knowledge about what works best. New knowledge is obtained through learning.

Figure 18 summarizes what Diagnostic Mentoring is all about: the three-step process, the executive experience, the essential design decisions and the practice of the inner game (see Chapter 20), which mobilize all of your resources to make the shift to better management.

With this introduction, it is up to you to initiate your Diagnostic Mentoring with your team. It's how you ultimately get to better management.

- Use *Agile by Choice* to initiate the process with traditional managers
- Use *People-Centric Management* to show what enabling managers can do
- Continue with Chapter 3, *The Enabling Operating Environment*, to learn about the new way to manage in today's dynamic and data-driven environment.

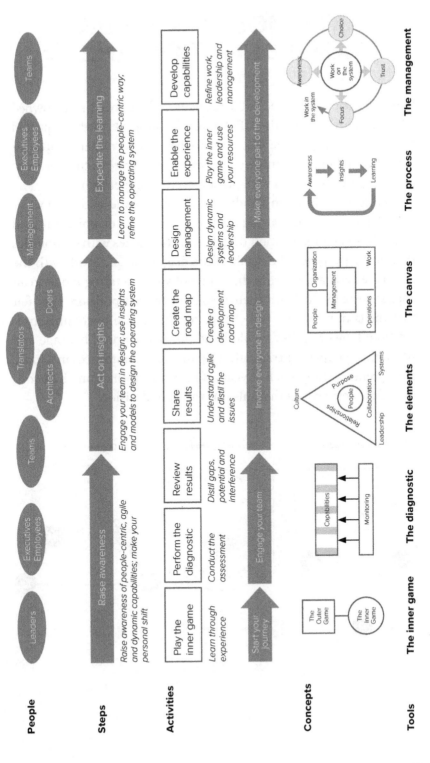

FIGURE 18: DIAGNOSTIC MENTORING

CITY MOBILITY – A BIG TRANSFORMATION AHEAD

In wise anticipation of the full deregulation of the government-owned city transport system, the CEO asked for support on the expected transformation. Imagine that you have been a government employee for life, and then, suddenly, you are asked to operate in the free market, going head-to-head with private-sector competition.

The leadership team conducted the diagnostic with 25 executives (Figure 19). The starting point is a traditional exploitation- and control-driven organization that delivers outcomes with capabilities that fit the purpose. The result of the diagnostic and work with the executives was a shift from the control-based operating mode to an engagement mode. With their dominant market position, they felt that the context would not change much, despite upcoming competition. However, they would build on their cultural heritage and strengthen people-centric leadership to engage employees in a more entrepreneurial approach. A year into the transformation, their continued success proved that this was the right decision.

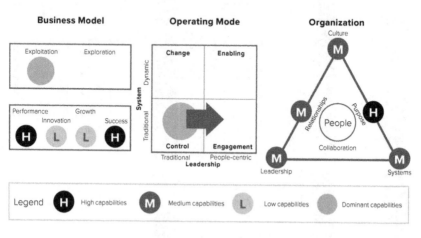

FIGURE 19: CITY MOBILITY

Why would they engage in Diagnostic Mentoring? First, because it was an evolutionary transformation approach that left ample room for individual leadership and solutions. Second, the data-based foundation allowed the leadership team to monitor progress with both an intermediate and a post-transformation diagnostic. Third, the external consulting cost (diagnostic and mentoring) to support the project was far below that of any traditional change project.

DIAGNOSTIC MENTORING

Diagnostic Mentoring is the systems approach for managers to work *on* the operating system through learning, based *on* their experience.

KEY CHAPTER IDEAS

- Work *on* the system enables work *in* the system (good management)
- The systems approach comes with a diagnostic, a model and a process
- Three steps — raising awareness, acting on insights and fast learning — guide the transformation to the new way to manage

ACTION AGENDA

Use Diagnostic Mentoring for your transformation to better management. Engage Diagnostic Mentors with the experience and tools to get there fast.

FURTHER READING

Michel, L (2021). *Agile by Choice: A Workbook for Leaders*. London: LID Publishing.

CHAPTER 3

THE ENABLING OPERATING ENVIRONMENT

Chapter 3 separates the individual and the institution to gain a deep understanding of flow, potential, sources of interference and the enabling operating mode. The enabling operating environment is *what* better management is all about. Diagnostic Mentoring guides you and your team on the way there.

A SCHISM

With *Diagnostic Mentoring,* we have so far discussed the people, management, work and operations dimensions of people-centric, agile and dynamic systems. Now, it is time to separate the individual and the institution for a better understanding of the enabling operating environment.

Today's work requires collaboration and cooperation. As most work involves more than one person, we need to expand our view beyond people and managers. Instead, we should reimagine them all as executives who make decisions in today's knowledge era. To continue the conversation about better management and discuss operating modes, we need to introduce a schism: a critical juncture that splits the executive into leadership (the individual) and systems (the institution).

Executives do not operate in isolation. They work with their management teams, lead people and worry about the functioning of their organization. While 'work *in* the system' is the focus of the *People-Centric Management* book, *Diagnostic Mentoring* turns to 'work *on* the system' and the need for people-centricity and agility in a dynamic context. Figure 20 splits the idea of a single executive into a dualistic view of the individual and the institution.

The Individual: Leadership	The Institution: Systems
The glass is half full or half empty	The glass may need to be twice as big
Work *in* the system	Work *on* the system
People development	Dynamic systems development
Heroic view: leaders as heroes	Post-heroic view: collective minds
Hard: can hardly be changed	Soft: can be changed (contrary to popular belief)
Source of people-centric thinking	The condition that creates the opportunity

FIGURE 20: THE INDIVIDUAL AND THE INSTITUTION

This schism helps us further dig into the sources of people-centric thinking, while at the same time talking about the conditions required to apply better management. As an executive, you have the duty and right (accountability/responsibility) to shape your conditions and those of every individual in your organization.

But, beware: in conflict, the institution always wins. System defects are always personalized. The dramaturgy of failure is always the same. Step 1: people note an institutional interference or error (the 'what *is*'). Then, Step 2 kicks in. The error falls back on the individual (this is the 'what *should be*'). That's why you should simultaneously care about leadership and systems.

We cannot discuss the institution, operating systems and work on the system without a deep understanding of the individual and how he or she impacts design. This is why we first turn to the individual.

Separating the individual and the institution is a deliberate Diagnostic Mentoring action, to dig into the foundations of the enabling operating environment.

THE INDIVIDUAL

Individuals play the inner game to cope with the challenges of the outer game (Figure 21). They make decisions: understand, think, act, engage and adhere. They accept responsibility and are accountable for their results. They source their motivation from a combination of individual responsibility and the opportunities and systems offered by the institution.

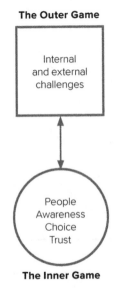

FIGURE 21: THE INDIVIDUAL

To capture relevant opportunities, people must deal with the personal challenges (the inner game) and external challenges (the outer game) they've set out to tackle (Gallwey, 2000). This bridges the outer game to the inner game of work. In that sense, the outer game represents the internal and external challenges people face when they perform. The bridge is needed to ensure that minimal interference occurs from the individual and the organization. Interference limits potential and reduces overall performance.

Individuals — people — are the centre of attention in Diagnostic Mentoring. The goal is to create a work environment that enables people to perform at their peak.

FLOW

Flow (Csikszentmihalyi, 1990) is a concept that's related to the inner game. It is a personal zone where challenges, skills and performance converge, creating a state in which a person performing an activity is fully immersed, has energized focus, and feels full involvement in and enjoyment of the activity. It is Self 2 in action, without the interference of Self 1. Figure 22 shows this defining moment — the 'flow zone.'

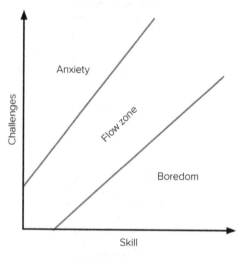

FIGURE 22: FLOW

"Flow also happens when a person's skills are fully involved in over-coming a challenge that is just about manageable, so it acts as a magnet for learning new skills and increasing challenges," Csikszentmihalyi (1990) explains. He continues, "If challenges are too low, one gets back to flow by increasing them. If challenges are too great, one can return to the flow state by learning new skills ... The best moments in our lives are not the passive, receptive, relaxing times ... The best moments usually occur if a person's body or mind is stretched to its limits in a voluntary effort to accomplish something difficult and worthwhile."

Flow is a defining moment. It's when our mind switches from the material world (matter) to the quantum world (energy). It's being *in the here and now*; the past and future collapse into the present. It's where time is infinite and eternal, and space has unlimited dimensions. To reach flow, we need to leave the physical world — to step outside our body — to become a *self*, with infinite possibilities. In this way, we access our true potential. Reaching the state of flow in the here and now requires practice. Awareness and focus of attention are the techniques used to get there.

Flow occurs when we switch from the beta state (thinking mind) to the relaxed and creative alpha state. Most of the day, our brains are governed by the frequency of beta waves. We are awake and our senses are aware. At times, we switch to the alpha state, in which we are quiet, relaxed, creative and intuitive, without thinking and analysing. We're essentially dreaming. In the beta state we focus on the environment, whereas in the alpha state the focus is on us, the inner self.

Too much challenge, not enough safety: Anxiety is everywhere in the workplace, as everyone has too much to do and not enough time to accomplish it. It is the classic situation of losing focus. Everyone and everything demands our attention. One way to ease this situation is to reduce the amount of unnecessary interference from Self 1, concerning things like perfection, over-control and avoidance of risk. Limiting that interference frees up attention capacity for Self 2. Staying focused is the only way to work effectively and efficiently.

Too little challenge, too much safety: When a job demands too little of us, or a task is perceived as routine or unimportant, our focus can be taken over by a sense of boredom. We perceive that we are undervalued and that our capabilities are unused, and this shuts down the receptors of the nervous system, resulting in a condition of non-alertness. This leads to disengagement, with the conclusion that work is boring. Self 2 goes to sleep. The solution is to either bring challenges into work or find more meaningful work to do. Self 2 focus occurs when these inner conflicts are resolved or when all agendas are aligned.

The flow experience, and being able to reach flow more often, is one of the goals of an enabling operating environment, better management and Diagnostic Mentoring.

STRESS AND BOREDOM

Stress interferes with performance and creativity. In situations where stress dominates, the 'prefrontal' (reflective) part of our brain turns off and the rear 'sensory cortex' (reactive) area is activated. This means that in strongly stressful situations, reactivity dominates over reflectiveness. However, with only a little stress, the reflective mode dominates.

Stress switches our mind and body into survival mode. The primitive (sympathetic) nervous system is activated. Blood flow prioritizes the reactive (rear) part of the brain over the reflective (front) portion, and we become primed to use routine and habit in order to react quickly. All our sensing mechanisms — seeing, hearing, feeling, smelling — are on alert. Our energy consumption is quite high, with almost no capacity for creativity or new things.

In stressful situations, Self 1 interferes with Self 2. Boredom is a product of too little stress, which reduces performance, and anxiety results from too much stress, with the same effect. Figure 23 compares male and female stress. Men and women start from different stress levels and have different needs when it comes to optimal performance.

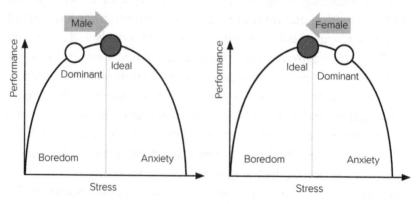

FIGURE 23: STRESS

In simplified terms, men's dominant stress level is slightly on the boredom side. For optimal performance, they need a little push to increase their stress and performance. Women's dominant stress level indicates slight hyperactivity. For them, the ideal level of stress for optimal focus and performance comes from experiencing less pressure. Knowing this difference has huge implications for leadership and the design of the ideal work environment for the inner game. Losing focus moves a person's stress level toward the dominant position, and regaining lost focus moves it in the opposite direction. To regain focus, women need trust and men need motivation.

Better management establishes a work environment that enables people to manage stress in ways that help them perform at their peak level.

THE PERFORMANCE LOOP

Peak performance is a reinforcing loop (Figure 24). With little interference, people can unlock their talents to take on greater challenges. With this, they reach the flow zone, where performance is at its peak. That fuels their ability to play the inner game even better, which closes and reinforces the performance loop.

When people apply their inner game techniques, they have full access to their talents and skills. The inner game helps them better deal with internal and external interference and address greater challenges. These are the conditions where flow occurs; one arrives at the state where skills and challenges match. Staying in the flow zone requires that people continue to apply and refine their inner game techniques. The positive reinforcing loop ('R' in Figure 24) closes, with better performance as the result.

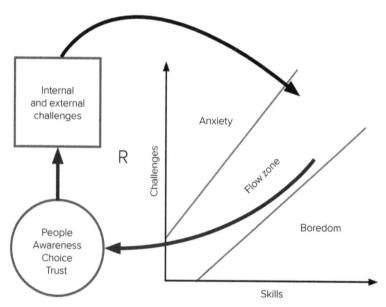

FIGURE 24: THE INDIVIDUAL PERFORMANCE LOOP

When anxiety or boredom prevail (internal challenges) or external challenges interfere, the loop turns negative and reinforces itself. In the context of greater internal and external challenges, it is more difficult to apply the inner game techniques. As a result, people can't apply their skills or challenges may appear too formidable. Both effects prevent people from reaching the flow zone. The negative reinforcing loop closes, with poorer performance as the result.

There's a critical tipping point between the positive and the negative loop. The positive loop keeps us out of anxiety and boredom. It requires little interference and provides conditions where the potential can be applied. With the negative loop, interference prevents the talent from applying its potential.

Two conditions help individuals fall into the negative loop trap: the inability to apply the inner game techniques and little interference from the external environment. The inner game technique is individual and many of the external factors are institutional.

Positive and negative loops can be weak or strong. Often, we don't notice the weak loops. We can easily handle them with our daily routines. Big loops, especially the negatives, require professional attention.

Diagnostic Mentoring makes the tipping points of stress and the performance loop visible, supports individuals' practice of the inner game, and develops the external organizational environment to facilitate the return to the positive loop.

SELF 1 AND SELF 2

The inner game[4] provides techniques to help people cope with greater challenges. Doubts, stress, fear, biased focus, limiting concepts and assumptions can distort our thoughts, decisions, behaviours and actions. This keeps us from operating at our full potential. The art of relaxing our distorting thoughts is called the inner game. Here is a brief introduction.

The inner game (Figure 25) is an organic and natural learning process based on experience. Attention and focus help us to learn by doing things, applying our own experience. This is in sharp contrast to learning by instruction. Instruction is external control. Most instruction compromises the natural abilities of the learner.

Self 1   Self 2

Focus
Awareness
Choice
Trust

FIGURE 25: THE INNER GAME

The voice of giving commands and making judgments is what we call 'Self 1.' 'Self 2' is yourself (Figure 26). Self 1 is the know-it-all who does not trust Self 2. Self 2 is the one who actually performs, although it is challenged by the mistrust implied by the judgment of Self 1. The self-doubt and over-control interfere with the natural learning process. Self 2 is the human being itself, with all its inherent potential and the innate ability to learn.

Self 1	Self 2
Interference that limits my potential	Everything that enables me to use my full potential
Doubts, stress, fear, bias, limiting concepts and assumptions	Resources, skills, attitude

FIGURE 26: SELF 1 AND SELF 2

Perception, response and results are part of every action we take. We have an image of what needs to be done. Then, we respond by performing. This produces the result, which is the action. Between perception (the image) and the action (the response) there is room for interpretation. Meaning is attached to every action, and often to the performer of that action. These meanings impact the actor's performance. Self 1 introduces distortion into every part of the action: distorted perception, distorted response, distorted results, distorted self-image. There must be a better way of dealing with the performer's distortions.

The context in which we perform, learn and work has a huge impact on how effective and satisfying our work is. The external context certainly matters. But, the inner game suggests that the space between our own ears matters even more. All our thoughts, feelings, values, assumptions, definitions, attitudes, desires and emotions matter when it comes to performing demanding tasks. When goals, obstacles and critical variables for success are clear, performance happens in a fulfilling way. However, when internal conflicts dominate — when thoughts and feelings pull in different directions — it's not easy to stay on track. Priorities become blurred, commitments are compromised, and doubts, fears and self-limitations rule. Figure 27 suggests three simultaneous interactions to consider.

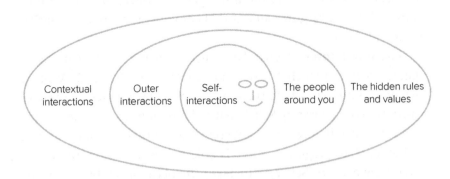

FIGURE 27: THREE PERSONAL INTERACTIONS

Self-interactions do not exist in isolation. They are influenced by the outer interactions we have with the people around us. For example, the quality of your relationships with your boss, your colleagues at work or your sports team impacts how you perform. An insecure boss may overuse control, which impacts the self-confidence of individuals and teams. This then limits both individual and team interactions and performance.

Another interaction also impacts how we work and perform: the conversation that silently happens in the back of your mind. It consists of the hidden rules, values and assumptions that arise from the culture of our context. Corporate culture, for example, shapes the way we think, behave and act, in a positive or negative way. While culture often is the source of all trouble, it is hard to change.

The self-interactions: Many things influence our thinking and get in the way of performance. As humans, we have ample skills, potential and room to think. But Self 1 interference, the invented self, is the voice that is fed by sources outside us and sows doubts that undermine us. Self-doubts lead to fear, judgments, over-control and internal conflicts that disrupt the inner environment in which we perform. This voice sounds like it is coming from a parent, a teacher, a boss or a friend who knows how to conform to the norms and rules within the context that determines the game we play. Self 1 is a voice that wants me, Self 2, to accept that it dictates what I think and do, independent of my own experience and understanding. Listening to Self 2 — the innate, natural self — is an essential challenge of the inner game. A harmonious relationship with Self 2 requires an internal conversation based on clarity, trust and choice.

The outer interactions: The purpose of the inner game is to quieten Self 1 such that it does not interfere with Self 2. Another person can hinder or help the process, either by augmenting Self 1's disruption or facilitating Self 2's natural functioning. The inner game works by introducing a different conversation than the one with Self 1. Rather than judgment, there is objective observation; things are what they are. For Self 2, trust takes the place of doubt or control. Manipulation is replaced by choice. The goal is to shift from a disruptive, confused and self-critical state of mind to one that is focused.

The contextual interactions: Fear, control and power are organizational viruses that can pervade a corporate culture. These invisible conversations have great influence on performance, as they may lead to stress and conflicts, often with unintended consequences.

Recognizing the relationships between the three interactions — the self-interactions, outer interactions and contextual interactions — enables you to change them. To accomplish productive, unhindered self-interactions, you must become aware of yourself, your team and (most challengingly) the context within which you operate.

Awareness, choice, trust and focus of attention help you deal with interference, both self-made and external:

- **Non-judgmental awareness is incredibly powerful,** but too often many of our managerial sensors are on mute
- **The choice of how to perform an action should reside with the performer,** but organizations need to establish boundaries on choice, or people may exceed their allotted space to manoeuvre
- **Trust in Self 2 is the fastest management concept,** but most organizations are built on mistrust
- **Focus of attention** is the key to learning and performance, but we continue to aim at everything that moves

TRUSTING SELF 2

When you are in the flow and rhythm of Self 2, you are inherently satisfied. It gives you the feeling that everything is working and things are coming together. When you experience that state, you naturally try to keep it. Or, if you lose it, you try to make it return. This usually does not work instantly.

When we lose focus, there is conflict between Self 1 and Self 2. What can we do? If we use Self 1 strategies to control Self 2, we will strengthen the taskmaster causing the conflict. If we try to resist Self 1, the interference gets stronger. If we focus on Self 2, we delay its return.

The way to succeed is to trust in Self 2. Acknowledging Self 2 means that you give it any attention you want to. As attention is a scarce resource, giving more attention to Self 2 reduces the attention given to Self 1. Simultaneously, this opens up the resources that you have available from Self 2.

IGNORING SELF 1

Self 1 is creative and subtle in the strategies and techniques it uses to interfere. And, it's easy to use Self 1 to distract anyone else's Self 2. The examples of successes are endless. Self 1's whispers are just around the corner. Some mean them well; others use them to their own advantage. Whether it is to undermine confidence or build up an ego, all they have to do is to command a certain amount of attention from their victims. The only way to make the inner game beneficial for all parties is to make the decision to tune out Self 1. Focus is both the best defence and best offence against interference from Self 1.

The distinction between Self 1 and Self 2 helps to identify the potential and interference that originate from *within* people and those that come from *the outside,* created by challenges and the organizational context.

INTRODUCING BARRY

Let me introduce you to Barry (Figure 28). He or she is the master of interference, but means well. Barry keeps the performance potential loop from exploding.

FIGURE 28: BARRY

Hi, I am Barry. I am with you today. Anytime. Anyplace. Intentionally. Willingly. Irrevocably.

I am your 'Chief Executive Officer' and live in the prefrontal cortex of your brain. May I call you by your first name? I think I will. As your friend (most of the time), I love to play. Let's have fun together. Think of me as your personal St Bernard companion. I have a lot to offer:

- I am always with you
- I have booze in case you need it
- I need a lot of attention
- I am amiable and need space
- I come in typical Swiss style

Imaginary Barry represents your Self 1, sits in your head and is part of you and your performance. When Barry is quiet, there is high focus and free flow. Your talents are engaged, and performance is at its peak. Barry is busy with himself. However, when Barry is active, he distorts your focus and prevents your flow. Barry uses your time, gets your attention and consumes all your energy. Good for Barry; bad for you and your performance.

Barry means well. He keeps you from overusing your potential and energy, preventing the reinforcing performance-potential loop (R) from exploding or imploding (Figure 29).

With the balancing loop (B), interference keeps you from exploiting the potential. More interference means less potential. In reverse, less interference means more potential and better performance.

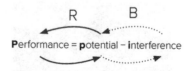

R   B

Performance = potential − interference

FIGURE 29: REINFORCING AND BALANCING LOOPS

The uncontrolled positive loop is a frequent source of burnout. Barry interferes and prevents you from getting in trouble. Barry is your imaginary balancing loop. Therefore, take good care of Barry.

Sometimes you, your self-interactions and inner conversation are the catalyst for Barry to become active. Sometimes it's your team (your outer interactions) or work environment — your institution with the contextual interactions. Barry knows the difference and decides on where and how to become active. Your strategy must be to trust yourself and ignore Barry for most of the time. But, always maintain the dialogue with Barry. He keeps you out of trouble. The inner game is the technique to do that.

Understanding the potential and acknowledging Barry are important parts of Diagnostic Mentoring. Barry is one source of interference. The institution is another source. Barry is in your hands. Unless you are the owner or manager, the institution is not. That's why we now need to look at the institution.

THE INSTITUTION

Most work requires more than one participant. That's why we need institutions. Institutions come as organizations that serve different purposes and are driven by different motives.

Figure 30 bridges the institution's operating system and the context at work to show the challenges of the outer game that people and the institution accept. "The greater the external challenges accepted by a company, team or individual, the more important it is that there is minimum interference occurring from within," explained Gallwey (2000). In this light, the job of the leader is to create a work environment that limits the negative effects of Self 1 so that Self 2 can accept greater challenges. But, Gallwey added, "Resistance to change within the corporation is rooted in the prevailing command and control corporate culture" (Gallwey, 2000).

For the purpose of Diagnostic Mentoring, let's call the institution work.org. For you and Barry to perform well, work.org's operating system and management must have a design that fits the challenges of the institution. The ideal design for significant challenges is the enabling operating mode. With this, the people who work at work.org can perform effectively, innovation takes place, and the institution grows. The operating system and the ability to deal with the challenges create a reinforcing loop that delivers performance, innovation and growth.

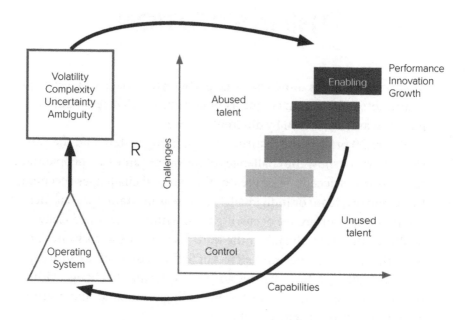

FIGURE 30: THE INSTITUTIONAL PERFORMANCE LOOP

For work.org, the flow zone corresponds to management fitness or agile maturity levels, two concepts that will be discussed in Chapters 8 and 20. Both competency models indicate increasing levels of capabilities to deal with challenges. They are indicative of higher levels of performance, innovation and growth.

When work.org operates in a control mode, it is unable to deal with a dynamic context. As a result, capabilities are unused and the operation delivers mediocre performance, little innovation and no growth.

In a work environment with little interference, the operating system helps people unfold their potential, with performance, innovation and growth as the results. As we will see later in this chapter, the enabling mode presents the characteristics of an operating system with little interference, where people can exercise their full potential.

That's why a large part of Diagnostic Mentoring focuses on understanding the potential, and the design of management and organization that minimizes interference. An enabling operating environment is designed to minimize interference and focus on supporting people's potential.

WHEN BARRY AND I MEET WORK.ORG

With little interference from work.org, Barry and I operate in the flow zone and perform at our peak. Consequently, work.org gets work done, resulting in institutional performance, innovation and growth. Figure 31 shows the reinforcing loops between Barry, work.org and me. The operating system establishes a work environment that facilitates the application of inner game techniques. As such, Barry, work.org and I are able to deal with greater challenges. The positive performance loop dominates.

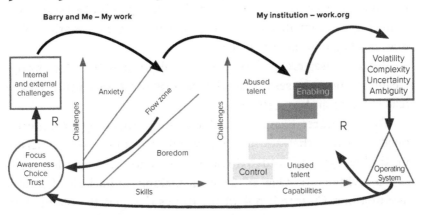

FIGURE 31: THE POSITIVE PERFORMANCE LOOP

Likewise, Figure 32 shows the example of the negative performance loop. If, for various reasons, the operating system is infected, work.org's combination of capabilities and challenges gets out of balance.

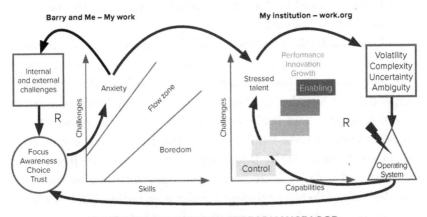

FIGURE 32: THE NEGATIVE PERFORMANCE LOOP

Barry and I, and all others at work.org, feel that our talent gets abused. The operating system has a design that forces leaders to put pressure on people without respecting current capabilities. Pressure creates stress and diminishes performance. Pressure also leads to anxiety. People are afraid to expose themselves or tackle challenges that involve risks. With pressure, internal and external challenges grow, which makes it more difficult for people to apply the inner game — the techniques that bring about peak performance. At worst, people mentally, and perhaps even physically, resign. Getting out of the context of a toxic culture, flawed leadership or broken systems is a much greater challenge than making sure that the negative spiral does not begin in the first place.

When viruses creep into an organization, it is time for spring-cleaning. These viruses might take the form of a toxic culture, flawed leadership or broken systems.

Toxic culture: Examples include faulty operating procedures, business values that are not clearly linked to outcomes, cynicism, upward delegation, outdated reasons for centralized decision-making, a technocratic view of decision-making and a lack of shared assumptions. Culture is one of the things that gets the blame. But, culture is an outcome — it's a feature that cannot be changed directly. A toxic culture creates subtle dissonances that are hard to detect. Fixing culture requires altering systems and leadership through workshops, mentoring and/or corporate programmes that are well crafted and professionally orchestrated. A defective culture's roots always lie in flawed leadership or broken systems. So, the task is to fix leadership or systems first.

Flawed leadership: Examples include excessive control, busyness, lack of time, disproportionate attention to detail, senselessness, obsessive focus on numbers and minimal added value. Normally, organizations hire the best and train them to stay that way, or to fit given templates. Bad leadership normally comes in counts of one. If otherwise, we have a different problem for which the only fix is replacement of an entire leadership team. As such, the flaw can be located and isolated, as it normally resides with one person (or a small group of them). Replacing a leader is an option, but it normally comes too late. And viruses spread. An immediate reaction is evident.

Fixing a leader takes time, and toxins might still spread for a while. It is expensive and the likelihood of success is questionable, despite the promises of a huge 'leadership-fixing' industry. Coaching or training flawed leaders is ineffective. Performance problems can be fixed where there is a will to learn. Behavioural problems (or a mixture of performance and behavioural problems) require a different course of action.

Broken systems: Examples include bureaucratic or non-existent routines, formalism, faulty design, revisiting past decisions, slow implementation that hampers decision-making, rules infected with the 'viruses,' and ineffective tools. Normally, it is a specific set of systems that cause flawed leadership. Common culprits include management by objectives, incentives, budgeting, resource allocation and communications. When any of these is broken, it affects the entire organization. Systems viruses have huge leverage. Human resources, financial officers, risk officers, governance officers, and all other support officers are often the cause rather than a symptom. They may be individually optimized but not aligned. Fixing systems is critical and affects the entire organization, so it is often a risk. But, not doing anything is not an option. It is comparatively cheap to fix broken systems. It is a free choice and it can be done quickly. Yet, simply fixing the toolbox might not be good enough. It might require a new design, for example, to fundamentally rethink the way you lead the organization.

The symptoms of a broken operating system are everywhere. The causes often lie with the tools, routines or rules that govern the prevailing management model. All of these are signs of a toxic culture that's missing energy or is lacking in flow experiences. The result is crippled creativity and stagnation.

Diagnostic Mentoring decodes these viruses, designs better management and healthy organizations, and installs an operating system that supports peak performance throughout the institution. The enabling work environment limits interference — it removes a toxic culture, flawed leadership and broken systems.

LOGISTICS
– THE FIRST 100 DAYS

Usually, CEOs have 100 days to sort out what needs to be fixed. In this case, a much faster answer was required. Increased global competition, with ongoing cost-cutting and multiple in-process change programmes, was our first-day observation. With this, 25 executives from around the world participated in the diagnostic, and helped roll out a subsequent transformation programme.

The diagnostic results revealed a number of truths (Figure 33). The organization was unprepared to face the most serious challenges, and the leadership team had stalled, with little constructive response to the prevailing situation. They were waiting for the order from above. A low level of agile maturity was reflected in faulty (or nonexistent) leadership, and systems that could not cope with a challenging context. Strong relationships among the existing team did not make the situation any easier. 'We know how things are done around here!' was the general attitude.

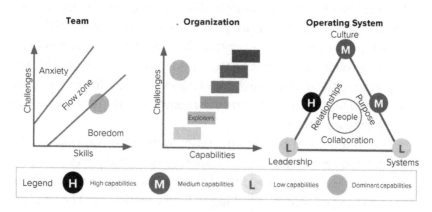

FIGURE 33: LOGISTICS

After the immediately-needed shake-up of the leadership team, a decision was made to completely redo the firm's operating system and build agile capabilities. Within 20 days, the ongoing change projects were stopped, and a fundamental rework of all managerial systems was initiated. Parallel to that, the CEO started working to build a fresh, new team that would move quickly to proactively address the company's challenges. The company's action came literally at the last minute, if not already too late.

THREE
CAPABILITIES

For management to perform at a high level of fitness, and organizations to operate at agile maturity in a challenging market context, three capabilities are needed (Figure 34):

- **People-centric** management (*People-Centric Management*, Michel, 2020)
- **Agile** organization (*The Performance Triangle*, Michel, 2013)
- **Dynamic** operating system (*Management Design*, Michel, 2017 2nd Ed.)

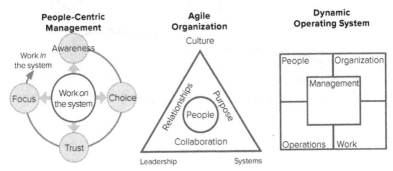

FIGURE 34: THREE CAPABILITIES

Being people-centric is a necessary management attribute if an organization is to benefit from talented people who possess skills, knowledge and a high-performance attitude. People-centric management follows the principles of self-responsibility, delegation, self-organization and focus of attention. Such enabling management is in sharp contrast to traditional management, where authoritarian control and command prevail.

The people-centric ecosystem (Figure 35) consists of enabling systems and supporting leadership that function as a positive loop, with our old friend Barry and sufficient resources to balance out the ecosystem. Leadership and systems enable people to apply inner-game techniques that allow them to fully use their talent. With an enabling environment, people are able to face down ever-greater challenges. The reinforcing loop sets in. Barry and a toolbox of resources ensure that the positive or negative reinforcing loop remains within limits.

Work *in* the system aims to support both the reinforcing and the balancing loop. People-centric leaders work with systems that help people quieten Barry down, fully apply their capabilities and use their resources wisely. People-centric management means responsible leadership and supportive systems.

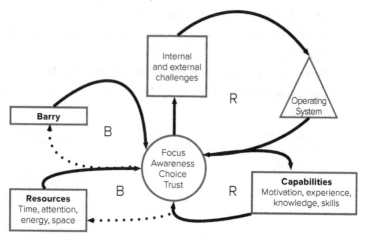

FIGURE 35: THE PEOPLE-CENTRIC ECOSYSTEM

As such, people-centric management requires work *on* the system. That work consists of making sure systems and leadership meet the needs of people, helping them play the inner game — dealing with Barry, and ensuring the effective use of resources and capabilities. Effective use implies the productive utilization of time, attention, energy and space. Doing this all effectively also means that there's room (and budget) to refuel limited resources. Doing this will help build out the organization's stores of experience, knowledge and skills.

Agile is the necessary feature of organizations in support of people-centric management. Agile creates a work environment where people serve their customers in ways that generate positive returns for the organization and its stakeholders.

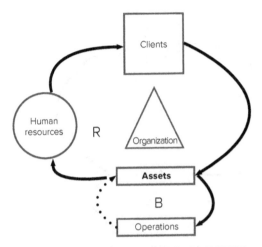

FIGURE 36: THE AGILE ECOSYSTEM

The agile ecosystem (Figure 36) consists of an organization with a shared culture, interactive leadership and an effective operating system. Managers use the operating system to make investment decisions on assets and human resources. People with the right talents satisfy customers, who ultimately come back and want more. Returning customers add to the growth of assets that can then be reinvested. Organizations with the right operating systems have assets that require investments. Agile means that there is a shared culture, interactive leadership and a supportive operating system. None of these three elements come for free. The need to continuously invest balances the reinforcing loop of organizations that nurture customers who come back.

Dynamic is the feature of operating systems that enables people to cope with the challenges of VUCA. The ability of people, the organization, work, operations and management to address a challenging environment better than the competition drives growth and considerably reduces costs and operational risks.

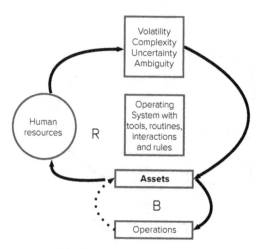

FIGURE 37: THE DYNAMIC ECOSYSTEM

The dynamic feature of an operating ecosystem (Figure 37) consists of rules, routines and tools that facilitate interactive leadership. Meaningful interactions and the diagnostic feature of systems enable people to deal with greater challenges. Such operating systems with dynamic features come with tools that can handle volatility, routines that deal with complexity, interactions for uncertainty and rules for dealing with ambiguity. The dynamic features of an operating system require the specific design of the rules, routines, tools and interactions. Design is a deliberate investment in an operating system that enables people, the organization, work, operations and management to handle adversity better than others. And that is a true competitive advantage.

In a people-centric, agile and dynamic operating context, Barry is out of work. He is quiet and lets you perform. People can reach their flow state more often without interference from Barry and 'the organization.' They can play the inner game and perform at their peak with the outer game. That operating context comes with a high level of managerial fitness, agile maturity throughout the organization, and the dynamic features of the operating systems. Making it so is a deliberate choice every manager has to make.

People-centric, agile and dynamic are the features of an enabling operating environment. Diagnostic Mentoring ensures that these features become part of better management.

OPERATING MODES

Operating modes offer choice. This chapter offers four operating modes as a powerful response to the challenges and opportunities of the new dynamic business environment. Each mode comes with the capabilities that support the choice, and they are designed for different outcomes.

These four modes combine specific capabilities based on the principles, means and systems of your choosing. Shifting the levers creates a variety of alignment options (Figure 38).

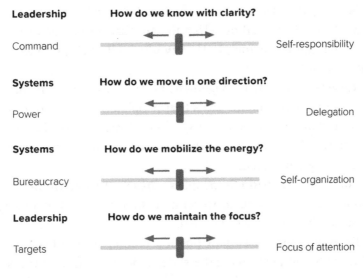

FIGURE 38: ALIGNMENT OPTIONS

Here is a brief introduction to what the principles mean.[5]

With the **command** principle, managers tell people what they should be doing. The underlying assumption is that employees cannot think and act for themselves, so they need to be controlled by managers. It's an assumption whose time has passed, but still dominates management practice.

Self-responsibility assumes that people have all the skills and knowledge to think, decide and act on their own. It's a capability that most people own. With accountability for work, most people grow.

Power is the principle in which hierarchy dominates. Managers at the top decide and client-facing employees implement. It's the classic hierarchical division between thinking and doing.

Delegation requires that decisions and actions be decentralized to where the knowledge resides and where the skills are. This requires that managers let go of traditional control, in order to assume new control at a higher level.

In **bureaucracies**, people follow detailed procedures to get things done. While they ensure efficiency, quality and consistency, they fail when context changes. No work can be done without routines. But, they should not get in the way of doing what makes the best sense.

Self-organization is the principle by which the organization of work is determined by self-sufficient teams that get work done. It's a demanding principle that works well with knowledgeable, skilled people.

Targets represent management by objectives, with detailed and prescriptive performance goals that people have committed to. Just because that's 'what we've always done' doesn't mean that it works well all the time. Targets are the cause of significant interference in modern organizations.

Focus of attention is people's capacity to determine what is important and what needs to get done first. It's a skill that everyone possesses. It just needs to be used.

By design, there are many possible combinations of these levers, achieved by simply moving the sliders. However, from our research we know that four combinations of capabilities are needed to cover most business cases.

For this discussion, we need a deeper understanding of what we call operating modes. They present four distinct ways to manage people and organizations. First, we select systems and leadership as the controls that facilitate management. Second, we separate traditional from people-centric and dynamic managerial responses. The result of these combinations is four operating modes, as mapped in Figure 39 with the enabling mode as an example.

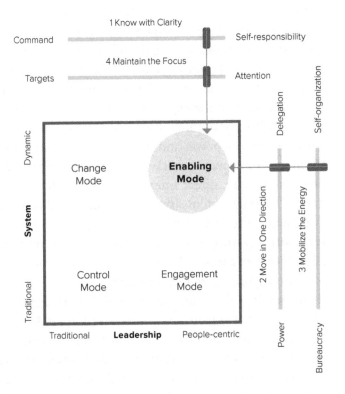

FIGURE 39: ALIGNED OPERATING MODES

Leadership and systems anchor the framework, with four operating modes: control, engagement, change and enabling. With systems, organizations respond to the changing, VUCA-challenged business context. Leadership is the answer to the need for knowledge among people in the changing work environment.

- **Control**: In a stable environment where knowledge is concentrated at the top, traditional management and institutional control dominate. The thinking and doing are separated, which justifies traditional, bureaucratic control. Traditional management applies direct control through narrow targets. Interactions focus on disseminating strategy and ruling performance. Decisions are made by leaders and narrow targets maintain the focus to keep people on track.
- **Engagement**: In a knowledge-driven environment with little change, the engagement mode dominates. People (the ends)

are tightly controlled by traditional means. People-centric leadership supports self-responsible people guided by broad direction. Management aligns individual interests through visions, beliefs, boundaries and values. As Simons (1995) observes, "In the absence of management action, self-interested behaviour at the expense of organizational goals is inevitable." Self-responsibility and broad direction are balanced with hierarchical power and institutional bureaucracy.

- **Change:** In a dynamic market environment with centralized decision-making, direct intervention through change dominates. Dynamic systems (the means) meet traditional ways to lead people (the ends). Change modes operate through a market control setting where managers alter the resource base, align interests through incentives and restructure accountability in response to market changes.

- **Enabling:** In a dynamic context with knowledge distributed throughout the organization, the enabling mode dominates. People-centric leadership (the ends) and dynamic systems (the means) match. Traditional rules-based management approaches are not effective. Under these conditions, enabling modes support fast decision-making and proactive, flexible action, which together lead to robust outcomes.

Diagnostic Mentoring offers a choice with a clear preference for the enabling operating mode for most organizations in today's operating environment.

THE ENABLING MODE

Enabling is the best choice for businesses that want to operate based on people-centric management, agile organization and a dynamic operating system.

In a dynamic context with knowledge distributed throughout the organization, the enabling mode (Figure 40) dominates. People-centric leadership (the ends) and dynamic systems (the means) match.

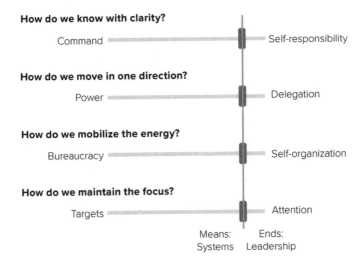

How do we know with clarity?
Command — Self-responsibility

How do we move in one direction?
Power — Delegation

How do we mobilize the energy?
Bureaucracy — Self-organization

How do we maintain the focus?
Targets — Attention

Means: Ends:
Systems Leadership

FIGURE 40: ENABLING MODE

Self-managed workgroups and wider spans of control decrease the importance of direct managerial influence and increase the interpersonal influence and lateral coordination to direct and motivate work. This requires peer control as the process, where peers direct attention, motivate and encourage performance.

Enabling mode organizations require people-centric managerial competencies and a talent base that favours creativity and continuous innovation. Learning, and access to knowledge through networks, is as essential as their approach to continuously reassessing their resource base. Change is ongoing, but not as a disruptive process. It is the dynamic systems capability that makes these organizations agile and nimble.

The enabling operating mode is the choice of better management. The following chapters expand the concept with people-centric principles, agile capabilities and dynamic systems to make the enabling operating mode work. The enabling mode is the ultimate response to the business context in the 21st century.

THREE TRIGGERS

Three triggers initiate the transformation to the enabling operating mode. We often hear from executive teams that they 'need to be more people-centric, agile, dynamic.' Unless you've already made that decision, here are three triggers to help you get going. They ask for a change in the design of leadership and systems:

- **Interference and unused potential**: when your organization lacks performance
- **Faulty operating mode**: when your leadership and systems are stuck in old modes
- **Change in context**: when your business environment has changed

INTERFERENCE AND UNUSED POTENTIAL

When interference and unused potential limit performance (Figure 41), it's time to consider the people-centric shift. You notice interference when your leadership requires lots of time to fix what should be normal. When fluctuation increases, it's time to look at unused potential.

Interference stems from erroneous systems, faulty leadership or a virus-infected culture. All three require a fix. The fix may need a shift to people-centric — for example, tools in the toolbox that don't fit create undesired behaviours. Or, self-responsibility and detailed performance targets don't fit. The results default to control, which limits motivation and engagement.

Unused potential is a major cost driver. It doesn't make sense to hire the best talent and then limit their engagement. Systems and leadership are a frequent cause of such inefficiencies. For example, control-oriented leadership may drive efficiency, but it limits creativity. As we noted earlier, when people take orders, they will follow these orders but do no more. As a result, organizations miss out on the creative potential and, eventually, the innovation capacity.

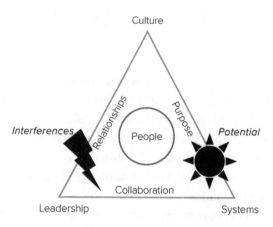

FIGURE 41: INTERFERENCE AND POTENTIAL

What do you fix first: leaders, culture or systems? Imagine that you've decided to make the shift to people-centric, agile and dynamic. Where do you start your intervention?

Culture? It is an outcome that requires interventions in leadership and systems. Over time, this will result in an effective culture.

Leadership? This is where most fixing starts. But, why would you train leaders to come back in on Monday morning only to find themselves in the same mess?

Here is what works best: First, fix systems, and then train leaders to use them interactively. Over time, this will establish a strong shared culture. Remove systems interference before developing leaders.

In their *Harvard Business Review* article, 'Why Leadership Training Fails — and What to Do About It,' management consultants Michael Beer, Magnus Finnström and Derek Schrader (2016) make the following point: "The problem was that even well-trained and motivated employees could not apply their new knowledge and skills when they returned to their units, which were entrenched in established ways of doing things. In short, the individuals had less power to change the system surrounding them than the system had to shape them."

Systems that define roles, routines and rules have a strong impact on individuals' mindsets and behaviours. If the system does not change, it will set people up to fail.

FAULTY OPERATING MODE

When your business functions in the wrong operating mode, you can expect interference to take over and opportunities to be lost.

The degree of external challenges and the distribution of knowledge are the two triggers that determine the choice of your operating mode.

Rules-based and engagement-based modes work in a stable environment. A dynamic environment needs dynamic capabilities. And, knowledge-based management is rooted in the engagement mode, with people-centric capabilities. Context and operations need to match.

CHANGE IN CONTEXT

When VUCA conditions change, it's time to adjust your operating mode.

For example, fixed performance targets and volatility don't go together. In a fast-changing context, annual goals prevent people from adapting to the change. Remember, targets are agreed upon, so they represent a contract between the employee and the organization. It's unfair to ask an employee to bend a contract and accept a disadvantage in order to follow the change. A system that works well in a stable environment may turn against employees and the organization when the context changes.

How do you know? Over the last 20 years, we've learned that it makes sense to diagnose your context and the operating system for viruses and unused potential. Such diagnosis offers a neutral outside perspective, with clarity on what requires change and how to initiate that development.

I also understand why it's hard to leave traditional approaches. Few leaders are willing to abandon their comfort zone for the chaos of uncharted territory. It's a risk. And the Dunning-Kruger Effect (Dunning, 2011) points to many leaders overestimating their own capabilities, and those of their organization, in making the shift. As a leader, self-confidence is essential; it is part of any leader's DNA. But, overconfidence and being risk-averse are like boomerangs. Demotivation and the feeling that change is impossible spread like a virus in teams. That leader gets very lonely, giving rise to the conviction that it's the leader who has to do all the work. And so, there we are, stuck in a vicious circle.

The enabling operating mode is better management, and it's every manager's primary job. Diagnostic Mentoring is the guide for managers and their teams to work *on* the system and develop the enabling mode. Clarity on the specific trigger initiates the transformation.

SPECIALTY FOODS
– EXECUTIVE TRANSITION

Leaving a great legacy is more an art than a science. The founder had long passed retirement age and was searching for ideas on how to build a management team that could take over. Founders and entrepreneurs are alike in the sense that they know how to manage. They are present every day and in constant contact with their employees. With these conversations, they convey their story and spread their motivation through an entire organization. Going forward, systems need to replace part of that personal touch.

The diagnostic results (Figure 42) with 25 key leaders uncovered what it would take to replace the founder and CEO with a leadership team. The decision was that the process to prepare for the transition needed a team approach.

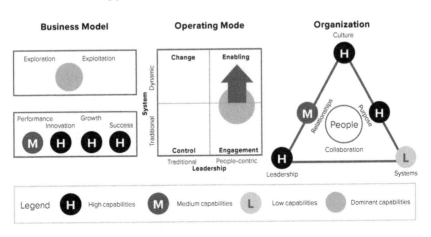

FIGURE 42: SPECIALTY FOODS

Thirty-five executives conducted the diagnostic and participated in the subsequent team workshop. With superb outcomes, a dominant enabling mode and high scores on organizational capabilities, the table stakes for the start were high. Only systems needed work. It's not that they were erroneous; they were non-existent. Over the lifecycle of the firm, it never felt necessary to establish an operating system that enabled leaders to function without the founder present.

The process of developing systems had to first ensure that the basics for management of a company were put in place. This included measurement, strategic planning, performance and risk management. Second, the design of these systems needed to support the enabling mode, with delegated decision-making authority and self-organization at its core. That would then shift the business model even further to the exploration mode, without losing the core implementation capabilities.

The two-day team workshop established the shared intent with all leaders. They created the agenda for a one-year development road map, where the missing systems were to be developed on the go. Rather than going through a concept phase, we supported the client performing the management processes as they were needed — essentially, on-the-job training. After a year, I received a report that the founder was only seen once a month going through the factory. The newly established executive team was in charge.

THE ENABLING OPERATING ENVIRONMENT

The new way to manage comes from the enabling mode. To make sense of enabling management, we need to separate the needs of the individual and those of the organization. However, getting there requires everyone to participate.

KEY CHAPTER IDEAS

- Barry helps us separate Self 1 and Self 2. Flow helps us avoid boredom and stress
- Work.org introduces potential and interference in the search for peak performance
- People-centric, agile and dynamic capabilities are needed for better management
- Four operating modes offer a choice. Enabling is the better choice
- The enabling mode characterizes the desired features
- Getting there is everyone's responsibility

ACTION AGENDA

Use the insights from the individuals' and institution's views to raise awareness for the enabling operating mode.
Be aware of potential, interference, assumptions and principles.

FURTHER READING

Michel, L (2020). *People-Centric Management: How Managers Use Four Levers to Bring Out the Greatness of Others.* London: LID Publishing.

PART II

AGILE ORGANIZATION

Part II introduces Diagnostic Mentoring Step 1: Raise Awareness, to identify the dimensions and elements of an agile organization with the Performance Triangle model. Part II initiates the learning journey with the diagnostic that makes intangibles visible and ready for discussion. It offers the observation points that direct the focus to critical issues requiring managerial attention.

CHAPTER 4

RAISE AWARENESS

Chapter 4 introduces Diagnostic Mentoring Step 1: Raise Awareness, of the transformation journey with diagnostic feedback, the canvas and the Performance Triangle model. The chapter offers an overview of the people, organization, work, operations and management dimensions that will help us identify the interference and the potential. We further introduce the executive briefing that we'll use to challenge assumptions, identify useful principles and start addressing the gaps.

CAPABILITY MONITORING

Are current capabilities in support of people-centric, agile and dynamic? Step 1 diagnoses current operations, and the context, to understand what needs to become people-centric, agile and dynamic.

Monitoring is the discipline to observe and alter capabilities. By observing (scanning) capabilities, potential faults and malfunctions can be spotted at an early stage. By becoming aware of critical signals, potential design requirements can be identified. With this, leaders can decide whether or not to address the issues. As such, monitoring initiates changes in capabilities.

Distance, new perspectives, critique and multi-voice input are integral parts of the monitoring. Taking a step back, observing and challenging the use of capabilities compensates for the risks of getting locked in. And so, organizations need to review their tools, routines and behaviours in view of their specific context.

Monitoring is risk management. The use of managerial tools and processes is selective. For every context, leaders select the specific systems that support them in managing their organization in that specific context. When the context changes, the toolbox also needs to change. Diagnosing systems, leadership and culture prevents organizations from misapplying tools, ignoring critical events or being threatened by changes in their operating context.

Taking an arms-length stance, observation and critique of design and capabilities helps compensate for risks, such as thoughtless reproduction of organizational designs and capabilities through path dependency, structural inertia and lock-in. Early warning systems, including monitoring and reflection, can help reduce these risks. This first step, raising awareness, is such an early warning system.

People-centric principles, agile capabilities and dynamic systems are not directly observable. They require indirect measurement. Monitoring as institutionalized, rules-based reflection is a non-routine practice. If such monitoring is to succeed, it must be kept open; it must not become subject to closed-down routinization. Only then is it possible to detect extraordinary signals that call the validity of current design and capabilities into question.

Monitoring must include the internal and external environment. While internal factors can be identified, external factors are wide open and largely without boundaries. Crises are regularly preceded by weak signals. The interpretation of weak signals requires skills (Ansoff, 1980).

Design scanning and observation should follow systematic methods for generating, modifying and improving capabilities. The monitoring routines themselves need to be updated repeatedly to prevent traps and path-effects. Professional agile insights diagnostics ensure effective monitoring, with continuous investments in the tool to prevent these traps.

It is important to encourage all units, subunits and individual members of an organization to actively participate in capability monitoring. Providing a supportive context and social climate is therefore a key task for effective monitoring. Leadership briefings establish the context and set the rules for a non-political approach to design monitoring.

Capability monitoring is too costly to own and perform in-house for most organizations. Consequently, it makes sense to use an outside supplier with expertise, experience and investment in professional diagnostics.

Step 1: Raise Awareness comes with the following:

The diagnostic: a professional set of tools to review capabilities.

The executive briefing: the feedback session with the executive in charge to review the potential and sources of interference, and to challenge assumptions and principles.

The canvas: the one-page recording tool for capturing structured conversions.

This step uses the Performance Triangle model to identify agile capabilities.

WHERE TO START

The scale of an organization-wide transformation task can be huge. Successful transformations I've seen hardly ever start with a budget or from the top. But, as I have said, agile, people-centric and dynamic are capabilities that permeate an entire organization. As such, limited department or team efforts to transform to new capabilities have little chance of survival.

So, where to start? What are the characteristics of successful transformations? The following is what we have learned from organizations we've accompanied on this journey.

It's starts with the idea. Often, the idea comes from an individual who sees the need for a positive approach and seeds the thought. That person can come from anywhere in the organization. Most often, though, that champion is someone from middle management, positioned close to where the decision is made and connected to people on the ground.

- **It can be anywhere**. Do you need to start at the top, in the middle or with a department? Experience tells us that agile development must range across an organization where people need to collaborate. That can be a department, a geographic unit or a larger organization, as a 'how.' And, it must have the right, and the ability, to change systems, leadership and culture.
- **Diagnosis establishes awareness**. Apart from providing the data for the transformation, diagnosis creates awareness of what is and what matters. This is an essential condition for people to contribute with their ideas.
- **Motivation comes from participation**. Dynamic capabilities are context- and organization-specific. People-centric is individual to every leader. Hence, engaging leaders and employees in evaluating and developing agile is a must.
- **Design creates prototypes**. Dynamic capabilities are specific and in need of tailoring. Copy and paste does not work. People-centric, for most, is untested ground. It requires a decision on mindsets, skills and tools. That decision is all about design. Prototypes help keep options open and refinement loops going.

- **It's a development, not a project**. People-centric principles require agile design and development, based on an organic and people-centric approach. Traditional project management is built on traditional management, with control and command in mind. It's the best way to kill the idea at square one. Having said that, agile development is focused and disciplined. Progress will be assessed, and feedback helps steer adjustments based on what's been learned.
- **Top management must support it**. The transformation changes management from traditional to people-centric. And, the accountability for managerial systems lies with management. It's a responsibility that cannot be delegated. Top management must establish the umbrella, the frame and the mindset for the transformation.
- **A mentor can help**. Because there is nothing new in this world, external experience can help accelerate the development. Reflection, diversity and interaction with people from different backgrounds stimulate the conversations and energize the development. I believe that most organizations possess the capabilities to make the transformation. Occasional mentoring keeps the development on track.

Keeping these characteristics in mind will help you figure out what the transformation might look like in your organization.

INITIALIZE DIAGNOSTIC MENTORING

We have identified Diagnostic Mentoring as a team effort, decided on the triggers that require action and determined where to start. With this, here are the initial steps to engage in Diagnostic Mentoring:

1. **Purpose**: Articulate the purpose of the intervention.
2. **Diagnostic Mentor**: Engage a mentor to support you and your team.
3. **Diagnostic**: Identify the diagnostic that fits the challenge.
4. **Participants**: Identify the diagnostic participants.
5. **Leader**: Determine a project leader.
6. **Timing**: Decide on when to start and end the assessment.
7. **Plan**: Establish the schedule for Steps 1 and 2.
8. **Invitation**: Draft the email invitation to participants and send it off.

Purpose: Insufficient business results and missing alignment with strategy are the most prominent triggers of Diagnostic Mentoring.

Diagnostic Mentors: These are experts who come with the business experience of many capability design and development projects, in all sorts of organizations.

Participants: The diagnostic requires very few participants to yield statistically significant results. The number of participants should be determined by the size of the team that needs to be engaged in the entire process.

Leader: Executives should assign an internal project leader with the task of managing the overall transformation. We call this individual an *agile supervisor*. Appendix 2 outlines the job profile.

Timing: In our experience, 10 days, from start to finish, for all participants to conduct the diagnostic offers the best returns. It takes 10-25 minutes to conduct the diagnostic.

Plan: Step 1: Raise Awareness, and Step 2: Act on Insights, can be scheduled in great detail. Step 1 normally takes about 14 days. Step 2 requires another seven days. Experience tells us that companies should complete Steps 1 and 2 in a maximum of three weeks. Many have done it faster.

Invitation: It is good practice to initiate the project and the assessment with an email that's sent by the executive in charge to all participants, with the following content: purpose, timing, next steps and contacts for help.

The transformation to better management with a diagnostic raises expectations among participants. This is why it's worthwhile to leverage the experience of experts who maintain professional diagnostic tools designed for specific purposes. Diagnostic Mentors are trained and certified to support their clients from start to finish.

THE DIAGNOSTIC

Capability monitoring with a professional, research-based diagnostic tool creates awareness and the necessary insights for managers to develop people-centric, agile and dynamic capabilities.

The questions force participants to step back, observe from a distance and challenge the current management and organization in a non-threatening environment. As institutionalized reflection and non-routine monitoring, the diagnostic detects weak signals and serves as an early warning system.

The diagnostic is an online questionnaire for managers and employees that takes less than half an hour to complete and is available with 33, 47, 59 and 102 questions. Unlike traditional employee surveys, the diagnostic yields significant results with as few as seven participants. It's therefore not necessary to involve an entire organization, which would only create false expectations.

The diagnostic is extensively documented in *The Performance Triangle* book (Michel, 2013) with definitions of all factors, their visual presentation, their foundation in research, examples, business cases and tips for crafting the right design. The diagnostic has been extensively tested in practice and validated through independent research (Nold et al., 2018).

Seven dimensions combine agile organization, people-centric management, dynamic capabilities and outcomes:
- **Agile organization**: Maturity, 11 Performance Triangle elements
- **People-centric management**: 10 people-centric levers, 20 Leadership Scorecard elements
- **Dynamic capabilities**: four dynamic levers, speed, agility, resilience, 15 Leadership Toolbox elements
- **Outcomes**: Performance, innovation, growth

Thirty 'result reports' support every part of the process, in the form of executive summaries, workbooks for workshops, technical reports for the design, and guides for agile and people-centric development.

Figure 43 contrasts the AGILITYINSIGHTS Diagnostic with traditional cultural assessments and employee surveys.

The Diagnostic offers the non-routine assessment of dynamic capabilities.

Culture Assessments evaluate gaps with predetermined culture attributes.

Employee Surveys identify faulty behaviours and flawed leadership.

The Diagnostic	Culture Assessments	Employee Surveys
Holistic and systemic model	Fixed, simple models	Traditional control tool
For the CEO and business leaders and their teams	For organizations and their leaders; HR loves it	For leaders and teams, often driven by HR
Performance, innovation and growth	Organizational development	Leadership and employee development
Scalable set of standardized questions that allow for benchmarking	Fixed set of simple questions with the ability to benchmark	Tailored questions, which often means copy & paste from other material
Foundation in behavioural economics and system dynamics	Questions to fix leadership and work along pre-determined spiral themes	Questions are based on current issues for an input-output mindset
Dynamic capabilities	Culture	Satisfaction and engagement
Identify patterns	Evaluate gaps to given models	Evaluate gaps to set standards
Separate root causes from symptoms	Compare assessment results with given model behaviours and idealistic leadership	Focus on finding faulty behaviours and flawed leadership
Focus on development action	Establish desired models	Identify who is at fault
Science-based, practice-proven and extensively tested	Published models, research-based and well-tested	With few exceptions, situational survey questions
AGILITYINSIGHTS, sold through exclusive certified Diagnostic Mentors	Culture consulting and headhunting firms; sold through subsidiaries and consultants	Consultancies and global survey establishments; sold through their consultants
Global benchmarking on all factors	Maintain comparative benchmarking databases	Some with large benchmarking databases, others with none

FIGURE 43: DIAGNOSTIC TOOLS

Conducting the diagnostic creates awareness and establishes a shared understanding of the context and the issues that require attention. Participating in the diagnostic is a first intervention. Answering the questions triggers the thinking about *how we do things here* and what better management looks like. Therefore, engaging people in the diagnostic and the following steps means using the knowledge and brain power throughout the organization to work *on* the system.

THE EXECUTIVE BRIEFING

The executive briefing is a 1- to 3-hour feedback meeting for a closed circle of executives who require first-hand insight into the diagnostic results. The intent is to help them control the process, filter the information and shape the direction of the transformation journey.

The executive briefing initiates the thinking about management and organization at the top. For most executive teams, taking time to discuss *how we do things around here* is a luxury and the exception. Few executive teams take time to reflect on management and organization. The executive briefing serves exactly that purpose.

During this briefing, a Diagnostic Mentor shares the diagnostic results and guides the conversation, with participants talking through the potential, sources of interference, assumptions and prevailing principles. The conversation focuses on 'what is' but can extend to 'what should be.'

One of the important outcomes of the executive briefing is agreement on what diagnostic information needs to be shared with all participants and across the broader organization. There are situations where filtering out discussion of certain issues is needed to limit risks, protect people and prevent preconceived notions.

Appendix 3 offers a standard agenda for the executive briefing. The canvas — which we describe below — supports facilitation of the meeting and serves as the recording tool for the conversations.

THE CANVAS

The canvas tool helps us facilitate the executive briefing conversation and all other interventions. It captures five dimensions in a template, with questions you can use to document your understanding of the diagnostic results. The five dimensions originate from the Performance Triangle (see Chapters 5-8). The four management levers come from *People-Centric Management* (Michel, 2020). As such, the canvas combines the agile and people-centric models with a facilitation tool. Figure 44 shows the alignment of the Performance Triangle model with five frames.

Five pairs of questions guide the diagnosis, the sense-making and the learning. Within each pair, the first question is about work *on* the system, while the second question guides your work *in* the system. The switch from question one to question two prepares you to transition from your individual journey to one you'll make with your team and the entire organization.

- **People**: How do I engage people? How do we know with clarity?
- **Organization**: How do I coordinate work? How do we move in one direction?
- **Work**: How do I mobilize the energy? How do we mobilize resources?
- **Operations**: How do I enable development? How do we maintain the focus?
- **Management**: How do I manage the organization? How do we lead in the people-centric way?

The canvas comprises your notes for your agile journey. Use it as follows:

- **Assumptions, principles and potential** (green Post-it notes) and **sources of interference** (red Post-its): the diagnostic offers the relevant observation points
- **Gaps** (yellow Post-its): the difference between your current situation and your desired situation reflects the gaps that require your attention

- **Key issues** (dark blue Post-its): the themes you've decided to work on spotlight your focus areas
- **Initiatives** (grey Post-its): these translate key issues into initiatives that help you address the gaps
- **Road map** (bright blue Post-its): this weaves schedules and resources initiatives into a programme that will ensure that your organization makes the transition to better management

The canvas is a template that can be used as a poster, for a team to work with in a workshop setting. The use of coloured Post-it notes helps separate the above steps.

Copy and use the canvas from Appendix 4 to facilitate your conversations around creating awareness for better management.

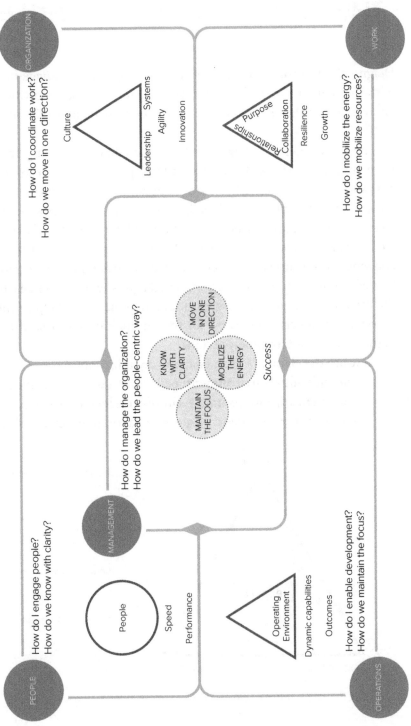

FIGURE 44: THE CANVAS FRAMES

THE PERFORMANCE TRIANGLE

Diagnostic Mentoring creates awareness for better management with the help of the Performance Triangle model. The following is an overview of the elements we'll look at in more detail in Chapters 5-8.

The Performance Triangle models the enabling operating environment (Figure 45), with culture, leadership and systems at its corners and success on top. Effective agile actions require a culture that creates shared context. Leadership is interactive, to facilitate the conversations around purpose, direction and performance. Systems work diagnostically, with focus on those aspects that matter most, allowing for self-directed action on deviations from the chosen path. Shared context, people interactions and diagnostic controls make up the capabilities of an agile organization. Together, they help people detect weak signals early, allow for the interpretation of that information, and facilitate timely action.

Here are the elements of an enabling organization:

- **The individual environment**: people with the inner game
- **The operating environment**: culture, leadership, systems
- **The work environment**: purpose, collaboration, relationships

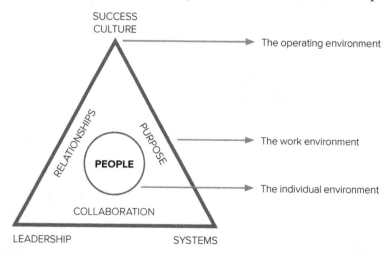

FIGURE 45: THE ENABLING OPERATING ENVIRONMENT AND ITS ELEMENTS

The individual environment. People are at the centre of the triangle. Awareness, choice, trust and focus are the means for people to perform at their peak. They are the capabilities that enable speed. When people apply these four capabilities, leaders can delegate work at the client front. As a result, decisions are made where the work is being done, which accelerates decision-making and action.

The operating environment. The corners with leadership, systems and culture enable agility. Interactive leadership is about the personal interaction between leaders and employees. Diagnostic systems offer the rules, routines and tools to get work done. Culture represents the invisible guide and organizational glue. When leaders connect and interact with employees, systems offer guidance and feedback, and culture establishes strong bonds; agile is at its peak.

The work environment. Purpose, relationships and collaboration establish resilience. When people find purpose in what they're doing, collaborate across boundaries and connect to build relationships that enhance their knowledge, organizations can resist any external shocks. They are resilient.

In Chapters 5-8, we will use the Performance Triangle model to identify the potential and any possible sources of interference to agile, and to challenge current assumptions and principles that prevail in your organization.

LEADERSHIP EVERYWHERE

Better management means leadership everywhere (Figure 46). The organization sets the context for distributed leadership. That's why raising awareness for speed, agile capabilities and resilience touches everyone in organizations.

It is increasingly recognized that companies need to be fast, agile and resilient. Speed represents the ability to implement strategy quickly. Agility provides the capacity to consistently change without having to change. Resilience adds stability, as the capability to absorb, react to and potentially reinvent the business model. Speed, agility and resilience represent dynamic capabilities. Their purpose is to enable the organization to reconfigure its resources in order to quickly adapt to a changing environment.

The inner game is the technique that every individual applies to become agile. Individual agility allows managers to delegate decisions to the client front, which speeds up decision-making. As a result, the CEO and the board will appreciate peak performance everywhere.

A shared culture, interactive leadership and dynamic systems are the elements that enable organizational agility. It's everyone's task to work on the system and make the organization agile. It certainly is every manager's primary job. As a result, the business has what it takes to become a truly innovative organization. In return, the CEO and the board have a chance to make innovation part of their strategy.

Everyone needs to care about purpose, collaboration and relationships. Together, this will make organizations more resilient. As a result, growth becomes part of the strategy.

Performance, innovation and growth are the scoreboard for the CEO and the board. It's their responsibility to ensure that everyone assumes leadership, with a focus on outcomes.

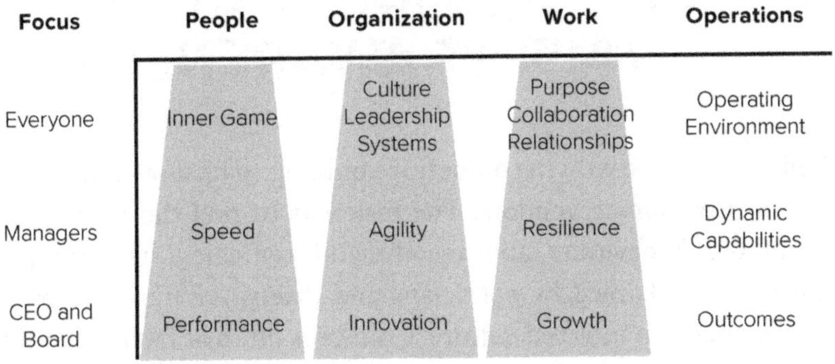

Focus	People	Organization	Work	Operations
Everyone	Inner Game	Culture Leadership Systems	Purpose Collaboration Relationships	Operating Environment
Managers	Speed	Agility	Resilience	Dynamic Capabilities
CEO and Board	Performance	Innovation	Growth	Outcomes

FIGURE 46: LEADERSHIP EVERYWHERE

Raising awareness for agile is everyone's task. The diagnostic, the executive briefing, the canvas and the Performance Triangle model help you and your organization to start the journey to reach agile maturity.

CITY ADMINISTRATION – RAISING AWARENESS

This is a case we won in competitive bidding against several employee satisfaction survey vendors. The task was to find the root of faulty employee behaviours and recommend remedies. The symptoms were, as proclaimed by politicians and extensively reported by local newspapers, an infected culture. Culture is often at fault when things go wrong. We were able to go to the root causes and suggest a subtle change that made all the difference.

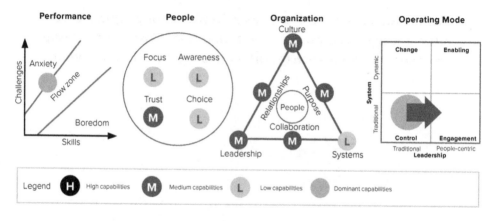

FIGURE 47: CITY ADMINISTRATION

With the diagnostic results (Figure 47) of work with 1,250 leaders and employees, the story effectively explains itself.

Elected officials responsible for the city government applied pressure to municipal administrators, gently supported by the media echo chamber. As a result, every official feared they'd be the next to take a beating in the press. Over the years, this impacted all employees, with a work environment that featured low performance, little focus, no awareness and no choice. Leaders tightened the control-based operating mode in ways that stalled every initiative, all performance and any risk taking.

The fix was simple but risky. We publicly presented the case — on TV — recommending that the elected politicians support city management and engage in a people-centric way of leading. Then we used a team workshop with the leaders of all departments to raise awareness of the critical linkages between operational modes and people performance, and guided them through that transformation. In fact, all of the leaders made a positive change. It is also interesting to observe that few of the politicians actively supported the change, but they did not get re-elected. Yes, it is always culture and leadership, but the root causes go deeper. We successfully made that case.

RAISE AWARENESS

Raising awareness for better management is the first step in Diagnostic Mentoring. It establishes the base and creates awareness within the team.

KEY CHAPTER IDEAS

- Three triggers initiate Diagnostic Mentoring
- Managers often have a distorted view of their organization's capabilities
- Capability mentoring with diagnostic tools creates awareness and insights
- The canvas tool helps us facilitate the conversations

ACTION AGENDA

Use the diagnostic to raise awareness for the agile feature of better management.

Share your diagnostic results in the executive briefing.

Document your conversations about the results with the canvas.

FURTHER READING

Michel, L (2013). *The Performance Triangle: Diagnostic Mentoring to Manage Organizations and People for Superior Performance in Turbulent Times.* London: LID Publishing.

CHAPTER 5
PEOPLE

People are every manager's first priority. The diagnostic raises awareness of the *people* elements — the individual environment of agile organizations. The natural inner-game techniques help people learn fast and perform at their peak. With the insights from the diagnostic and Chapter 5, review what people need in order to deliver performance, and identify the potential and sources of interference in the individual environment using the people elements of the Performance Triangle.

THE INDIVIDUAL ENVIRONMENT

For greater agility, people need to be the centre of your attention. This is informed by the European Humanism movement of the 18th century, which held that humans were responsible, critical, self-developing individuals. They want to contribute, learn and grow. However, there's no such thing as *the* image of mankind. We are all different, unique and, for the most part, irrational beings. But, this generalization helps us better deal with the fissure between what people need to perform well and the current reality of control in most organizations.

Humans engage through a sort of self-control mechanism, called self-responsibility. Awareness, choice, trust and focus of attention are the elements of how they activate their control mechanism. It's always there; managers can only interfere with it. It's the people themselves who must allow the mechanism to perform. They do this with the help of Barry, who's both our friend and the mortal enemy of peak performance.

In *Levers of Control* (2005), Professor Robert Simons of the Harvard Business School states: "To unleash this potential [knowledge workers] managers must overcome organizational blocks. Management control systems play an important role in this process." Over the years, organizational 'viruses' have seeped into many firms, introducing interference in the form of faulty leadership, erroneous systems or an infected culture, preventing people from performing at their peak. Or, as framed by Gallwey (2000): "The greater the external challenges accepted by a company, team or individual, the more important it is that there is minimum interference occurring from within."

Performance and creativity require degrees of freedom, self-responsibility and the ability to focus. These are things that are not naturally given in organizations, even though every responsible leader would insist that 'everything is under control.' Control is the key word for the lack of understanding of what performance is all about. Humanism, propounded by the Enlightenment philosopher Immanuel Kant, introduced the notion of "Humans as the end, not the means." This means that people should not be used to reach higher goals. Creativity, freely interpreted, requires fairness (equality), individualism and an elevated sense of the purpose of work. Kant calls these the attributes of a modern society.

FIGURE 48: THE INDIVIDUAL ENVIRONMENT

Four elements (Figure 48) offer insights into the individual environment, with **speed** as the operation's dynamic capability and **performance** as the outcome:

- **Awareness**, to understand and know with clarity
- **Choice**, to move in one direction
- **Trust**, to act and mobilize the energy
- **Focus**, to stay on track

Translated into the reality of today's organizations, this means that responsible employees require choice, trust and purpose to perform. The enabling mode assumes that people are self-motivated and want to get things done fast. This calls for providing them with observation points to focus their attention. Greater awareness means they sense early signs and have a significant degree of freedom to react to them. Choice is the foundation for responsibility. Once people have made their choices, they will need to be trusted to maintain the right focus. The inner-game techniques translate knowledge into action and require an enabling working environment.

Awareness, choice and trust help people focus their attention on what counts. The result is flow — the state in which learning, performance and creativity are at their peak (Csikszentmihalyi, 1990). It shifts control to the learner and redefines the role of the leader as a coach.

AWARENESS

Awareness involves learning by translating observed data into information, without making a judgment about it. It is about having a clear understanding of the present. Non-judgmental awareness is the best way to learn. Leaders have a choice between self-confident awareness and disengagement through outside control.

Awareness combines skills, knowledge and experience. Awareness is about knowing the present with clarity. Outside awareness is instruction. As a leader, you have an important policy choice to make between learning and instruction. Making this choice requires an understanding of how to provide direction and learn. It is a choice between being a coach who supports others' learning or a manager who tells people what to do.

The observation of a neutral but critical variable helps you to perform and improve upon an activity without any instruction. Watching your left foot during your golf swing helps you keep the proper balance without any distorting instruction. It's like magic — by using a critical performance variable at work, people steadily improve their performance. Learning takes place and performance improves. As a mentor, your only responsibilities are to maintain non-judgmental observation, provide opportunities to learn and ensure that people maintain their focus.

Awareness is part of the inner game: it is a synthesis of the insights we get from focused attention. Whatever the light of focus shines on becomes knowable and potentially understandable. As such, awareness helps people operate in a complex environment.

With this introduction and the information in Figure 49, think about the following:

- What is your awareness score? What does it mean?
- How does awareness enable people to play the inner game and perform?
- Where is the potential, and where does interference arise, relative to collectively knowing with clarity?

Question. The assessment statement for this element:

I have access to relevant information and ask for feedback to gain clarity on important things.

Evaluation. The answer is scored as follows:

0 = Strongly disagree, 25 Disagree, 50 Neutral, 75 Agree, 100 Strongly agree.

Meaning. The score indicates the following known symptoms:

- **Alert**. A high score means high awareness through neutral observation and non-judgmental feedback
- **Obstructed**. A medium score means blurred signals, lots of 'noise' and limited or faulty feedback
- **Blocked or false**. A low score means that signals are on mute, and limited or faulty feedback leads to faulty behaviours and disengagement

Interpretation. Linkages to other elements offer insights and root causes:

- **Leadership Scorecard**: Information, Sense-making
- **Leadership Toolbox**: Measurement, Information & Feedback, Performance Indicators

Sources

- **Model**. *The Performance Triangle*, pages 129-131
- **Process**. *Management Design* (2nd Ed. 2017), pages 46-47, 142-143
- **Application**. *People-Centric Management*, pages 60-69
- **Exercise**. *Agile by Choice*, pages 112-119

Facilitation. Use Post-it notes and the canvas for the answers:

What are the assumptions and principles? Use green Post-it notes.
Where is the potential? Use green Post-its.
What are the instances of interference? Use red Post-its.

FIGURE 49: AWARENESS INSIGHTS

CHOICE

Choice is the prerequisite for responsibility. It is the choice to take charge and move in the desired direction. Choice means self-determination, whereas rules are determined from the outside. Leaders need to decide between offering choice through delegation versus the power play of controlling what people do.

Choice is about moving in the desired direction. Without choice, there is no free will. Making a choice requires options and an awareness of the pros and cons, as well as the consequences, of the choice. Purpose without choice is meaningless.

People want to have choice. Whether they have opportunities to contribute is strongly linked to the amount of room they have to move and act. But, having room to move requires space. Every space is defined by its boundaries. Without boundaries, there is no space. A lack of room to move is the same as a lack of opportunities to perform. Creating room to move means eliminating blockages, such as rules, procedures and targets.

Choice means self-determination. It requires space with clear boundaries. Not providing choice means outside determination, with rules and prescriptions. It amounts to telling people what they should do and how they should do it.

Choice is another element of the inner game: it consists of deliberate decisions that follow our desires. It means pursuing what we like and saying no to the things that aren't relevant to us. Choice is the prerequisite for self-responsibility — the principle that brings all the joy of being human. Choice is needed to operate in an ambiguous environment.

With this introduction, and the information in Figure 50, think about the following:
- What is your choice score? What does it mean?
- How does choice enable people to play the inner game and perform?
- Where are the potentials for, and possible sources of interference with, collectively moving in one direction?

Question. The assessment statement for this element:
I have sufficient choice on what I need to do and how I perform those tasks.

Evaluation. The answer is scored as follows:
0 = Strongly disagree, 25 Disagree, 50 Neutral, 75 Agree, 100 Strongly agree.

Meaning. The score indicates the following known symptoms:

- **High**. A high score means self-determined work with high degrees of freedom and space for creativity
- **Formalized**. A medium score means limited choice and work that is determined by others, with a narrow space for creativity
- **Missing or interfered with**. A low score means no choice on how to get things done. Others determine what is important

Interpretation. Linkages to other elements offer insights and root causes:

- **People-centric levers**: Self-responsibility, delegation
- **Leadership Scorecard**: Direction, shared intent
- **Leadership Toolbox**: Strategy, strategy conversation

Sources

- **Model**. *The Performance Triangle*, page 132
- **Process**. *Management Design* (2nd Ed. 2017), pages 46-47, 142-143
- **Application**. *People-Centric Management*, pages 72-81
- **Exercise**. *Agile by Choice*, pages 120-125

Facilitation. Use Post-it notes and the canvas for the answers:

What are the assumptions and principles? Use green Post-it notes.
Where is the potential? Use green Post-its.
What are the instances of interference? Use red Post-its.

FIGURE 50: CHOICE INSIGHTS

TRUST

Trust means speed and performance. It is the cheapest management concept ever invented, and the foundation for every business transaction. With trust, there is no need for any renegotiation of contracts when things change. Leaders need to decide between trusting self-organization and the mistrust that's inherently built into bureaucratic procedures. But, trust must be earned. The best way to earn trust is by delivering on promises.

Trust becomes important when you let go of certain mental control. When Barry spreads doubt, the flow is broken. Doubts lead to confusion and the paralysis of action. When you are focused, you're conscious of your purpose, fully engaged in the present, and Barry's voice is not heard. The more you trust yourself, the less doubts and uncertainties will interfere with your performance and actions. Trust in Self 2 means that it's *you* who performs by engaging your full talent. If we trust ourselves, trust will take control.

Trust is a prerequisite for self-organization. Leaders must have trust in teams that organize themselves. And, teams must trust their own abilities in an uncertain context. Trust is the only way to cope with high uncertainty.

With trust, there is no need to wait for bureaucratic systems, such as objective agreements, to be modified in order to get things done. Trust directly reduces the time required to act and enhances flexibility. With trust, people exchange critical information that is essential for the survival of a business. To achieve speed and agility, leaders need to let go, trust and reduce control. Trust compensates for the impossible need to have everything under control: it makes us ready to let go and reduce control because we expect others to be competent and willing.

Trust is another part of the inner game. It is needed to mobilize resources in times of uncertainty. Trust is the source of speed in organizations.

With this introduction and the information in Figure 51, ask yourself these questions:

- What is your trust score? What does it mean?
- How does trust enable people to play the inner game and perform?
- Where are the potentials for, and possible sources of interference with, collectively mobilizing the energy?

Question. The assessment statement for this element:
I trust myself and my team, and I can mobilize the resources to get things done.
Evaluation. The answer is scored as follows:
0 = Strongly disagree, 25 Disagree, 50 Neutral, 75 Agree, 100 Strongly agree.
Meaning. The score indicates the following known symptoms:
• **High**. A high score indicates high trust and confidence in personal capabilities. People are responsible for what they are doing • **Formalized**. A medium score means limited trust and confidence in capabilities. Often times, control dominates self-determination • **Missing or interfered with**. A low score means mistrust in a control-dominated environment
Interpretation. Linkages to other elements offer insights and root causes:
• **People-centric levers**: Delegation, self-organization • **Leadership Scorecard**: Implementation, shared agenda • **Leadership Toolbox**: Plans & reviews, performance conversation
Sources
• **Model**. *The Performance Triangle*, pages 133-134 • **Process**. *Management Design* (2nd Ed. 2017), pages 46-47, 142-143 • **Application**. *People-Centric Management*, pages 84-93 • **Exercise**. *Agile by Choice*, pages 126-131
Facilitation. Use Post-it notes and the canvas for the answers:
What are the assumptions and principles? Use green Post-it notes. Where is the potential? Use green Post-its. What are the instances of interference? Use red Post-its.

FIGURE 51: TRUST INSIGHTS

FOCUS

Focus means self-initiated attention to what matters most. It is a conscious act of concentration that requires energy. It's difficult to stay focused over a period of time. Leaders need to decide between self-initiated focus of attention and target-oriented goal achievement.

Focus is energy channelled toward a specific outcome. Focused people can concentrate despite the many distractions that come up every day. Rather than just reacting to a specific interference, focus helps us to stay on track and pursue our goals. Our activities are directed toward a specific purpose. Focused behaviour does not emerge by chance. It is a deliberate mental act and follows personal discipline.

Focus is a limited resource. Focus is self-initiated attention to what matters most. It is a conscious act of concentration that requires energy. The challenge for people is to maintain focus over a period of time. Managers have a choice between self-initiated focus of attention and goal achievement following detailed performance targets.

Focus is a resource and part of the inner game. It involves paying attention, concentrating so as to focus on the things that matter to us, and learning quickly.

With this introduction and the information in Figure 52, think through the following:
- What is your focus score? What does it mean?
- How does focus of attention enable people to play the inner game and perform?
- Where are the potentials for, and possible sources of interference with, collectively maintaining the focus?

Question. The assessment statement for this element:
I am able to focus my attention on important things without interference.
Evaluation. The answer is scored as follows:
0 = Strongly disagree, 25 Disagree, 50 Neutral, 75 Agree, 100 Strongly agree.
Meaning. The score indicates the following known symptoms:
• **Bundled**. A high score indicates self-initiated learning and concentration on important things. However, a narrow focus might lead to missed opportunities • **Blurred**. A medium score means limited learning takes place and people are distracted. This often results in narrow goal orientation rather than focus • **Distracted or wrong**. A low score means there is distraction and focus on the wrong things. Both lead to underperformance. The most frequent cause is faulty goal orientation rather than lack of focus
Interpretation. Linkages to other elements offer insights and root causes:
• **People-centric levers**: Self-organization, attention • **Leadership Scorecard**: Beliefs and boundaries • **Leadership Toolbox**: Engagement and governance
Sources
• **Model**. *The Performance Triangle*, pages 136-137 • **Process**. *Management Design* (2nd Ed. 2017), pages 46-47, 142-143 • **Application**. *People-Centric Management*, pages 96-105 • **Exercise**. *Agile by Choice*, pages 146-153
Facilitation. Use Post-it notes and the canvas for the answers:
What are the assumptions and principles? Use green Post-it notes. Where is the potential? Use green Post-its. What are the instances of interference? Use red Post-its.

FIGURE 52: FOCUS INSIGHTS

RESOURCES

The skilful application of the principles of the inner game is the prerequisite for people to effectively mobilize their resources and succeed with the challenges of their outer game. Focused attention, time and energy are critical resources on your journey to agile and beyond.

The most talented people are able to use their resources most effectively and efficiently. They combine extraordinary motivation and the ability to improve quickly to release productive energy. Focus of attention is about the ability to learn, and time creates the momentum to turn motivation into energy.

The idea is to invest as little time and attention in management as possible, while getting the most out of the energy expended. Time and energy are limited resources. Energy is a resource that requires refuelling.

Energy is the power that emerges when people combine readiness, commitment and engagement. It is a limited resource with some stretch. Energy can only be redirected, not created or removed. But, humans don't always have access to full energy. It needs to be renewed and refuelled when it's been used up. Refuelling is an investment that takes time. And, the energy level cannot be sustained at 100% all of the time.

Focus of attention is a resource that's related to effectiveness. The human capacity for attention is also limited. The task is to concentrate on those things that offer the most value. The challenge is to reach a high level of focus and sustain it at that level. This mental process consumes a considerable amount of energy, but it results in the release of productive energy.

Time is a resource that is commonly related to efficiency. People have a limited amount of time available. We cannot change time. Time is the only resource that cannot be enlarged, copied or stored. But, how we invest our time, and whether we use it wisely, makes a big difference. The challenge is to reach controlled momentum, where time and energy merge to create flow.

With the people-centric ecosystem (Figure 35) we have included resources as a balancing loop. It is therefore clear that focus of attention, time and energy are the critical resources. Focus of attention is the willpower with which people reach clarity. Time creates momentum, and energy is the power to perform and get things done.

CAPABILITIES

It's easy to say, 'We only hire the best talent.' But, who then hires all the untalented people? Nobody would reasonably do that. So, then, what is talent?

When we talk about talent, we assume that people have the necessary skills for peak performance. But, talent is much more than that. Talent requires beyond-average motivation and the ability to improve quickly. Both motivation and learning separate superior talent from people with the right skills. In this light, it becomes obvious that people with talent need opportunities to apply their skills and an environment where they can perform at their peak.

Motivation and learning are shared responsibilities. Self-responsibility is the source of motivation. It requires an organization that has made the choice of agile to ensure that self-responsible people can use their potential, and that interference is within limits that individuals can handle. Learning also is shared between the individual and the institution. It requires a willingness to learn and the opportunity to learn. In this way, organizations that make best use of their talent make the choice of agile and offer opportunities to learn.

Experience, motivation and skills are part of knowledge. Aristotle explained 2,000 years ago that three types of knowledge are required. *Techne*, craft knowledge, is about learning to use tools and methods to create something. *Episteme* is scientific knowledge that uncovers the laws of nature. *Phronesis* is knowledge of judgment; the perspective and wisdom necessary to make decisions. These three kinds of knowledge require different types of leadership.

Better management combines techne, episteme and phronesis. Much of managing is about techne, the use of routines, rules and tools to solve problems. Many of the problems require episteme. The assumption is that there's a right way of doing things. In that sense, better management evolves as an episteme problem. Phronesis, then, is about how one uses the principles and insights to make decisions.

Talented people will develop the skills to apply better management. They are aware that the final script for better management will never be written, and they're motivated to use their experience and responsibility to deliver better management performance in the moment, at their very best, to solve real live problems.

SPEED

The inner game is the technique people use to translate knowledge into action. The result is speed as a dynamic capability in organizations.

Self-responsibility is the people-centric principle by which people have control over what they do and how they do it. They have the choice and therefore can make decisions, act and behave with speed, avoiding the cumbersome detours that come with traditional hierarchy. They assume accountability for delegated responsibilities.

Trust is the fastest management concept to achieve. When people trust each other, there is no need for contractual arrangements to get things down. Trust replaces systems such as target setting, which slow things done rather than make them happen more quickly.

Learning is the solution for time-critical action in dynamic situations. The inner game, with awareness and focus of attention, is all about learning and performance.

Speed is strongly correlated with performance. Our research confirms that people engaged in the inner-game techniques far outperform people without these capabilities. For organizations as a whole, this means speed as a capability that drives performance.

We therefore conclude that people who use the inner-game techniques in an environment that allows for self-responsible action are the real drivers of speed in organizations. As such, speed is the dynamic capability that helps organizations succeed in a volatile environment.

Speed needs the balance of control. Mario Andretti, the former Formula 1 racing world champion, once said: "If you have things under control, you simply don't go fast enough." Speed involves risk. Self-responsible people who play the inner game possess the accelerator pedal and know the right balance between speed and taking too much risk. The intelligent use of their knowledge and skills — and awareness of their resource limitations — are the controls that counter-balance speed.

Diagnostic Mentoring measures speed as the average of the four inner-game techniques: focus of attention, awareness, trust and choice.

With this introduction, and the information in Figure 53, consider the following:

- What is your speed score? What does it mean?
- How does speed contribute to overall outcomes?
- Where are the potentials for, and possible sources of interference with, speed?

Question. The assessment statement for this element:
The average of the focus, awareness, trust and choice scores.
Evaluation. The answer is scored as follows:
0 = Strongly disagree, 25 Disagree, 50 Neutral, 75 Agree, 100 Strongly agree.
Meaning. The score indicates the following known symptoms:
<ul><li>**High, well balanced**. A high score means people have the means to perform at their peak</li><li>**Medium, struggling**. A medium score means interference prevents people from using their full potential. Performance likely suffers</li><li>**Low, unbalanced**. A low score means people don't use their potential. They're bored, stressed or work in an infected environment</li></ul>
Interpretation. Linkages to other elements offer insights and root causes:
<ul><li>**People-centric levers**: Self-organization, attention</li><li>**Leadership Scorecard**: Beliefs and boundaries</li><li>**Leadership Toolbox**: Engagement and governance</li></ul>
Sources
<ul><li>**Process**. *Management Design* (2nd Ed. 2017), pages 94-95, 142-143</li><li>**Application**. *People-Centric Management*, page 149</li><li>**Exercise**. *Agile by Choice*, pages 90-131</li></ul>
Facilitation. Use Post-it notes and the canvas for the answers:
What are the assumptions and principles? Use green Post-it notes. Where is the potential? Use green Post-its. What are the instances of interference? Use red Post-its.

FIGURE 53: SPEED INSIGHTS

PEAK PERFORMANCE

Performance is a key element of *The Performance Triangle*. People who perform at their peak require a work environment that enables them to play the inner game and use their knowledge and resources wisely.

Performance is the result of people engaging their full potential in what they do. This requires minimum interference from Barry, the external environment and the organization. That's why the individual environment, populated by people, is in the centre of the triangle. People-centric management requires agile organization — a context with little interference that can impede the potential.

People are every manager's first priority. When priorities are set that way, performance is the desired outcome. Chapter 5 demonstrated how the inner game enables speed and performance within the context of a supportive agile work environment and organization.

The inner game is the technique that drives performance.

With this introduction, and the information in Figure 6 as part of the results conversation, ask yourself this:

- What is your performance score? What does it mean?
- How does performance contribute to overall outcomes?
- Where are the potentials for, and possible sources of interference with, performance?

ENERGY – NO TIME

The story starts on a Saturday morning, when I unexpectedly got an email from the CEO of that regional energy supply company. "I cannot get my work done," he wrote, explaining that he needed to better organize his office. I followed up with a call, but was told by his executive assistant: "Sorry, the boss is busy. He has no time. But, there is a 30-minute slot in three weeks' time."

Another three weeks passed, and we finally had a chance to discuss his problem. During that call, cartoon images of a manager hidden behind stacks of paper on his desk ran through my mind. We talked things through, and I was retained to help with the office-organization problem, utilizing our diagnostic process.

My first visit confirmed my cartoon image. The desk was full of paper. The first thing I got to see was the project portfolio: a multi-page document with one line per project. We then ran the diagnostic with 25 leaders, followed by a couple of personal interviews.

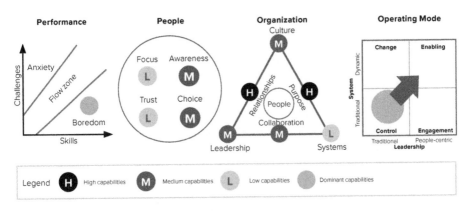

FIGURE 54: ENERGY

People were bored, overwhelmed with task lists or somewhat scared that they would not meet expectations. The organization was divided between those who had the CEO's trust (those on the anxiety side) and others who he didn't trust (they had no work to do and got bored). Disagreement on trust, a lack of focus and low performance was the result. The review of systems with the Leadership

Toolbox highlighted the very dominant control mode. Performance Management was the symptom, with detailed, multi-page personal performance targets that were in constant flux and challenges posed by day-to-day changes in priorities.

The cause of all of this was apparent: a CEO who failed to delegate, backed up by a system that always confirmed his case. The biggest challenge was to first explain that to those in charge. Unfortunately, that met with little success. My contract was terminated, and the CEO remained in charge of his poorly performing organization until just recently, when he retired.

Interestingly enough, I soon came across the same dysfunctional story, with a similarly controlling, untrusting CEO, in another regional energy company. Think there might be a pattern emerging here?

How long will it take for the realization to sink in that times have changed? It's a VUCA environment out there. Power and control have lost their effectiveness, completely and unquestionably. Untrusting leaders cannot be trusted.

PEOPLE

Diagnostic Mentoring creates awareness of the 'people' elements of better management, and of what people need to perform at their peak. People come with talent, inner-game principles and resources.

KEY CHAPTER IDEAS

- Being aware of the essential skills people need to perform is the first step toward better management
- People come with talent and potential. Good management engages their full talent and potential
- The inner game uses awareness, choice and trust principles to deal with the outer challenges of work
- Time, attention and energy are the key resources of knowledge workers
- Focus, choice and trust are the principle catalysts for speed in organizations
- Peak performance needs potential and little interference

ACTION AGENDA

Diagnose the critical people elements to raise awareness of people's potential. Search for the causes of interference.

FURTHER READING

Michel, L (2020). *People-Centric Management: How Managers Use Four Levers to Bring Out the Greatness of Others*. London: LID Publishing.

CHAPTER 6

ORGANIZATION

Organization is every manager's second priority. The diagnostic makes the organization elements visible, for a conversation about how they support people to perform at their peak. Chapter 6 explores the culture, leadership and systems corners of the Performance Triangle in light of their agile features. An operating environment with agile features has everything that organizations need for innovation.

THE OPERATING ENVIRONMENT

Greater agility requires an operating environment that enables people to perform and act fast. The Performance Triangle offers the model for superior agility and innovation.

Culture, leadership and systems frame the corners of the triangle. Superior decision-making and effective actions require a culture that creates shared context. Leadership needs to interact and facilitate the conversation around purpose, direction and performance. Systems that work diagnostically direct attention to the issues that matter most to the business, and allow people to act in a self-directed manner.

There are three ways to influence what people do:

1. Culture works like an invisible compass. It embodies the values and norms around how to do things that people embrace.
2. Leaders can directly influence people through interaction and interference. They can tell them what to do and how to do it. Leadership interaction is heavy work. It requires energy and time.
3. Systems — governing strategy, mission, objectives and the like — direct and influence people. Systems work like autopilot. Once set, they serve their purpose and influence people.

All three ways of influencing human behaviour need to be in balance.

A shared culture, interactive leadership and dynamic systems make organizations agile. They help people detect weak market signals early from feedback data, allow for the interpretation of that information, and facilitate timely action to address it. These are the features of an agile organization and the foundation for innovation.

FIGURE 55: THE OPERATING ENVIRONMENT

Three elements (Figure 55) offer insights in the operating environment, leading to **agility** as the operating system's dynamic capability and **innovation**. As we've said, these elements include:

- **Culture**, the shared understanding, intent, agenda, beliefs and norms
- **Leadership**, the sense-making, strategy, performance, contribution and risk conversations
- **Systems**, the information, strategy, implementation, beliefs and boundary rules, routines and tools

Interactive leadership is about the personal interaction between leaders and employees. Dynamic systems offer the rules, routines and tools to get work done. Culture represents the invisible guide and glue. When leaders connect and interact with employees, and systems offer guidance and feedback — with culture at the centre of it all, establishing strong bonds — then agile is at its peak.

The following sections on culture, leadership and systems create awareness of the organizational elements — the operating environment of an agile organization.

CULTURE

The culture of an organization creates shared context, enables or inhibits knowledge exchange, and defines the invisible boundaries of collaboration. A vibrant culture establishes shared context as the common ground, with a mutual agenda, language, thought models, relationships and purpose. Shared context is all about a shared mindset: the behaviour of individuals based on common thinking and shared norms. The organizational culture becomes the invisible force that, like gravity, shapes all interactions within the universe in which the organization exists.

We agree with the assertion that culture has both visible and invisible components, underlying beliefs, values and shared assumptions that shape collective thoughts. They can be observed through the decisions, behaviours and actions of the people in the organization. Culture has a stabilizing effect on the organization and helps people make things meaningful and predictable.

Each organization has a unique culture that evolves over years and is reinforced as people absorb, repeat and pass along what works. There may be an infinite number of dimensions that make up the culture of an organization, but we've identified five attributes that seem to be nearly universal. They thrive, unseen, in the minds and actions of employees at all levels. These attributes help form a shared context within the organization.

These five culture elements, which establish a shared mindset, include (Figure 56):
1. **Shared understanding** to know with clarity
2. **Shared intent** to move in one direction
3. **Shared agenda** to mobilize the energy
4. **Shared aspirations** to maintain the focus
5. **Shared norms** to maintain the focus

Shared Mindset

Culture

Relationships

Purpose

People

Collaboration

Leadership   Systems

FIGURE 56: SHARED MINDSET CULTURE

Understanding. Do leaders and employees share an understanding of where the organization is and where it's going (or attempting to go)?

Intent. Do leaders and employees share a common intent on how to move the organization forward, to meet goals and objectives?

Agenda. Do leaders and employees share a common agenda outlining what needs to be done to move the organization forward?

Aspirations. Do leaders and employees share a common sense of energy, and possess the resources needed to implement strategy?

Norms. Do leaders and employees share a common set of norms of behaviour needed to maintain the chosen focus?

It is important to note that changing culture is more than changing individual mindsets. It's about the collective behaviours as a sort of habit system. Such systems can only be changed by action, experience and feedback, attained through experience, rather than the cognitive abstractions of new values. This is why culture is an outcome, with systems and leadership as its triggers.

With this introduction and the information in Figure 57, consider the following:

- What is your culture score? What does it mean?
- How does your culture enable people to perform?
- Where are the potentials for, and possible sources of interference with, a shared mindset?

Question. The assessment statement for this element:

Leaders and employees share the same understanding of how work is performed.

Evaluation. The answer is scored as follows:

0 = Strongly disagree, 25 Disagree, 50 Neutral, 75 Agree, 100 Strongly agree.

Meaning. The score indicates the following known symptoms:

- **Sustainable**. A high score means the team has a shared mindset and agenda
- **Mediocre**. A medium score means the team has a limited shared mindset and agenda
- **Toxic or missing**. A low score means the team has no shared mindset or agenda

Interpretation. Linkages to other elements offer insights and root causes:

- **Leadership Scorecard**: Shared understanding, intent, agenda, aspirations and norms
- **Leadership Toolbox**: Values

Sources

- **Model**. *The Performance Triangle*, pages 77-92
- **Process**. *Management Design* (2nd Ed. 2017), pages 64-65, 144-145
- **Application**. *People-Centric Management*, pages 142-143
- **Exercise**. *Agile by Choice*, pages 47-51

Facilitation. Use Post-it notes and the canvas for the answers:

What are the assumptions and principles? Use green Post-it notes.
Where is the potential? Use green Post-its.
What are the instances of interference? Use red Post-its.

FIGURE 57: CULTURE INSIGHTS

LEADERSHIP

Leadership is a key component of the triangle. In today's organizations, be they a small group in a traditional structure, a community or an ecosystem, leadership is exercised wherever it influences other people's thinking, behaviours, decisions and actions. Leadership is not necessarily tied to traditional positions with power in hierarchies.

Effective leaders in agile organizations interact with people on a personal level, relate to others to facilitate meaningful collaboration and establish a supportive work environment based on a culture of trust. In the broadest sense, leadership is communication and interaction with others at all levels, vertically and horizontally, throughout an organization. We suggest that leaders in any organization develop effective communication and interaction skills that are natural and unique to them.

The traditional notion is that the culture of an organization is shaped at the top of the management hierarchy and cascades downward. We generally accept this belief. However, in many organizations we've seen a huge disconnect between what top executives *think* is going on and what the rank and file employees actually believe.

Leaders and managers at all levels must recognize that their actions and behaviours are being observed and interpreted by employees through the lens of their own beliefs and values. Many leaders, perhaps inadvertently, fail to connect with employees, and they communicate conflicting values and beliefs throughout the organization. Employees will rarely approach the CEO and say, 'You said this, but we actually did that. Which is it, and what's going on?' The result is that employees are left to develop their own interpretation, which is in many cases inconsistent with organizational goals.

Leading requires fluency in things that are probably unnatural for most of us. Teaming and interaction mean that leaders take interpersonal risks. True teaming requires a sense of psychological safety, and stepping back to see others' perspectives. It's about losing traditional control to gain real control.

Leadership is a complex and indefinable quality, but we've identified five unconscious (and rarely discussed) attributes that contribute to strengthening the culture and performance of the organization.

Five conversations can be had, as interactions to exercise leadership control (Figure 58). They are as follows:

1. **Sense-making discussion**, to understand and know with clarity
2. **Strategy conversation**, to think and move in one direction
3. **Performance conversation**, to act and mobilize the energy
4. **Contribution dialogue**, to engage and maintain the focus
5. **Risk dialogue**, to adhere to and maintain the focus

FIGURE 58: INTERACTIVE LEADERSHIP

So, what's covered in these conversations?

- **Sense-making.** Do leaders and employees have the ability to sense changes in internal and external environments, and interpret their meaning?
- **Strategy.** Do leaders and employees have an understanding of why the organization has established strategic goals, and are goals founded on lessons from the past?
- **Performance.** Do leaders and employees have a clear understanding of whether the organization is on track, what needs to be done to remain on track, and how to achieve superior performance?
- **Contribution.** Do leaders and employees have a clear understanding of what they can do to move the organization forward? As part of that, do leaders clearly understand their role?
- **Risk.** Do leaders and employees have a clear understanding of the potential risks, and the ultimate level of risk the organization can tolerate?

People-Centric Management is *high-touch* interaction with people. Remember, leadership is a contact sport. Yet, when you show up, it's often seen as interference — almost as an unwelcome interruption. Employees should be worrying about clients, not leaders. It's therefore important to show up as encouragement. Encouragement shows that we are all here, together, to focus on the client. Leadership presence is important.

With this introduction and the information in Figure 59, consider this:

- What is your leadership score? What does it mean?
- How does your leadership enable people to perform?
- Where are the potentials for, and possible sources of, interference with interactive leadership?

Question. The assessment statement for this element:

Leaders and employees share the same understanding of how work is performed.

Evaluation. The answer is scored as follows:

0 = Strongly disagree, 25 Disagree, 50 Neutral, 75 Agree, 100 Strongly agree.

Meaning. The score indicates the following known symptoms:

- **Interactive**. A high score means productive conversations on direction, performance, beliefs and boundaries
- **Busy**. A medium score means limited conversations on direction, performance, beliefs and boundaries
- **Missing or flawed**. A low score means no, or false, conversations on direction, performance, beliefs and boundaries

Interpretation. Linkages to other elements offer insights and root causes:

- **Leadership Scorecard**: Systems
- **Leadership Toolbox**: Sense-making discussion, strategy conversation, performance conversation, contribution dialogue, risk dialogue

Sources

- **Model**. *The Performance Triangle*, pages 147-166
- **Process**. *Management Design* (2nd Ed. 2017), pages 64-65, 144-145
- **Application**. *People-Centric Management*, pages 136-138
- **Exercise**. *Agile by Choice*, pages 47-51

Facilitation. Use Post-it notes and the canvas for the answers:

What are the assumptions and principles? Use green Post-it notes.
Where is the potential? Use green Post-its.
What are the instances of interference? Use red Post-its.

FIGURE 59: LEADERSHIP INSIGHTS

SYSTEMS

Systems are located at the lower-right corner of the triangle. They represent the institutional toolbox, with rules, routines and resources that set the stage for rigorous and disciplined leadership. It's about systems support implementation with the right balance of freedom and constraint. Supporting collaboration between people and systems provides the fuel to power the formation of beliefs and decisions. This is essential for identifying purpose. In addition, systems set boundaries to achieve the desired balance between entrepreneurship and efficiency.

Systems are both influenced by and influence the culture and leadership practices that shape the decision-making process. When we talk about systems we aren't just talking about IT systems, but the rules and routines that shape the input and output from computerized tools. Everyone reading this chapter is familiar with the phrases 'garbage in, garbage out' and 'what gets measured, gets done.' However, we contend that such thinking is just scratching the surface of the complex dimension we call *systems*. What managers and employees do with the output from IT systems, and how that output shapes decisions and behaviours, is rarely considered.

Similarly, we've witnessed many examples of systems developed in prior decades being used to drive decisions today, despite the fact that the business dynamic — and the wider world around us — have changed dramatically. We have seen many instances where managers created systems to generate relevant data needed to solve some problem, or give the organization an edge, 20 years ago. The problem was solved, partially with the aid of the data, and the company gained an edge over competitors.

Today, though, managers are making decisions using information that is no longer relevant, because their approach was established decades ago and the competitive dynamics have changed significantly. What was relevant and meaningful 20 years ago may not be today, leading to regrettable decisions. It therefore becomes imperative for leaders to constantly evaluate whether the old rules, routines and tools being used to drive decisions are still relevant, and whether they shape desired behaviours.

We have identified five questions, the answers to which provide insight into unconscious and rarely examined beliefs, values and shared assumptions that either inhibit or enable the effectiveness of systems.

The system of work and the system of management are interconnected. Changing the system of work will not yield performance if the operating system that governs it remains flawed.

These five diagnostic systems (Figure 60) support people to get work done with the benefit of:

1. **Information** — to understand and know with clarity
2. **Strategy** — to think and move in one direction
3. **Implementation** — to act and mobilize the energy
4. **Beliefs** — to engage and maintain the focus
5. **Boundaries** — to adhere to and maintain the focus

FIGURE 60: DIAGNOSTIC SYSTEMS

Information. Do leaders and employees at all levels have access to timely and relevant information, to keep them abreast of what's going on inside and outside the organization, and help them make informed decisions?

Strategy. Do leaders and employees clearly understand the rules of the game and what's needed to move in one direction?

Implementation. Do leaders and employees throughout the organization clearly understand what's needed to mobilize the energy and implement the strategy?

Beliefs. Do leaders and employees at all levels have a shared ambition to adhere to the focus, as determined by the strategy?

Boundaries. Do leaders and employees have a firm understanding of boundaries or limits to their decisions or authority?

With this introduction and the information in Figure 61, think about the following:
- What is your systems score? What does it mean?
- How do your systems enable people to perform?
- Where are the potentials for, and possible sources of interference with, dynamic systems?

Question. The assessment statement for this element:
Our systems help leaders and employees effectively get their jobs done and perform in a dynamic context.
Evaluation. The answer is scored as follows:
0 = Strongly disagree, 25 Disagree, 50 Neutral, 75 Agree, 100 Strongly agree.
Meaning. The score indicates the following known symptoms:
• **Dynamic**. A high score means reliable systems that are intended to support people performing in a dynamic context • **Bureaucratic**. A medium score means limited systems, which creates friction rather than enabling collaboration and purpose • **Missing or broken**: A low score means erroneous systems, which prevents collaboration and purpose
Interpretation. Linkages to other elements offer insights and root causes:
• **Leadership Scorecard**: Information, strategy, implementation, beliefs and boundaries • **Leadership Toolbox**: : 15 rules, routines and tools
Sources
• **Model**. *The Performance Triangle*, pages 177-196 • **Process**. *Management Design* (2nd Ed. 2017), pages 64-65, 144-145 • **Application**. *People-Centric Management*, pages 139-141 • **Exercise**. *Agile by Choice*, pages 47-51
Facilitation. Use Post-it notes and the canvas for the answers:
What are the assumptions and principles? Use green Post-it notes. Where is the potential? Use green Post-its. What are the instances of interference? Use red Post-its.

FIGURE 61: SYSTEMS INSIGHTS

AGILITY

Interactive leadership, dynamic systems and a shared culture with delegation as the principle are the enablers of agility in organizations.

Agility is all about sensing opportunities early, taking action and continuous change throughout an integrated organization. Dynamic systems with key performance metrics and feedback processes enable that flexibility and adaptability.

Agility promotes self-organized work in teams with delegated decision-making, greater flexibility, effective adaptation to external change, improved problem-solving and intensive innovation as its benefits.

Leadership is interaction, and next to systems it is the most important managerial control mechanism. Leaders who see the need to change, and decisively act on it, can directly influence people. With this, the organization has an active and nimble response to changes in the environment.

A shared culture gives people the ability to act based on broad direction. This enhances the agility of organizations. Agility therefore requires implicit leadership that facilitates knowledge sharing, seeks consensus, trusts people, delegates more, and provides an environment for people to maximize inherent tacit knowledge (Nold, 2012).

Agility balances with stability. Imagine a coiled spring, representing agility. The spring can only be agile if it is fixed on one end. That anchoring is similar to stability in an organization. For agility to work, it needs to be balanced with stability. The stability comes from the shared culture, interactive leadership and an operating system that enables people to perform and act flexibly.

With this introduction and the information in Figure 62, think about this:

- What is your agile score? What does it mean?
- How does your organization's agility enable people to perform?
- Where are the potentials for, and possible sources of interference with, a shared mindset?

Question. The assessment statement for this element:
The average of the systems, leadership and culture scores.
Evaluation. The answer is scored as follows:
0 = Strongly disagree, 25 Disagree, 50 Neutral, 75 Agree, 100 Strongly agree.
Meaning. The score indicates the following known symptoms:
• **High, well balanced**. A high score means the organization has well-developed agile capabilities. The challenge is to keep it up • **Medium, limited**. A medium score means the organization has room to improve agility. The task is to work on culture, leadership and systems • **Low, unbalanced**. The organization lacks the capabilities for agility. It is important to fix this, in order to compete in a dynamic environment
Interpretation. Linkages to other elements offer insights and root causes:
• **The Performance Triangle**: Leadership, systems and culture • **Outcomes**: Innovation
Sources
• **Model**. *The Performance Triangle*, pages 29-33 • **Process**. *Management Design* (2nd Ed. 2017), pages 94-95 • **Application**. *People-Centric Management*, pages 139-141 • **Exercise**. *Agile by Choice*, pages 47-51
Facilitation. Use Post-it notes and the canvas for the answers:
What are the assumptions and principles? Use green Post-it notes. Where is the potential? Use green Post-its. What are the instances of interference? Use red Post-its.

FIGURE 62: AGILITY INSIGHTS

INNOVATION

Agility with culture, leadership and systems sets the stage for knowledge workers to use their creativity as a means of achieving higher levels of innovation throughout the organization. There is a strong linkage between knowledge work and innovation. Furthermore, innovation is directly related to value creation in organizations.

Innovation relates to the enabling mode. With respect to innovation, our research for *Diagnostic Mentoring* confirms that organizations operating in a people-centric and dynamic operating environment far outperform those in control, change or engagement modes. These organizations favour self-responsibility, delegation, self-organization and focus of attention over traditional control and command approaches.

People align and become creative with an operating environment where culture provides the invisible compass, where leaders interact to influence what is being done, and when systems offer choice, are based on trust, create awareness and help focus attention.

With this introduction and the information in Figure 7, ask yourself:

- What is your innovation score? What does it mean?
- How does your organization's innovation contribute to outcomes?
- Where are the potentials for, and possible sources of interference with, innovation?

MUSIC
− RETURN TO INNOVATION

Sometimes when I walk into a company, I immediately feel the spirit. With this particular client, within a second I sensed an entrepreneurial team that was desperate to get back on a successful path. Unfortunately, the past 15 years were hard for the company and its employees. From a headcount of 2,500 in the year 2000, today just 150 employees are left. It's the hardcore loyalists who want to make it work, against all odds.

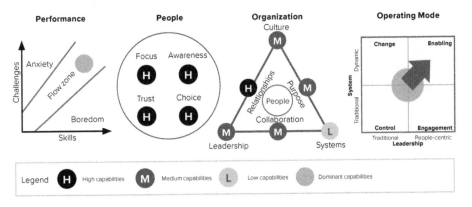

FIGURE 63: MUSIC

The diagnostic results (Figure 63) reflected the initial impression: people who are highly motivated and able to perform, and an organization that struggles between efficiency and innovation, with leaders who do everything and more. The only way this company was able to survive was to radically innovate its products and services, without losing their unique offering: the highest quality musical instrument on the market. All they needed in order to return to a place of innovation and success was to trust themselves.

With the diagnostic results and the team workshop, we helped them rebuild confidence. Our innovation expert worked with the leadership team, through role-playing personas, to identify pockets of innovation opportunities. It became clear that the company would continue to pursue its shift to the enabling mode.

The diagnostic and our workshops confirmed that they were and still are on the right track. Success has returned, with new products for a digital market.

ORGANIZATION

Diagnostic Mentoring creates awareness of the elements of an agile organization and what context people need in order to perform. Culture, leadership and systems frame the context as the Performance Triangle. They are the elements that determine agility and innovation.

KEY CHAPTER IDEAS

- Being aware of what makes an organization agile is the first step toward better management
- Shared intent, a shared agenda and shared norms establish culture over time
- Leadership is interaction with people
- Systems determine people's behaviours, actions and decisions
- Agility is largely the result of a shared culture, interactive leadership and an operating system that enables people
- Agility and innovation are strongly correlated; one needs the other

ACTION AGENDA

Diagnose the critical organizational elements to raise the awareness for agile and innovation.

FURTHER READING

Michel, L (2013). *The Performance Triangle: Diagnostic Mentoring to Manage Organizations and People for Superior Performance in Turbulent Times.* London: LID Publishing.

CHAPTER 7
WORK

Work is every manager's third priority. The diagnostic raises awareness of the elements that shape the work environment of individuals and teams. Chapter 7 identifies purpose, collaboration and relationships as the sides of the Performance Triangle and determinants of resilient features of organizations. The resilient work environment establishes the foundation for internal growth.

THE WORK ENVIRONMENT

Purpose, collaboration and relationships represent the three sides of the Performance Triangle (Figure 64). Their configuration sets the stage for a resilient organization with an operating system that has the potential to enable growth from within.

People need three things to perform: to find purpose in what they do, collaborate with others and connect with others to gain more knowledge.

Purpose, relationships and collaboration are the bonding elements of every organization. For superior decisions, knowledge work requires purpose. It is the driving force behind motivation.

Knowledge workers use internal and external relationships to share and expand their knowledge, to create value for clients. Only knowledge that is shared and applied has value for any organization. New technologies facilitate the transfer of knowledge in a way that generates new knowledge.

Many knowledge-related tasks in an organization require more than one individual for their completion. It is the combined knowledge and the shared experiences of collaboration that stimulate creativity, innovation and growth.

Resilience results from a deep sense of purpose, trusted relationships among stakeholders and collaboration to share knowledge. With these capabilities, organizations have a better chance of withstanding external shocks and change.

FIGURE 64: THE WORK ENVIRONMENT

Three elements offer insights in the work environment, with **resilience** as the operating system's dynamic capability and **growth** as its outcome.

- **Purpose** — the meaning people attach to work
- **Relationships** — the connectivity among people
- **Collaboration** — the ability to work across diverse teams

With strategies for deep meaning, strategies for strong connectivity and strategies for effective cooperation, organizations can shape their work environment.

The following sections on purpose, relationships and collaboration create awareness of the elements of the work environment, as well as options, with strategies, to establish a resilient organization and better management.

PURPOSE

Purpose connects systems and cultures to people. However, as the philosopher and sociologist Jürgen Habermas said, "There is no administrative production of purpose" (1988). What we often hear when the climate changes is that when people lost sight of the purpose of their work, companies started a discussion on motivation. When people experience their work as meaningful, they contribute with greater energy. They're fully present — physically, mentally and emotionally. Purpose is created individually, subjectively. It is always 'me' that provides purpose to the world. It is called sense-making, not 'sense-giving'. Purpose cannot be delivered; it needs to be found or 'produced' individually.

As a leader and an employee, ask yourself:

- Do people have a strong, shared sense of higher purpose?
- Does the purpose that motivates people inspire them to go above and beyond the minimum expectations?
- What is the impact my organization has on customers and society?
- How am I uniquely contributing to that purpose?

Individuals search for purpose. But, in tough times, purpose needs reinforcement. Agile techniques enable purpose at scale.

STRATEGIES FOR DEEP MEANING

Meaning offers purpose. Meaning comes from systems with explicit beliefs and boundaries (vision, mission, offering and goals). And, it's enabled by a culture with implicit values and standards that help people find purpose, gain awareness, become motivated, get creative and unlock their talents. With purpose, they identify opportunities, stick with them, and deal with complexity and volatility. Four purpose modes (Figure 65) can be used to identify the nature of 'meaning' in your organization.

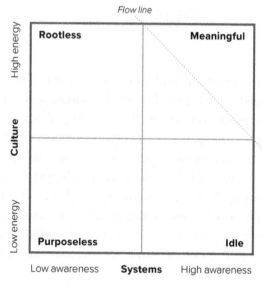

FIGURE 65: PURPOSE MODES

Here is what the strategies mean:

Rootless purpose: low awareness, high energy; thoughtless, haphazard change reigns Productivity and 'being busy' are often mixed up; action dominates Intensity of work is often ineffective and needs ongoing justification Themes and initiatives keep changing and ignore reality	**Meaningful purpose**: high awareness, high energy; people find purpose in what they do People are motivated, convinced, creative and contribute Awareness, accountability and self-determination prevail Vision, values and direction provide meaning
Purposeless meaning: low awareness, low energy; demotivation draws on energy People are unmotivated, have no choice and are busy all the time They lack resources, routine work dominates and complexity takes over Initiatives are blocked and direction is confusing	**Idle purpose**: high awareness, low energy; the lack of energy kills motivation People and teams are exhausted, and constantly sapping energy Defensive reactions prevail and are part of the culture Risk and boundaries dominate decisions and action

Strategies for reaching the flow line (in Figure 65) with purpose include knowing with clarity, raising awareness and helping people find purpose. The solution involves the following:

- **Build awareness and nurture a productive culture**: Use agile systems with vision, values, strategy and routines to reduce complexity, and tools that can handle volatility

- **Remove interference:** Fix erroneous systems and then marshal leaders to help people find purpose. The fix is systems with agile features

With this introduction and the information in Figure 66, ask this:
- What is your purpose score? What does it mean?
- How does purpose enable people to perform?
- Where are the potentials for, and possible sources of interference with, purpose?

Question. The assessment statement for this element:
We are able to find purpose in what we do, establish a clear identity and fully commit to our work.
Evaluation. The answer is scored as follows:
0 = Strongly disagree, 25 Disagree, 50 Neutral, 75 Agree, 100 Strongly agree.
Meaning. The score indicates the following known symptoms:
• **Meaningful**. A high score means that people find purpose, are excited and are energized to contribute • **Formalized**. A medium score means that people find it hard to see purpose in what they do • **Missing or distorted**. A low score means that people are demotivated and don't find purpose in what they do
Interpretation. Linkages to other elements offer insights and root causes:
• **Performance Triangle**: Systems and culture • **Leadership Scorecard**: Strategy, vision, mission
Sources
• **Model**. *The Performance Triangle*, pages 125-127, 196-197 • **Process**. *Management Design* (2nd Ed. 2017), pages 184-187 • **Application**. *People-Centric Management*, pages 65 • **Exercise**. *Agile by Choice*, pages 37-46
Facilitation. Use Post-it notes and the canvas for the answers:
What are the assumptions and principles? Use green Post-it notes. Where is the potential? Use green Post-its. What are the instances of interference? Use red Post-its.

FIGURE 66: PURPOSE INSIGHTS

RELATIONSHIPS

Relationships are the cornerstones of every business transaction. In individualized, people-to-people business relationships with external stakeholders, trust and agreement between employees and the organization are essential. As such, 'relationship capital' is essential to the value of a company. But, good relationships come at a price. They impose a challenge on every leader of an organization. Relationships also relate to interpersonal connectivity. The greater the number of connections among people in an organization, the more restrictions and boundaries they place on one another. This limits their freedom of movement and their ability to perform. As a result, relationships and connectivity must be tuned to the optimum level.

Relationships are an important means for addressing the challenges in an ambiguous context. Connected people with diverse knowledge make better decisions in any context, and with a variety of outcomes, than one lonely manager might.

As a leader and employee, ask yourself:

- Do people have healthy relationships that build trust and agreement among employees and external stakeholders alike?
- Do the relationships among employees and stakeholders facilitate knowledge sharing and growth?
- How do I make it easier for employees to connect with their colleagues?
- How do I deepen relationships to build social glue?

Individuals connect and build relationships. Agile techniques enable relationships at scale.

STRATEGIES FOR STRONG CONNECTIVITY

Connectivity facilitates relationships. It comes from leadership: interactions and a culture that support people with direction, offer choice, delegate authority, use knowledge and foster continual learning. Remember, knowledge is the only resource that grows with use.

Connectivity helps people select the right opportunities and deal with ambiguity. Four relationship modes (Figure 67) can be used to identify the nature of connectivity in your organization.

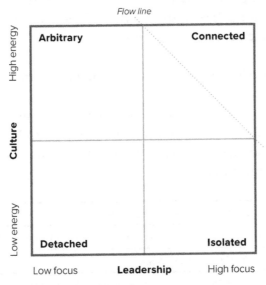

FIGURE 67: RELATIONSHIPS MODES

Here is what the strategies mean:

Arbitrary relationships: low focus, high energy; people are busy with scattered initiatives. People are always busy and need ongoing motivation. Teams miss opportunities, or the right time. Leaders are blind to inefficiencies	**Connected relationships**: high focus, high energy; creative people with choice build knowledge. Employees have choice in how to do things. They get the right things done. Leaders interact, offer clarity and support learning
Detached relationships: low focus, low energy; people are isolated and mediocrity prevails. People stand in each other's way for no reason. Teams resist change and are mobilized by others. It's hard to escape the negative spiral	**Isolated relationships**: high focus, low energy; leaders keep people busy. Employees use up resources with long hours. There is no capacity for anything else. Teams work on projects in the dark, with little impact

Strategies for reaching the flow line and building reliable relationships include moving together in one direction, enabling choice and building relationships between people to enhance knowledge. The solution involves:

- **Strengthening the focus and energizing the culture**: Use agile systems (build for creativity and innovation) and rethink the culture (desired behaviours, decisions and actions)
- **Removing interference**: Fix erroneous systems, eliminate viruses from the culture (see Tool #1 for more on viruses) and vaccinate the culture against new infections

With this introduction and the information in Figure 68, ask these questions:

- What is your relationship score? What does it mean?
- How do relationships enable people to perform?
- Where are the potentials for, and possible sources of interference with, purpose?

Question. The assessment statement for this element:
We can rely on relevant relationships to support our work and to enrich our knowledge.
Evaluation. The answer is scored as follows:
0 = Strongly disagree, 25 Disagree, 50 Neutral, 75 Agree, 100 Strongly agree.
Meaning. The score indicates the following known symptoms:
• **Intensive**. A high score indicates strong internal and external relationships that enable people to connect and share their knowledge • **Formalized**. A medium score indicates limited internal and external relationships, with disconnects and limited sharing of knowledge • **Missing or disrupted**. A low score indicates blocked internal and external relationships, with no knowledge sharing
Interpretation. Linkages to other elements offer insights and root causes:
• **Performance Triangle**: Leadership and culture • **Leadership Scorecard**: Implementation, shared agenda
Sources
• **Model**. *The Performance Triangle*, pages 167-173, 173-175 • **Process**. *Management Design* (2nd Ed. 2017), pages 184-187, 190-191 • **Application**. *People-Centric Management*, page 77 • **Exercise**. *Agile by Choice*, pages 56-69
Facilitation. Use Post-it notes and the canvas for the answers:
What are the assumptions and principles? Use green Post-it notes. Where is the potential? Use green Post-its. What are the instances of interference? Use red Post-its.

FIGURE 68: RELATIONSHIPS INSIGHTS

COLLABORATION

Collaboration is an issue because of complexity, which increases with size and scope. We keep adding functions, geographies, departments, services, client groups and other structures to our organizations. In a complex and networked world, where knowledge matters, collaboration is more important than ever. Every structure creates barriers between people who need to work together, such as limited or distorted information flows. In addition, there is a need to resolve the fundamental cooperation problem of employees and organizations having different, often conflicting, goals.

Collaboration is an important means to address the challenge of an uncertain environment. Collective knowledge and many diverse minds are better than individuals at dealing with uncertainty.

As a leader and employee, ask yourself:

- Do employees and stakeholders share unique knowledge and work together toward common goals, to achieve success in their everyday activities?
- Do people demonstrate trust, creativity and patience when working together as unexpected events occur?
- How do I encourage people to connect and collaborate?
- Who are the people I need to cooperate with to get work done? Where do I get support in that endeavour?

Individuals naturally collaborate. Engage agile techniques to scale collaboration in organizations.

STRATEGIES FOR EFFECTIVE COOPERATION

Cooperation enhances collaboration. Cooperation comes from systems (rules, routines and tools) and leaders (who connect people) that facilitate collaboration. Trust helps mobilize resources and turn opportunities into value, despite uncertainty. Four collaboration modes (Figure 69) can be used to identify the nature of cooperation in organizations.

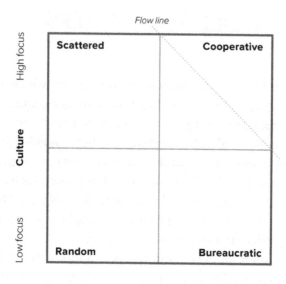

FIGURE 69: COLLABORATION MODES

Here is what the strategies mean:

Scattered collaboration: low awareness, high focus; private agendas determine work People move in different directions and miss opportunities Teams miss out on synergies and only follow orders Leaders follow their own agendas	**Cooperative collaboration**: high awareness, high focus; trust mobilizes people and resources People connect to share and collaborate with others Teams address important themes in the right way Leaders provide resources and trust teams
Random collaboration: low awareness, low focus; people cooperate where there is trust People don't know what's important and who to go to for information Teams work in isolation without getting things done Leaders are uncertain and out of their depth, and tend to keep their heads down	**Bureaucratic collaboration**: high awareness, low focus; systems are in control People need to navigate around bureaucracy to get things done Routines and rules have taken control Leaders are torn between many priorities

Strategies for reaching the flow line of superior collaboration include mobilizing energy, building trust and facilitating collaboration. The solution involves the following:

- **Build awareness and focus attention on collaboration**: Use agile systems (with 'management by objectives' that works,

rules and routines, and collaboration tools) and marshal leaders to work in the system (see Chapter 1)
- **Remove interference:** Fix erroneous systems, remove faulty leadership and train leaders the agile way

With this introduction and the information in Figure 70, consider the following:
- What is your collaboration score? What does it mean?
- How does collaboration enable people to perform?
- Where are the potentials for, and possible sources of interference with, collaboration?

Question. The assessment statement for this element:
We can freely collaborate and exchange information across organizational boundaries for synergies and leverage.
Evaluation. The answer is scored as follows:
0 = Strongly disagree, 25 Disagree, 50 Neutral, 75 Agree, 100 Strongly agree.
Meaning. The score indicates the following known symptoms:
• **Intensive**. A high score means that collaboration across boundaries and sharing of knowledge takes place • **Formalized**. With a medium score, collaboration and sharing of knowledge are controlled by leaders, which is a bottleneck • **Missing or disrupted**. Low scores mean that silos prevent collaboration and the exchange of information
Interpretation. Linkages to other elements offer insights and root causes:
• **Performance Triangle**: Systems and culture • **Leadership Scorecard**: Beliefs, contribution dialogue, shared aspirations
Sources
• **Model**. *The Performance Triangle*, pages 95-99, 198-199 • **Process**. *Management Design* (2nd Ed. 2017), pages 184-187, 188-189 • **Application**. *People-Centric Management*, page 89 • **Exercise**. *Agile by Choice*, pages 56-69
Facilitation. Use Post-it notes and the canvas for the answers:
What are the assumptions and principles? Use green Post-it notes. Where is the potential? Use green Post-its. What are the instances of interference? Use red Post-its.

FIGURE 70: COLLABORATION INSIGHTS

RESILIENCE

Purpose, relationships and collaboration with self-organization as the principle support the resilience of organizations.

The 'work environment' defines how we establish goals as a bonding element in relationships. It is the trigger for collaboration and provides clues to the meaning of work. Narrow targets limit the options, whereas broad direction opens up multiple ways to connect, cooperate and find meaning.

Resilience is about the robustness of systems. It has a stabilizing effect, through social controls and absorptive capabilities. Organizations reach greater levels of resilience through purpose, relationships and cooperative strategies.

Organizations with high resilience are able to reinvent themselves and find new business models that preserve the core. Relationships bring new knowledge to the firm; collaboration expands beyond traditional boundaries; purpose inspires entrepreneurial behaviour. This combination strengthens resilience and offers growth opportunities.

Resilience needs the balance of renewal. By itself, resilience is a conserving capability. Only through its counterpart, renewal, can it reach growth capacity. Renewal means new knowledge, intense collaboration and a deep sense of purpose.

Diagnostic Mentoring measures resilience as the average of the purpose, collaboration and relationship scores.

With this introduction and the information in Figure 71, consider these questions:

- What is your resilience score? What does it mean?
- How does your organization's resilience enable people to perform?
- Where are the potentials for, and possible sources of interference with, resilience?

Question. Resilience is calculated as:

The average of the purpose, collaboration and relationship scores.

Evaluation. The answer is scored as follows:

0 = Strongly disagree, 25 Disagree, 50 Neutral, 75 Agree, 100 Strongly agree.

Meaning. The score indicates the following known symptoms:

- **High, robust, balanced**. A high score means a robust organization with capabilities to withstand external shocks. The task is to maintain them at that level
- **Medium, limited**. With a medium score, the organization risks fighting new challenges with yet another project to fix the gaps. The task is to invest in resilient capabilities
- **Low, fragile**. A low score indicates a lack of any defensive mechanisms. With the smallest change or shock, the organization is at risk. The task is to invest in resilient capabilities, and to do so quickly

Interpretation. Linkages to other elements offer insights and root causes:

- **Performance Triangle**: Leadership and culture
- **Outcomes**: Growth

Sources

- **Process**. *Management Design* (2nd Ed. 2017), pages 94-95
- **Application**. *People-Centric Management,* page 149
- **Exercise**. *Agile by Choice, page*s 56-69

Facilitation. Use Post-it notes and the canvas for the answers:

What are the assumptions and principles? Use green Post-it notes.
Where is the potential? Use green Post-its.
What are the instances of interference? Use red Post-its.

FIGURE 71: RESILIENCE INSIGHTS

GROWTH

Purpose, relationships and collaboration have the capacity to absorb and renew. Our research for *Diagnostic Mentoring* confirms a strong relationship between resilience and growth.

An organization where people find purpose in what they do, can collaborate across organizational boundaries and gain new knowledge can likely weather any storm. Employees find new business opportunities that contribute to growth.

People engage and grow when purpose and self-responsibility are the sources of motivation; they can gain knowledge and they learn from others. Organizations exist because there's almost no work any more that can be completed solely by one person. Work happens in teams, where people collaborate and contribute.

With this introduction and the information in Figure 8, ask yourself:

- What is your growth score? What does it mean?
- How does your organization's growth contribute to outcomes?
- Where are the potentials for, and possible sources of interference with, growth?

MINING
– GET HEROIC LEADERS
TO COLLABORATE

The new, female CEO of a traditional company in a male-dominated industry known for heavy gear and questionable people-management decided to change the way her company operated. The starting point was a corporate organization that managed a portfolio of 150 independent divisions. As the price of some of its products dropped fast, many operations lost their profitability.

The task was to review corporate management in line with the new CEO's agenda for more of a *people* focus, and with more care and respect for the environment. The idea was to engage 80 leaders of local operations in a series of workshops organized by a leading executive development firm to create a shared agenda around these themes. As part of that initiative, all executives involved conducted a diagnostic that then served as the agenda for the workshops.

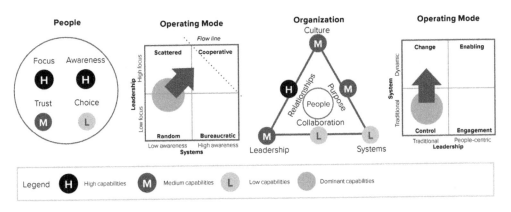

FIGURE 72: MINING

The diagnostic results (Figure 72) show the familiar patterns of a conglomerate where the divisions have a life of their own: little feedback, poor awareness, random collaboration, systems that do not support corporate or local management, and a control mode that dominates.

While the chances of changing the dominating mode in such an industry are slim (if not downright illusory), collaboration became the prevalent topic across all workshops. The idea was to identify areas of potential cooperation, which would help lower costs in the relevant areas.

The workshops ended with the 80 managers agreeing to more than 50 initiatives. This amounted to a significant call for change, driven by the businesses themselves. Together with the redesign of key corporate processes and an annual management cycle, the new CEO was able to change the way the corporation operates.

WORK

Diagnostic Mentoring creates awareness of the elements of the work environment and fosters a resilient organization. Purpose, relationships and collaboration link the corners of the Performance Triangle. They are the elements that determine resilience and growth.

KEY CHAPTER IDEAS

- Being aware of the essential aspects of work is the first step toward better management
- Purpose needs to be found — it's called sense-making, not sense-giving
- Relationships offer the access to enhanced knowledge
- Collaboration is a matter of effective cooperation in teams
- In a resilient organization, people find purpose in what they do, connect with one another to enhance knowledge, and collaborate across organizational boundaries
- A resilient organization has the ability to achieve growth from within

ACTION AGENDA

Diagnose the critical work elements to raise awareness for what it takes to be resilient and grow.

FURTHER READING

Michel, L (2013). *The Performance Triangle: Diagnostic Mentoring to Manage Organizations and People for Superior Performance in Turbulent Times.* London: LID Publishing.

CHAPTER 8

OPERATIONS

Operations is every manager's fourth priority. The diagnostic raises awareness of the elements that constitute operations. Chapter 8 combines the people, organization and work elements into speed, agility and resilience, which together represent dynamic capabilities. Together, they frame capabilities and outcomes as part of operations. Agile maturity creates awareness of the elements and provides a benchmark.

DYNAMIC CAPABILITIES AND OUTCOMES

The Performance Triangle combines elements of the individual, operating and work environments into the system that operates the business. Managers use the operating system to develop the operation's capabilities, which deliver the expected outcomes.

Groups of people align through dynamic capabilities. It is that invisible force in the operating system of an organization that aligns employees around a central core, with information, direction, plans, beliefs and boundaries.

Speed, agility and resilience are the three elements of dynamic capabilities. Dynamic capabilities are configurations of resources (talent, routines, rules, competencies, structures, etc.) that enable organizations to continuously adapt to rapid changes in the environment. Such organizations enable people to perform the inner game and create the capabilities to cope with a volatile environment — the outer game. With increasing variety and interlinked dynamics in the environment, dynamic capabilities are a true competitive advantage.

Figure 73 shows how dynamic capabilities relate to outcomes. It's the operating system — with the individual, operational and work environments — that determines the nature of operations.

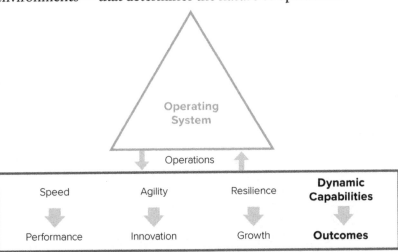

FIGURE 73: DYNAMIC CAPABILITIES AND OUTCOMES

These capabilities help organizations address changes in the environment without the negative effects of traditional change programmes. As such, they balance speed and control, agility and stability, resilience and renewal. This helps ensure that reinforcing loops and balancing loops are in tune with each other.

Performance, innovation and growth are key indicators for organizational outcomes. Awareness, choice and trust help people focus on what counts. The result is flow, where learning, performance and joy collide to deliver superior results. In an environment where people can unlock their creativity and create new knowledge, innovation is the outcome. The way we set goals and deal with stakeholders determines much of the internal growth capacity of a company.

Figure 73 is one of the key visuals for Diagnostic Mentoring. When speed does not match performance, we need to look at the individual environment. When agility and innovation don't correlate, the operating environment needs work. When resilience does not lead to growth, we need to search for clues to root causes with the work environment. As such, Figure 73 is a key snapshot to take note of.

REFUELLING ENERGY

There is no speed without control, there is no agility without stability and there's no growth without renewal. There are no dynamic capabilities without energy. It's therefore appropriate to ask who is responsible for refuelling energy: people or organizations?

There are different roles when it comes to re-energizing organizations: individual employee responsibilities, shared accountability and institutional authority. Figure 74 identifies the sources of motivation.

Motivation	Individual Self-responsibility	Institution Outside control
Readiness: want to do … Accountability lies with the individual	Responsibility, awareness, focus of attention, intrinsic contract	Purpose, extrinsic contract, awareness
Capability: able to do … Shared responsibility	Choice, skills, learning	Development, competencies
Opportunity: can do … Accountability lies with the institution	The institution offers the playing field, work, employment for the individual	Degrees of freedom (room to move), resources, process, tools (the system)

FIGURE 74: SOURCES OF MOTIVATION

- **Readiness**: Accountability lies with the individual. Responsibility is the driving force behind motivation: the intrinsic contract is a prerequisite for people getting things done. The extrinsic contract is an external-control tool that institutions use to motivate people to perform in the desired direction.
- **Capability**: There is shared accountability for capability, between the individual and the institution. The organization's mechanisms for competence-management define the talent's needs and offer development opportunities. But, for this to be effective, individuals have to make choices about learning.
- **Opportunity**: People need to be given scope and opportunity to perform. This is solely the responsibility of institutions. Leaders represent the institution and are accountable for creating a productive working environment, with adequate resources, rules and processes. Creating such an environment saves considerable managerial time and puts the focus on opportunities, rather than ineffective control.

AGILE MATURITY

The agile maturity level is a gauge that can be used to review the dynamic capabilities and intangible value of organizations. Agile maturity is calculated using the dynamic capabilities score (Figure 75) from the diagnostic. It produces a six-level ranking, from pioneers at the top to contestants at the bottom.

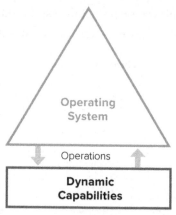

FIGURE 75: DYNAMIC CAPABILITIES SCORE

The six agile maturity levels in Figure 76 provide an indication of where organizations are in their shift to agile: contestants, exploiters, changers, enablers, performers or pioneers.

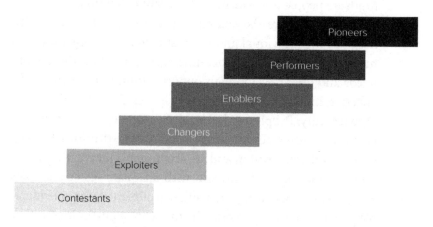

FIGURE 76: AGILE MATURITY LEVELS

This scale is the result of 15 years of research with the diagnostic and 250 organizations worldwide, in all industry sectors. It has proven to be a valuable tool, offering a benchmark for organizations and pointing to what can be achieved through various improvements. Given the strong correlation between dynamic capabilities, outcomes and success, the results are better than with organizations lacking these capabilities.

Pioneers are organizations designed in a way that helps ensure continuous evolution. They use dynamic capabilities to deliver superior outcomes. Decentralized decision-making, teamwork and active influence are the trademarks of a new way to manage — the agile way — with guided self-organization as one of its fundamental principles.

Performers are organizations designed to encourage a dynamic environment. They've built capabilities that help navigate a VUCA world, and that balance people's needs and organizational objectives. Coordination across boundaries, self-control and connectivity help them outdo their peers, even in a turbulent context, on performance, innovation and growth.

Enablers are organizations designed to engage well with people in a stable environment. They motivate employees based on self-responsibility, purpose and social control. They favour action-orientation and knowledge work. However, their implementation of the people-centric approach is insufficient to cope with a dynamic setting. The fix is to implement radically decentralized decision-making.

Changers are organizations designed to implement disruptive change. Whenever their leaders believe that change is required, they alter their structures and reallocate resources. As the context changes, they keep restructuring. The fix is always more control, direct managerial influence and relentless customer focus.

Exploiters are organizations designed to exploit their assets. They optimize processes to deliver at the lowest possible level of asset utilization. Many are quite successful in doing so. Consequently, their leaders are largely satisfied with the current situation. However, in dynamic markets, they don't have the capabilities to adapt quickly. They can fix their situation by tightening performance management and embarking on change.

Contestants are organizations that inherited a design based on operating in a stable environment. Often, their context and current capabilities don't match, and this reflects an infected culture, faulty leadership or erroneous systems. Typical but ineffective resolutions include fixing the culture, people and leaders. Contestants are stuck in bureaucracy.

With this introduction, your agile maturity level and the information in Figure 77, think about these questions:

- What is your agile maturity level? What does it mean?
- How does your organization's agile maturity contribute to outcomes?
- Where are the potentials for, and possible sources of interference with, agile maturity?

Metrics. Agile maturity is determined ...	
... through the average of the aggregate dynamic capabilities, the outcomes and the success score.	
Evaluation. The answer is scored as follows:	
A score lower than 55 for contestants, 55-60 for exploiters, 60-65 for changers, 65-70 for enablers, 70-75 for performers, higher than 75 for pioneers.	
Meaning. The score indicates the following known symptoms:	
Use the descriptions of the six levels to evaluate your agile maturity.	
Interpretation. Linkages to other elements offer insights and root causes:	
• **Performance Triangle**: culture, leadership, systems, success	
Sources	
• **Exercise**. *Agile by Choice, pages* 74-76	
Facilitation. Use Post-it notes and the canvas for the answers:	
What are the assumptions and principles? Use green Post-it notes. Where is the potential? Use green Post-its. What are the instances of interference? Use red Post-its.	

FIGURE 77: AGILE MATURITY INSIGHTS

PHARMA
– AGILE RESEARCH

The research department, with 2,500 employees, had not established a pipeline necessary to ensure the company's future profitability. The new head of the research division committed to changing that.

The idea was to work with the research leader on creating and implementing what he called his 'agile' agenda. He was determined that the division would become more agile in how it allocated resources to promising projects, and rebuild a solid project pipeline.

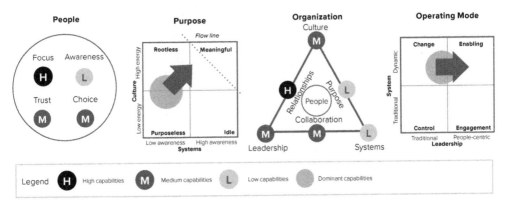

FIGURE 78: PHARMA

The first diagnostic results (Figure 78) indicated people with a distorted focus, who got work done based on trust. Purpose was invested in work they performed for the firm's research mission. But, the real honour came with getting favourably referenced for their academic work.

On the organizational side, with medium scores on leadership and culture and low scores on systems, agile maturity only reached the Changers level. This corresponded with the dominant 'change' operating mode.

The task became clear. On one hand, research management had to clarify its purpose and get control of those projects that got the funds. In line with that, it also had to make sure that a slew of secondary pet projects did not get the funds any more. Systems had to be reworked to support the agile approach to planning, allocating resources and implementing strategy. A second measurement clearly indicated that the road map was on track and had the right initiatives in place.

A year into the project, there were visible signs that the pipeline had become richer.

OPERATIONS

Operations combine the people, organization and work elements of an agile organization. Agile maturity is the tool to create awareness of the critical elements that create value in every operation.

KEY CHAPTER IDEAS

- Speed, agility and resilience are three dynamic capabilities
- Performance, innovation and growth are the outcomes
- Agile maturity levels indicate readiness in a VUCA world
- There are different responsible parties for the development of people

ACTION AGENDA

Diagnose the elements of operations with the agile maturity framework.

FURTHER READING

Michel, L (2020). *Agile by Choice: A Workbook for Leaders*. London: LID Publishing.

CHAPTER 9
MANAGEMENT

Management is the fifth priority. The diagnostic offers insights on people-centric levers and the elements of the Leadership Score-card. Chapter 9 combines choices on the operating model with requirements for the design of management. The scorecard extends the Performance Triangle to 20 elements. We begin this chapter by gaining a deeper understanding of people-centric attributes.

How do we *enable* people? (Note that 'control' is the technical term used throughout the management literature to explain influence, motivation, accountability and engagement. However, in the popular media, control is generally associated with negative features. That's why I use *enable* rather than *control* here. True, it's an opportunistic decision, but it aligns with the enabling mode.)

PEOPLE-CENTRIC ASSUMPTIONS

'Knowledge work' means that people — not just leaders — have the full ability to act and make decisions. Distributed decision-making requires a people-centric operating environment in which people can apply their full potential. This is in sharp contrast to the traditional principles of the 'controlling mode,' where interference prevents people from using their knowledge and experience to seize opportunities. In the enabling operating mode, the thinking and doing are united.

Knowledge work is made up of five control elements:

- **Understand**: Information and immediate feedback raise awareness of what is important. This helps people understand what matters and focuses attention. Superior understanding requires that sensors are not on mute and amplifiers work properly
- **Think**: Knowledge workers have a set of mental maps that help them make sense of situations and make decisions. The benefits for an organization come not only from individual thinking but also from collective thinking. The thinking requires an opportunity to create meaning and asks for a deliberate choice to move in one direction
- **Act**: This involves translating ideas into action. The task is to mobilize resources to get things done. People put their energy into things that they care about. And, energy requires action to be meaningful. Contribution requires the opportunity to apply knowledge, and to support and balance freedom and constraints. Superior contributions build on trust of people and in people
- **Engage**: Attention is a limited resource; energy is required to maintain it at a high level. Attention must be focused to prevent distraction from competing demands. A high level of engagement requires beliefs, motives and purpose
- **Adhere**: Energy adds pull and a positive tension to the boundaries of an organization. It helps traverse the stretch between safely staying within the boundaries and searching for opportunities outside the boundaries. This tension requires a balance between efficiency and entrepreneurship. A high level of adherence maintains a good balance

Figure 79 contrasts traditional and agile approaches to knowledge work, according to these five elements.

	Understand	Think	Act	Engage	Adhere
In a people-centric context ...	Use information to get work done	Make decisions	Are motivated by a sense of purpose	Have clear priorities	Are empowered and clear about norms
People use their potential	Unlimited information	Unlimited opportunities; encouraged to take risks	Increased pressures	Limited attention; limited resources	Growing temptations for outside the boundaries
In a traditional context ...	Information is limited to the top	Leaders make decisions	Leaders motivate for performance	Employees execute ...	... and control what gets done
People are bound by limitations	Lack of information	Lack of opportunities; fear of risk	Lack of purpose	Conflicting goals; lack of resources	Lack of boundaries

FIGURE 79: CONTRASTING KNOWLEDGE WORK

People-centric assumes a mindset where people want to contribute, develop and work in a goal-oriented way. This is in sharp contrast to traditional assumptions, where people are motivated, controlled and trained. Figure 80 illustrates the differences for employees and leaders.

People-centric assumptions

Knowledge employees ...
Want to contribute
Want to do things right
Want to achieve
Want to be creative and develop

People-centric managers ...
Ask questions and focus
Shape the environment
Support creativity
Establish relationships

Traditional assumptions

As compared to ...
Don't do anything on their own
Need to be developed
Need to be directed
Do what they are told

As compared to ...
Motivate and decide; tell people what to do
Judge and review
Sit at the top; provide instructions
Are responsible; have the power to change and set the rules

FIGURE 80: ASSUMPTIONS ABOUT WORK

In a people-centric context, managers have a new role: to create an environment where people can unlock their full talent.

PEOPLE-CENTRIC LEVERS

Now, it's time to change our perspective from the individual to management, to further explore the choice of people-centric. This section offers four levers that determine the dimensions of people-centric management (Figure 81). These levers translate the inner game into a management cycle. It's the people-centric replacement of traditional managerial control.

Business is about identifying and selecting opportunities, and transforming them into value. With people in mind, you can now use the four principles of awareness, choice, trust and attention to deliver value. Executives apply these four people-centric practices within their teams.

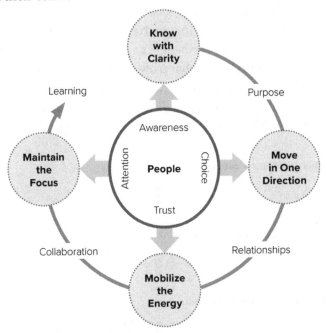

FIGURE 81: PEOPLE-CENTRIC MANAGEMENT

1. **Know with clarity**: raise awareness. Help people find purpose. Motivation stems from self-responsibility. Purpose replaces incentives. All leaders need to do for people is help them make sense of what truly matters. That's the best way to identify

opportunities and deal with complexity in your business. The lever serves the need to understand.

2. **Move in one direction**: enable choice. Encourage relationships to enhance knowledge. People-centric leaders delegate decisions and encourage relationships among people to enhance their skills and knowledge. Choice and direction are their means to bundle the energy, to help them select the right opportunities and move in one direction as their way to deal with ambiguity. The lever serves the need to think.

3. **Mobilize the energy**: build trust. Facilitate collaboration. People-centric leaders facilitate self-organization based on trust as the means to deal with uncertainty. They mobilize resources in ways that enable collaboration across organizational boundaries, turning opportunities into value. The lever serves the need to act.

4. **Maintain the focus**: focus attention. Enable learning. People-centric leaders use beliefs and boundaries to maintain the focus of attention on what truly matters. They know that focus enables learning as the means to unlock creativity and stick with chosen opportunities, despite the distractions of greater volatility. The lever serves the need to engage and adhere.

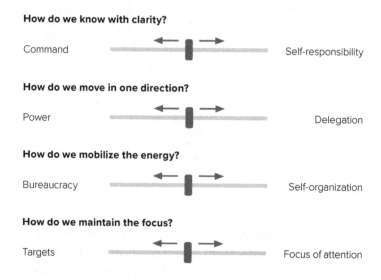

How do we know with clarity?

Command — Self-responsibility

How do we move in one direction?

Power — Delegation

How do we mobilize the energy?

Bureaucracy — Self-organization

How do we maintain the focus?

Targets — Focus of attention

FIGURE 82: FOUR PEOPLE-CENTRIC LEVERS

The four people-centric levers (Figure 82) offer a choice between traditional and people-centric management:

1. How do we know with clarity?
2. How do we move in one direction?
3. How do we mobilize the energy?
4. How do we maintain the focus?

Traditional management favours command, power, bureaucracy and narrow targets. People-centricity is about self-responsibility, delegation, self-organization and focus of attention. It requires a shift from left to right — from traditional to people-centricity.

Know with clarity helps with identifying opportunities. It represents the ability to raise awareness, understand and find purpose, despite complexity. Lever 1 identifies how we help people understand and find purpose, between traditional command styles and being agile through self-responsibility.

Move in one direction is the ability to select valuable opportunities. Choice requires the alignment of forces and connecting people around purpose and direction, despite ambiguity. Lever 2 identifies how people align to form teams, between applying traditional power and delegation.

Mobilize the energy refers to how we turn opportunities into value. It is the ability to trust our own resources and those around us, and to get things done despite uncertainty. Lever 3 identifies how we mobilize the energy to collaborate between traditional bureaucracy and self-organization.

Maintain the focus is about sticking with the chosen opportunity. It is the ability to focus attention and learn, despite volatility. Lever 4 identifies how we maintain the focus and learn, between traditional target setting and attention.

The four levers offer a choice between traditional and people-centric capabilities. The shift from tradition to people-centricity means a different way to work, organize and manage. It serves the purpose of helping people understand, think, act, engage and adhere.

THE LEADERSHIP SCORECARD

The Leadership Scorecard (Figure 83) summarizes 20 elements as observation points into a table intended to help leaders work *in* the system. The horizontal view of the scorecard represents the organization view (success, culture, leadership, systems) while the vertical view (information, strategy, implementation, beliefs and boundaries) establishes the management dimension.

The scorecard offers a template, with 20 questions to discuss the management view of the Performance Triangle. These elements become context-related and specific through the answers to these questions.

Effective information systems help raise awareness of, and help employees make sense of, what is important. This increases the agility of the organization, as employees can react to changes in the environment.

Clarity of strategy supports leaders in providing direction and establishing a shared intent. This enhances the overall alignment of the organization. Rigorous implementation and performance conversations establish the shared agenda, to address the capabilities of the organization. Strong beliefs enable the conversation about the contribution of every employee. This creates the shared aspirations and purpose, for higher motivation. And, it helps establish clear boundaries with a conversation about risks, to help the organization set its norms. As a result, the organization ensures that it is smart about how it uses its playing field.

With the Leadership Scorecard, the four levers combine with five systems and five leadership interactions to help achieve people-centric management: people understand, think, act, engage and adhere in line with the direction of the firm. 'Know with Clarity' helps people understand and raises their awareness. 'Move in One Direction' guides the thinking and offers choice. 'Mobilize the Energy' enacts responsibility to deliver value based on trust. 'Maintain the Focus' provides engagement and adherence elements to refocus attention when it gets lost.

In combination, systems, leadership and culture shape the intangible capabilities that determine success: responsiveness, alignment, core capabilities, motivation and cleverness.

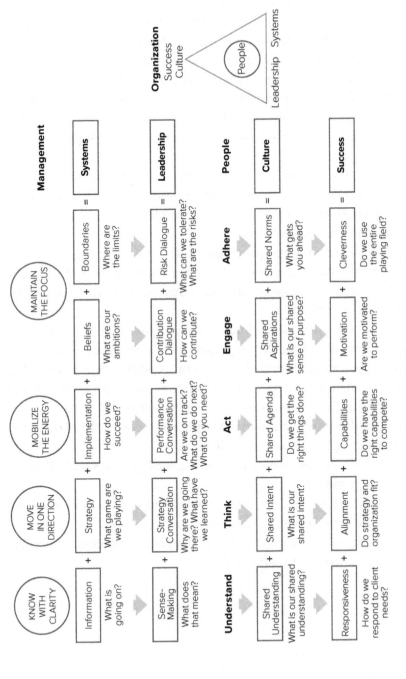

FIGURE 83: THE LEADERSHIP SCORECARD

Imagine driving a car. It takes five things to do that:

First, you need a dashboard that indicates how everything is operating and reflects how fast you're going. In organizations, this helps you make sense of information, to create the shared understanding of how well we are doing. → Supporting the ability to understand

Second, the navigation system directs you to the destination. In organizations, the conversation about the strategy creates a shared intent with the team on what direction to take. → Supporting the ability to think

Third, the engine and wheels translate the energy into motion. In organizations, this means implementation — putting the strategy into a shared agenda that plots out what's being done to get there. → Supporting the ability to act

Fourth, with the gas pedal, the driver controls speed. In organizations, acceleration happens through a conversation on beliefs: the vision, mission and individual goals that create pull. → Supporting the ability to engage

Fifth, every car needs brakes. They ensure that speed remains under control and enable the proper reaction to sudden, unexpected events. In organizations, this function resides within boundaries: the governance, structures and risk limits that clarify what is in and out of bounds. → Supporting the ability to adhere

With this introduction to the Leadership Scorecard and the information in Figure 84, ask yourself:

- What are the scores in your Leadership Scorecard? What do they mean?
- How does your scorecard support people to performance and the organization to succeed?
- Where are the potentials for, and possible sources of interference with, your scorecard?

Metrics. The Leadership Scorecard elements are determined ...
... through 20 individual questions.
Evaluation. The answer is scored as follows:
0 = Strongly disagree, 25 Disagree, 50 Neutral, 75 Agree, 100 Strongly agree.
Meaning. The score indicates the following known symptoms:
Use *The Performance Triangle* to review your scores with detailed descriptions of all culture, leadership, systems and success elements.
Interpretation. Linkages to other elements offer insights and root causes:
• **The Performance Triangle**: culture, leadership, systems, success
Sources
• **Model**. *The Performance Triangle*, pages 209-212 • **Process**. *Management Design* (2nd Ed. 2017), pages 150-151 • **Application**. *People-Centric Management*, pages 145-147
Facilitation. Use Post-it notes and the canvas for the answers:
What are the assumptions and principles? Use green Post-it notes. Where is the potential? Use green Post-its. What are the instances of interference? Use red Post-its.

FIGURE 84: LEADERSHIP SCORECARD INSIGHTS

FOUR PEOPLE-CENTRIC SHIFTS

In essence, the Leadership Scorecard is neutral: it supports traditional and people-centric management. For both, managers will shape it to serve their specific business and management models. For most organizations, the transformation from a traditional to an enabling scorecard requires a shift.

The people-centric shift splits into four parts: The purpose, relationship, collaboration and learning shifts (Figure 85). Each part comes with a distinct culture, distinct leadership and distinct systems, all based on people-centric principles.

From	To	Levers	Shifts
Command	Self-responsibility	Know with clarity	1. The purpose shift
Power	Delegation	Move in one direction	2. The relationship shift
Bureaucracy	Self-organization	Mobilize the energy	3. The collaboration shift
Narrow targets	Attention	Maintain the focus	4. The learning shift

FIGURE 85: FOUR SHIFTS

The purpose shift. The goal of the organization shifts from making money to delighting the customer. The role of the manager now is to help people find purpose, rather than telling them what to do.

The relationship shift. The relationship of individuals to their direct manager shifts to teams with delegated responsibility. And, with that pivot, the role of the manager is to offer direction and enable a supportive work environment, not to check on people's work.

The collaboration shift. Instead of work being coordinated by bureaucracy with rules, plans and reports, it's coordinated through self-organization and agile approaches.

The learning shift. Rather than preoccupation with goals, efficiency and predictability, now, transparency, learning, sharing and continuous improvement help teams maintain their focus.

The four shifts require work *on* the system with the following questions:
1. How do we shift from command to self-responsible, and know with clarity?

2. How do we shift from power to delegation, and move in one direction?
3. How do we shift from bureaucracy to self-organization, and mobilize energies?
4. How do we shift from narrow targets to wide direction, and maintain the focus?

The shift should start with storytelling, as it's a quick and inspirational way to make sense of what's happening to the wider team and organization. Rather than communicating and advocating the next change, you can establish credibility and trust by telling a story that touches lives. Storytelling translates abstract models and numbers into compelling images of the future.

THE PURPOSE SHIFT

The first shift is the story of people who know with clarity and find purpose. It's the shift from command to self-responsibility, with the goal of delighting the customer.

Command assumes that people need guidance to get things done. That guidance may range from detailed orders and control of actions to gentle observation. But, both remain part of the traditional control mindset. It comes with traditional 'plan, do, check and act' management skills that are guided by extensive performance measurement and information tools.

In contrast, self-responsibility builds on motivation. By definition, self-responsible people are motivated by the ability to say no to things. They're driven by purpose that guides their engagement. By agreeing to get things done by their own will, they'll apply their creativity and knowledge to better deal with greater complexity.

The first shift (Figure 86) enables people to find purpose. It requires a different mindset — a new set of skills and enabling tools that build on distributed knowledge for a dynamic era.

Capabilities	Shift to	Purpose
Mindset	Self-responsibility	Motivation
Skill set	Interactive sense-making	Feedback and clarity
Toolset	Understanding	Raise awareness, shared understanding

FIGURE 86: THE PURPOSE SHIFT

The shift from command to self-responsibility requires agile capabilities.

The shift of mind to self-responsibility. Self-responsibility is the prerequisite for motivation. It requires that leaders let go of traditional control modes. In a context where knowledge is widely distributed, agile assumes that people want to contribute and perform.

The shift to skills for feedback and sense-making. Motivated people demand purpose. They need feedback with information that helps them make sense of things. Agile demands active sense-making.

The shift to tools that deepen the understanding. Agile works with a toolbox that raises awareness of what matters most and creates a shared understanding.

Agility builds on a strong, stable foundation. And then, a successful shift to self-responsibility always builds on solid capabilities that enable people to know with clarity. The stability comes from skills and tools to assess market moves and performance indicators that offer reliable feedback. Without high quality diagnostic information, it's a risky shift and agility remains fragile.

THE RELATIONSHIP SHIFT

The second shift is for people to move in one direction and build relationships to enhance knowledge. It's a shift from power to delegated responsibility in teams.

Power originates from a mindset with an industrial background of low-skill work, where people need to be told what to do. It implies hierarchy and concentrated knowledge at the top. Relationships are formed through pre-set structures and formal authority. Power is exercised in many shades of grey, and it's important to note that power and authority are neither inherently bad nor good. There are times when power and authority are the only way to get things done fast.

Delegation assumes that knowledge is widely distributed and those who assume responsibility know what they're doing. Choice is left to those who assume delegated responsibility. The challenge comes from the need to move in one direction. Alignment with strategy must come from intensive conversations and sharing, which establish productive relationships.

The relationship shift (Figure 87) enables people to build relationships. It requires a new set of conversation and interaction skills that help transcend the shared intent throughout the organization.

Capabilities	Shift to	Relationships
Mindset	Delegated authority in teams	Connectivity & sharing
Skill set	Interactive strategy conversation	Employer brand
Toolset	Thinking	Choice, shared intent

FIGURE 87: THE RELATIONSHIP SHIFT

The shift from power to delegation requires agile capabilities.

The shift of mind to delegation. Relationships at eye-level work with distributed power, where people are accountable for their actions. Agile capabilities ensure that people move in one direction. As such, delegation offers a new and superior kind of control.

The shift to skills for strategy conversations. Delegation requires connectivity, sharing and interaction. Agile capabilities, with conversations about strategy, enhance the employer brand and, eventually, employee loyalty.

The shift to tools that support the thinking. While traditional strategy tools focus on analysis, agile tools support delegated thinking throughout the organization. They offer choice and simultaneously enhance bonding through a shared intent.

The shift from power to delegation does not mean that leaders lose control. Power is the stable platform from which the shift to delegation can be successfully made. Agile delegation demands interaction between leaders and employees on strategy and the way to get there.

THE COLLABORATION SHIFT

The third shift is the story of people who mobilize resources and collaborate across organizational boundaries. It's a shift from bureaucracy to coordination and collaboration in self-organized teams.

Bureaucracy builds on efficiency with leaders, rules and routines to coordinate work. It works well with repetitive tasks that remain the same and where little collaboration is required. But, we've also learned that trust is the *quickest-to-deliver* management concept around. Bureaucracy assumes a competitive environment where mistrust prevails. This is why there are alternatives to traditional bureaucracy.

Self-organization builds on natural trust and assumes that people at the client front are better equipped to coordinate where the work is being done. However, self-organization does not just happen. It requires energy from the outside, in the form of leadership. But, that leadership differs from traditional control. It comes with tools that enable teams to properly function in an uncertain environment.

The collaboration shift (Figure 88) enables people to collaborate with a new set of skills and tools that create trust and a shared agenda throughout the organization.

Capabilities	Shift to	Collaboration
Mindset	Self-organization	Resource flexibility
Skill set	Interactive performance conversation	Collaboration, value creation
Toolset	Delivery	Trust, shared agenda

FIGURE 88: THE COLLABORATION SHIFT

The shift from bureaucracy to self-organization requires agile capabilities.

The shift of mind to self-organization. It's a shift from fixed bureaucratic procedures to flexibility with resource allocation. Agile capabilities ensure that resources are available on demand.

The shift to skills for performance conversations. Interactions across organizational boundaries enhance collaboration. Agile, peer review-based conversations focus on value creation rather than goal achievement.

The shift to tools that focus on value creation. Traditional management-by-objectives systems are replaced by business plans and reviews owned by self-organized teams. Planning and reviews facilitate collaboration with a shared agenda, based on trust, and replace top-down bureaucracy.

The shift from bureaucracy to self-organization enables collaboration throughout the organization. Bureaucracy adds the stable platform, with rigorous routines, while self-organization provides the flexibility of combining resources. A successful shift builds on a stable platform.

THE LEARNING SHIFT

The fourth shift is the story of people who maintain the focus and learn. It's the shift from preoccupation with narrow targets to enabling teams to maintain their focus through learning, sharing and continuously improving.

Narrow targets limit the scope of action beyond team assignments or job descriptions. They're time-limited goals, set by managers to drive performance. Goal-setting may range from fixed targets established by leaders to a contract that's agreed upon with employees. Yet, it remains a tool that cannot cope with higher volatility. The negative effects of gaming the target-setting process are widely discussed in the professional literature.

Attention with broad direction, in contrast, offers space and enables people to focus on things that matter most to their clients. At the same time, focus of attention is a tool that helps people learn and improve upon what they're doing.

The learning shift (Figure 89) enables people to focus attention and learn. It requires a different mindset, with new tools that work well in a volatile environment where knowledge dominates.

Capabilities	Shift to	Learning
Mindset	Focus of attention	Accumulating knowledge
Skill set	Interactive contribution and risk dialogues	Entrepreneurial behaviours, decisions and actions
Toolset	Engagement and adherence	Focus, shared aspirations and norms

FIGURE 89: THE LEARNING SHIFT

The shift from narrow targets to attention based on broad direction requires people-centric capabilities.

The shift of mind to focus of attention. The primacy goes to seeing the whole rather than digging into all the detail. This is a shift away from goal-setting with detailed, fixed targets; it's aimed at enabling people to focus attention within the frame of a broad direction.

The shift of skills to contribution and risk dialogues. These conversations zero in on how to maintain the focus rather than how to aim at goals. Focus directly impacts performance, whereas goals are an intellectual construct with no direct relationship to action.

The shift to tools to engage and adhere. Focus of attention enables learning. Agile tools establish the boundaries of the playing field, with beliefs and norms that frame entrepreneurial behaviours and actions. Broad direction and beliefs stretch the boundaries, whereas norms ensure that no one steps over the boundaries.

The learning shift changes leadership from applying detailed targets to communicating broad direction in support of entrepreneurial behaviours and actions. It assumes, however, that leaders have given some thought to the direction. A successful shift to people-centric builds on the stable platform that helps people maintain their focus and continuously learn.

People-centric levers and the Leadership Scorecard are the means to the ends: they help people perform, align, engage and learn. Step 1: Raise Awareness, with the four shifts, is how you and your organization will get there.

INSURANCE –
REVIVING ENTREPRENEURSHIP

Over the last 20 years, a drive for total perfection in everything resulted in bureaucracy creeping into daily work and management routines. The resulting forms, procedures and reports diverted people's time and attention from creating value.

The diagnostic (Figure 90) with 80 executives worldwide revealed limited choice in a work environment driven by regimented systems and paperwork for everything, which dominated work life. HR had introduced *everything and nothing* for people-centric in a way that turned leaders into robots. There was a weekly schedule of leadership duties. It only took a new CEO to sense the proverbial dying frog in the water that was heating up.

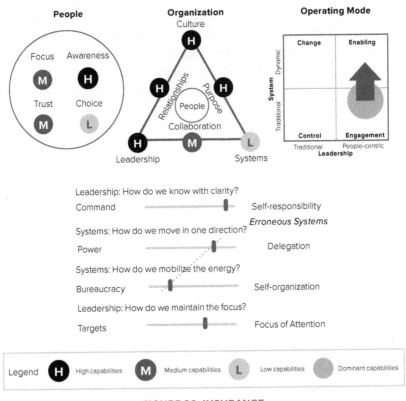

FIGURE 90: INSURANCE

Well-intended self-responsibility and delegation faced bureaucracy and target setting. When it came to management by objectives, many leaders and employees had started to ignore or alter the pre-determined process. The cause of all this was a dangerous mix of erroneous systems. Much of that was rooted in HR's desire for perfection. Just to note: the HR department and leaders earned much international praise for their work in the company.

To revive entrepreneurship, the 'fake' engagement mode first had to turn *real*, with systems that mobilized the energy rather than consuming it. Second, the shift to the enabling mode provided the systems that not only supported people's creativity and performance, but also helped the leaders better strategize, manage, lead and guide performance in a dynamic era.

While the remedy included the redesign of systems, the bigger part was to support leaders in their use of the new systems. One of the interventions was a live-streamed, concurrent team workshop in New York, Singapore and Zürich, with all leaders of the company. It energized the shift. Yet, it took another two years and many more workshops and seminars to fully make the transition — a changeover that was viewed as historic. It enhanced the brand, fortifying its reputation as an excellent employer. Entrepreneurship had returned.

MANAGEMENT

The Leadership Scorecard extends the Performance Triangle to 20 elements.

KEY CHAPTER IDEAS

- Understand, think, act, engage and adhere are the key people-centric attributes
- The four people-centric levers structure the Leadership Scorecard
- The scorecard includes 20 elements
- The horizontal view originates from the Performance Triangle elements
- The vertical view adds the managerial perspective
- Four shifts add people-centric features to the Leadership Scorecard

ACTION AGENDA

Diagnose the elements of the Leadership Scorecard with a managerial lens.

FURTHER READING

Michel, L (2017). *Management Design: Managing People and Organizations in Turbulent Times (2nd ed.)*. London: LID Publishing.

STEP 1: RAISE AWARENESS

Part II of *Diagnostic Mentoring* (Chapters 4-9) introduces Step 1: Raise Awareness. Figure 91 summarizes Step 1.

Purpose: Step 1 raises awareness of the critical agile elements of an organization, through diagnostic feedback.

Action: Use the diagnostic with the canvas to move from opinions to meaning. Conduct the executive briefing to identify potential and any possible sources of interference, and to challenge assumptions and principles.

Mentor: Orchestrates the diagnostic process, leads the executive briefing.	**Organization:** Conducts the diagnostic, learns about the results in the executive briefing.

Focus: Performance Triangle, Leadership Scorecard, potential, interference, assumptions, principles.

Tools: Diagnostic, executive briefing, canvas.

FIGURE 91: RAISE AWARENESS

Use Figure 92 to summarize your insights from the canvas.

	Potential, interference	Assumptions, principles
People		
Organization		
Work		
Operations		
Management		

FIGURE 92: RAISE AWARENESS - SUMMARY

PART III

THE DYNAMIC OPERATING SYSTEM

Part III introduces Step 2: Act on Insights, with choices on the dynamic operating system for better management. Part III continues the learning journey with the team workshop to identify gaps and key issues, followed by the expert briefing, which translates the issues list into a development road map with initiatives. The result is a plan with focus areas that address the leverage points.

ACT ON INSIGHTS

What operating system fits the business and context? In Chapters
5-9, we provided the logic to identify, select and align capabilities.
Now, Step 2 is about how to design the operating system with people-centric, agile and dynamic capabilities and intervene with the
insights from the diagnostic. Chapter 10 introduces the step.

DESIGN THINKING

As mentioned, the use of capabilities and design is selective. The decision on a specific design excludes other alternatives. For Diagnostic Mentoring, design is about the selection of managerial tools, routines and rules that make organizations agile. Design requires reflection and interactions. It is not free of politics. The setting for these conversations determines much of the design quality.

As we know all too well, organizations are not free of politics. There is ample bargaining over goals, interests and values. The three-step shift needs to combine design thinking with facilitation techniques into an intervention that helps bridge diverging views on how to manage and organize.

In our data-driven times, analysis has become the predominant way we look at the world. We're rationally compelled by the logic of the idea and assume that feelings will naturally follow. Logic and data combine to produce a cognitive 'sense of proof.' The academic and author Roger L. Martin said that in today's world, logic plus data provides proof, which generates emotional comfort, which leads directly to commitment (Martin, 2017). "The tricky thing about new ideas is that there is no data yet to analyse — otherwise the idea wouldn't be new," Martin wrote. "The absence of data undermines our modern commitment equation. For a new idea, the equation is likely to be: logic without data produces speculation, which results in emotional discomfort. ...And a consequence: an over commitment to exploitation over exploration."

Later, I will introduce systems theory, citing the work of scientist and educator Donella Meadows. Another foundation of systems thinking came from the social scientist Niklas Luhmann. His focus is on systems-based sociology. He claims that sociology — and with it, systems-based sociology — "ist die Wissenschaft des zweiten Blicks" (is the science of the second opinion). But, nobody depends on a second opinion. A second opinion is a luxury. Systems-based external descriptions are an important element of systems theory and practical in use. The challenge is that communication on alternatives often interferes with the self-creation and development tendency (*autopoiesis*) of systems. Rash pronouncements like, 'Enough conversation — it's time to act!' prevent people from exploring good alternatives.

Design thinking is the methodology that helps us find new ways of exploring the future and how we do things. It combines both logic and emotions. Commitment comes from a balance of the two.

Design thinking is about reflection and interaction. Reflection is a systems perspective that limits the resistance to change that's inherent in any individual's perspective. Guided interactions among participants deal with politics in organizations. They serve as a framework for action.

People-centric is new information and new knowledge for most leaders, employees and organizations. Design initiates the immediate learning. Effective learning of new knowledge and behaviours requires a supportive environment. Workshops where all participants are involved in the diagnostics create such an environment.

Building on agile methodologies, design thinking is a collaborative, customer-centric and iterative approach. For example, the team workshop is a setting where all participants apply their knowledge and insights to come up with alternatives for dealing with the challenges the diagnosis might reveal. The goal is to come up with a list of 5-7 things the team has decided to work on. The team workshop combines individual, team and organizational perspectives. It establishes the setting for interaction among leaders and employees that neutralizes the inevitable effects of bias, power and traps. Does any of this add value for our customers?

Authentic dissent through multiple perspectives is an important function of capability monitoring. This is why it's advisable to retain an outside partner with expert knowledge to balance valuable diverging views on the interpretation of diagnostic results. Creating a 'naysayer culture' is another important element of such workshops. An effective team workshop follows a strict set of rules for these conversations.

TEAM WORKSHOP

The team workshop is a large, group-facilitated session of 3-5 hours involving all participants in the diagnostic. The purpose is to learn and distil the gaps and key issues from the diagnostic results. A dedicated team workshop report supports the facilitation and the conversations.

The team workshop involves everyone who performed the diagnostic, in a collaborative setting, to help them understand and interpret the results. Its purpose is to use the collective knowledge, integrating the insights to generate a comprehensive laundry list of issues that require executive attention. This integration is important, as it shapes any group's sense of what a shared action plan should include. Often, this extends to more than one workshop, involving different groups of people.

The workshop establishes institutionalized rules through observation and conversation as an important part of dynamic capabilities. Context influences observation. This is why the workshop design establishes a context for all participants to share their observations and insights, based on self-reflection, combination and cooperation. Conversation styles provide for statements always being traceable back to diagnostic data, to ensure proper logic and help resolve conflicts through appropriate rules.

For most participants, this is a first-time conversation in a new field. Memory has the capacity to acquire fresh knowledge, to be recalled and applied. New knowledge is connected to existing structures. With more objects, patterns and concepts anchored in our brains, it is easier to digest new information on an existing theme. Learning about new fields is more difficult than learning in a known area. This is why the skills of a Diagnostic Mentor are required to facilitate learning in new fields.

An important outcome of the team workshop is a list of key issues. Think of this list as a flip chart with perhaps a five-item summary of issues the team committed to address, based on the diagnostic results.

The agenda follows a standard protocol, where the Diagnostic Mentor first shares the key results. Then, the team works in groups to distil the gaps and list the key issues. Next, every team presents their insights, which the Diagnostic Mentor aggregates into one comprehensive list.

Key issues answer the following questions in line with the canvas dimensions:

People: How do we enable people to play the inner game for superior speed and learning?

Organization: How do we establish a work environment for superior agility?

Work: How do we create purpose, connectivity and relationships for superior resilience and growth?

Operations: How do we develop dynamic capabilities?

Management: How do we create a toolbox for superior decision-making?

Appendix 5 offers a standard agenda for the team workshop. The canvas continues to support the facilitation of the meeting and serves as the recording tool for the conversations.

EXPERT BRIEFING

The expert briefing is a one-day workshop with internal company experts. The purpose is to translate the list of key issues into initiatives and a road map plan to develop the desired capabilities. A dedicated report supports the development conversations and facilitation of the expert briefing.

The expert briefing involves professionals from areas such as human resources, control, risk, organizational development, governance and compliance. They translate the laundry list into an actionable programme to address issues raised in the team workshop. The project leader then presents the results of this meeting to the executive team for approval of implementation. The purpose of this step is to formalize the shared action plan and initiate the communication to repeat and reinforce the story. It leaves the choice for action — and the energy to get things done — with the team.

In a 'fast action/immediate impact' environment, the extensive experience of a Diagnostic Mentor, and a reliable method for supporting staff professionals with the expert briefing, is essential in structuring an effective road map programme.

The agenda for the expert briefing is flexible. The setting needs to ensure that all experts can offer their advice on what development agenda and process works best for the organization. The Diagnostic Mentor brings in their expertise in developing large-scale development programmes.

Appendix 6 offers a standard agenda for the expert briefing. The canvas now serves as the protocol for all conversations. With a bit of experience, participants will recognize patterns that are specific to their organizations. Often, these patterns indicate either practices to omit or practices to encourage.

FROM INSIGHTS TO ACTIONS

Diagnostic Mentoring follows a three-step approach with eight action items.

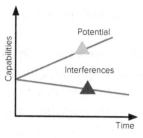

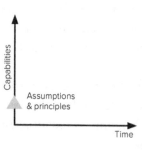

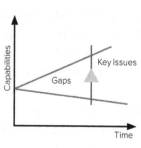

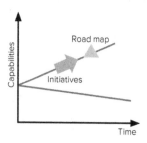

What are our current capabilities?

With the feedback on the diagnostic results from Step 1: Raise Awareness, the manager in charge reviews the capability potential and possible interference points during the executive briefing.

Simultaneously, the manager challenges current assumptions and principles that govern management and organization. That opens the next conversation:

What are the future capabilities?

Step 2: Act on Insights then identifies the gaps and key issues to close the gaps. Gaps are the differences between the desired future capabilities and the expected capabilities without any intervention. Capabilities that are not maintained will deteriorate over time. Key issues address the gaps as action items. The next question then is:

How do we develop the desired capabilities?

Step 3: Learn Fast is about identifying the initiatives that address the key issues. With the staff briefing, initiatives are then combined in a road map — a master plan that spells out who does what, and when. In most cases, the road map spans more than a year and effectively becomes the development programme for the entire organization.

With this overview, the next chapters focus on identifying the gaps and key issues.

VISUAL THINKING AIDS

Diagnostic Mentoring follows the principles of design thinking. In support of this, visual thinking aids (Figure 93) combine diagnostic information with models that facilitate the review of that information and the design of management. Over the years, 25 visual thinking aids have become part of various diagnostic reports to support Diagnostic Mentoring.

Visual thinking aids are grouped in seven dimensions of Diagnostic Mentoring. Dimensions represent homogenous aspects of organization and management, each of which requires dedicated management attention. Visual thinking aids combine various elements that each make up a story. With diagnostic information, these stories then come to be owned by those who focus their attention on developing better management.

Without pointing to the concept of visual thinking aids, so far we have discussed the dimensions of organization and parts of leadership. We've answered the questions: 'What are our current capabilities?' and 'What are the sources of interference, potential, assumptions and principles?'

Organization: the Performance Triangle, results and agile maturity.

Leadership: the Leadership Scorecard and leadership style.

Now we switch to two other questions: 'What are our desired capabilities?' and 'What are the gaps and key issues?' For this, we will likely come back to dimensions 1 and 2, and continue with the following:

Business: strategy, business model and challenges

Management: Operating modes, people-centric levers, management models, management levers, decision-making styles and context levers

Systems: Leadership Toolbox, operating models, 'the bridge'

Development: development paths, roles and systems levers

While dimensions offer the recommended sequence of visuals to build a consistent transformation story, the thinking aids are often combined in other ways to support presentations, workshops and teaching.

Three levels offer increasing depth of analysis and insights. Level 1 works well with the executive briefing and the team workshop. Level 2 is for the staff briefing. And, Level 3 is for experts in design and development.

FIGURE 93: VISUAL THINKING AIDS

	BUSINESS	ORGANIZATION	LEADERS	MANAGEMENT	SYSTEMS	DEVELOPMENT
LEVEL 1 Executive Briefing Team Workshop	Strategy & Business Model Outcomes & Success Expectations	Performance Triangle — Operations Flow — People Work — Organization	Leadership Scorecard	Operating Modes — People-Centric Levers Management		
LEVEL 2 Staff Briefing	Agile Maturity	Purpose — Collaboration Relationships	Leadership Styles	Management Models — Management Levers Decision-Making Styles — Context Levers	Leadership Toolbox — The Bridge	Development Paths
LEVEL 3 Design & Development	Fitness Levels				Operating Models — Toolbox	Roles — Levers

223

FOUR OPERATING SYSTEMS

The ultimate goal of Diagnostic Mentoring is to design, develop and implement an operating system that fits the needs of people and the context, and comes with people-centric, agile and dynamic features. Before we dig into the details of design, it is time to distinguish four dominant operating systems. While they never exist in pure form, they offer guidance for those on the way to deciding on their operating system.

Domestication is a distinctive feature of operating systems and, at the same time, a barrier to changing operating systems. Domestication translates explicit systems into implicit values, capabilities and behaviours that are deeply embedded in culture. Culture works like glue. This makes it hard to reconfigure operating systems.

It won't come as a surprise that managers and employees are expected to make quick decisions, focus their actions on what matters most and demonstrate entrepreneurial behaviours in everything they do.

Reality strikes, and offers something even more startling. In the context of our information-rich, dynamic environment, the requirements and expectations outlined above are virtually impossible to meet — people are distracted, struggle with decisions and miss opportunities. As such, managers and employees often have no choice but to act in a self-interested manner. As a consequence, talent is not effectively used and companies perform far below their potential. This challenge is endemic in the dynamic and knowledge-driven environment, in which we have become comfortably uncomfortable.

Systematic information overload, analysis paralysis, endless meetings, bias toward rationality, risk-aversity and blindly following rules dominate our ways of thinking and doing at work. This comes at the expense of disciplined decision-making, deliberate actions and behaviours aligned with company beliefs and boundaries. We know that this is the result of strong domestication.

In a virus-infected culture, faulty leadership and erroneous managerial systems lead to flawed decisions, missing action and undesired behaviours. The negative domestication spiral accelerates because of this deteriorating operating environment. Domestication is what we define as the behaviours and actions of leaders and employees that follow the habits and patterns determined by the organization's rules, norms and values.

On the positive side, a vibrant culture, interactive leadership and supportive systems enable fast decisions, actions with impact and the desired behaviours. These are the outcomes of an operating system with a deliberate design, leading to positively domesticated behaviours: these companies enable a high degree of individual effectiveness, where the talent is effectively used.

People follow given rules. They want to *do well*. That's why the operating system is so important. It domesticates how people decide, act and behave. It is deeply embedded in the organization's culture. With this comes the challenge of responding when the operating system requires change. Changing operating systems influences the rules, routines and tools people follow. Taking all of that into account, how can organizations jump-start positive domestication?

The idea of positive socialization starts with every individual's *return on management* (ROM). Harvard Business School Professor Robert Simons developed the concept in 1995, based on the fact that time, attention and energy are scarce resources for anyone. In order to achieve a high ROM, it's wise to carefully invest time and focus attention to generate a maximum amount of productive energy. We know that many leaders and employees struggle with this.

ROM = Productive energy released / time and attention invested

An operating system must yield a high ROM (Figure 94). It supports individual effectiveness, time, attention, energy and organizational effectiveness through efficiency, innovation and value creation.

Effectiveness	Exploitation	Exploration	Outcome
Individual	Time	Attention	Energy
Organizational	Efficiency	Innovation	Value creation

FIGURE 94: RETURN ON MANAGEMENT

Figure 95 positions four operating systems in line with the operating modes: control, engagement, change and enabling. Each has a different purpose and outcome that spans traditional and people-centric.

Managers can choose and mix four operating systems, depending on the specific managerial context in which their organizations operate.

FIGURE 95: FOUR OPERATING SYSTEMS

The changing environment and a tech-savvy generation's knowledge and talents force companies to be clear about the operating mode.

Four questions help us distinguish the four operating modes:

1. How do we engage people and know with clarity?
2. How do we make superior decisions and move in one direction?
3. How do we coordinate work and mobilize the energy?
4. How do we enable performance and maintain the focus?

Enabling operating systems call for self-responsible, collective decisions, with a focus on learning and development. In control operating systems, decisions are deferred to senior management, at the top of the hierarchy. Engagement systems facilitate collective debate and motivation, whereas with change systems, management takes corrective action. Figure 96 summarizes the features of the four generic operating systems.

Operation	Control	Change	Engagement	Enabling
Systems	Hierarchy and power	Management action	Individual knowledge	Learning and development
Context	Comparably stable environment	High uncertainty and pace	Knowledge- and technology- intensive	High complexity and ambiguity
How we understand and engage	Leaders motivate, extrinsic rewards	Stretched goals and incentives	Mastery and meaning	Self- responsibility and purpose
How we think and decide	Through hierarchy	By leaders	Debate and reason	Collective wisdom
How we act and coordinate	Processes and operating procedures	Change projects	Workshops and meetings	Self- organization, mutual adjustment
How we behave and motivate	Top-down goals and control	Aligned action	Self-interest	Wide goals, shared mindset

FIGURE 96: FEATURES OF OPERATING SYSTEMS

Operating systems come with a toolbox for leaders and employees that helps them use time effectively, focus attention and mobilize the productive energy.

The dominant operating system varies, depending on the business context in which a company operates. More often than not, companies unwillingly or unknowingly operate with mixed (or multiple) operating systems that vary within the organization. My research confirms that 45% of companies still operate in the control-based operating mode.

For example, a global pharmaceutical company I worked with used the engagement mode for its research and development function, while its manufacturing part applied the control-based system. The selection and design of the toolbox for each mode of operations is a senior executive task that requires experience.

In a highly regulated, safety-first context, the control-based operating systems may still be effective. Change-based operating systems are the norm in transaction-oriented and heavily technology-supported industries, such as insurance, banking and telecom. Engagement-based operating systems do well in knowledge-driven environments, such as educational institutions or professional-services businesses.

Counterintuitively, operating systems can be observed in a variety of settings that require both a high degree of flexibility and a rigorous set of operating procedures. This is certainly the case in the work of a commercial airline pilot, the emergency room of a hospital, a military unit in a combat situation or a firefighting company. These examples do not illustrate normal, everyday business operations, but looking at the extremes helps to make the point.

Nobody would ever go into a restaurant kitchen and ask for the specifics of a recipe before ordering a meal. It is expected that the chef knows what he's doing.

In an emergency room, we trust the exceptional skills of highly trained doctors, nurses and technicians who intuitively do what is right in that specific situation and context. They're trained to follow strict standards, but when the situation requires, it is their skills rather than the routines that save lives. Agility and capabilities beat rigorous routines.

In military combat or a firefighting situation, leaders can only provide broad guidance on how to go about handling a specific emergency. On the battlefield or at the scene of a fire, well-developed skills and intuition are required to do what is necessary. No command from above could ever be better at reacting quickly and flexibly to fit the situation. Soldiers and firefighters respond in the best way their intuition and trained behaviours allow. They've absorbed rigorous procedures on how to deal with emergencies, and can simultaneously exhibit flexibility and resilience.

Well-developed operating systems facilitate intuitive decision-making (the agile elements) and trained routine (the stable elements) rather than authority, blind action and *decision-by-paralysis*. And so, they allow for fast responses, permit flexible action and enable robust solutions.

ENGAGING SELF-RESPONSIBLE PEOPLE

The control-based operating system is what most of us know well. For the past 100 years, industrial-style leaders have been trained to motivate and control people. Moreover, despite the wealth of research proving that there's no meaningful relationship between bonuses and performance, extensive extrinsic and monetary rewards continue to dominate people management. Stretched goals tied to incentives are the predominant means of change-based operating systems.

The fact is that control-based systems achieve exactly what they're intended to: fulfilment of detailed objectives, and not one bit more. As management expert Peter Drucker once said: "Management by objectives works — if you know the objectives. Ninety percent of the time you don't." The engagement-based operating system demands personal mastery and meaning to engage people. We know from the philosophers of 17th-century European Humanism that self-responsible people are by definition motivated people.

The engagement-based operating system is built on the assumption that people are fundamentally motivated and, as such, the management task is to help employees find that purpose. As we said earlier, this is called sense-making, not *sense-giving*.

High-performance sports professionals around the world know that engaged people need four things to perform at their peak:

1. They must be able to focus their attention on what matters most to them.
2. They need a high degree of awareness of what's most important.
3. They trust their own skills and their environment.
4. They require choice.

Choice is a prerequisite for self-responsible behaviours. If you cannot say no, then you have no choice, and therefore cannot be self-responsible. Managers are well advised to give this careful thought.

As an example, a renowned leadership think tank I worked with decided to invest in 'people engagement' activities, as recommended by mainstream consultants. No doubt, their efforts resulted in a better place to work. But, the company lost on speed, agility and robustness. Meetings, town halls and more personal conversations augmented the sense of purpose, but what truly mattered to the organization was whether employees could fully apply their talent and focus on priorities, to actually get things done.

Insights from the diagnostic revealed the need to complement engagement activities with a toolbox for 21ˢᵗ century working practices. Less than two months after these practices were put in place at the organization, creativity increased, collaboration became a natural way of working, and relevant knowledge was shared and accumulated.

Self-responsible action and a deep sense of purpose enable people to use their time most effectively. As a result, organizations that embrace this approach get things done faster, and still have things under control, despite a more dynamic environment.

MAKING DECISIONS BASED ON COLLECTIVE WISDOM

With control-based operating systems, decisions are made through hierarchy. Delegated decisions always require the manager's signature, which means the boss always makes the decisions. We know that most leaders understand that this type of top-down control makes organizations slow, inflexible and fragile.

In change-based operations, it's always the leader who decides, assuming that they're the most qualified and most knowledgeable in the organization. As the academic and business management author Henry Mintzberg would put it, in these organizations, people are seen as re(movable) human resources, costly human assets and human capital. They aren't seen as human beings who add value to an organization.

In contrast, engagement-based operations favour debate, reasoning and committees. People are valued for what they add: knowledge and experience. It's just that filling calendars with endless meetings doesn't add to the agility of these companies.

Enabling operations favour decision-making through collective wisdom. Decisions are delegated to the most knowledgeable and skilled person. Rapid feedback ensures that individuals and organizations learn quickly, and continuously improve their decision-making and implementation of these decisions.

A high-tech utilities provider I work with successfully transformed from a CEO-driven, decision-making style to a collective approach. The challenges of the energy sector — with decreasing investment in traditional energy sources and more in riskier new sources — demands that companies continuously sense what is politically acceptable, judge what is possible and decide what is doable. As such, energy companies require ongoing sensing and debate, without 'losing it' to *analysis paralysis*.

With the help of the diagnostic, the CEO of this particular company was able to change his approach and began to mobilize knowledge and insights from his executive team. This quickly transformed his team into a body that used its collective wisdom and made the entire company more people-centric, without it getting locked into decisions without choices.

COORDINATING SELF-ORGANIZED WORK

With control-based operating systems, the coordination of work happens through detailed processes. Every time naturally connected parts fall apart, these companies install further operating procedures.

With the change-based operating system, managers initiate change projects to reconnect parts that have become disconnected through recently added structures and accountabilities. Workshops, meetings, alignment and role clarifications are the means to coordinate work with the engagement-based operating system.

The enabling-based operating system supports companies with decentralized businesses. Self-organized teamwork and ad-hoc project teams are favoured over strictly following plans and budgets.

Pharmaceutical firms I work with have long-established project teams that develop assets from research, development, distribution, marketing and sales as parts of their business. Functions allocate knowledge and experience throughout the course of flexible and temporary projects. People mutually adjust in a self-organized and purpose-driven manner to release their productive energy. In this way, they help their organization remain flexibly grounded, with a stable backbone.

Self-organized work and mutual adjustment helps employees focus their attention on what matters most. A high degree of agility comes from the fact that shifting focus within a shared purpose makes organizations flexible.

THRIVING PERFORMANCE THROUGH BROAD PURPOSE

Control-based operating systems apply rigorous individual management by objectives, with top-down goals and frequent performance appraisals. People in these modes spend a lot of time getting agreement on and conducting reviews of the performance objectives.

Change-based operations favour action orientation. In other words, valuable management time is dedicated to aligning value-adding projects and coordinating actions. These companies argue that implementation is what makes or breaks performance.

In engagement-based organizations, knowledge-driven employees follow their self-interest, making it difficult for management to get into balance with corporate intent.

People working in enabling-based systems support teams with a shared mindset and clarity, based on broad direction, with a strong, shared purpose. Managers help them understand and use their energy to apply their full talent.

The public transportation company we recently worked with (see page 56) had transformed from a government agency to an independent entrepreneurial unit. One of the legacies it brought along was the rigid management-by-objectives system that dominated most management conversations. It was good practice to be very detailed and concrete when it came to target setting. A review of the organization's Leadership Toolbox with the diagnostic revealed that rigorous and detailed routines made the entire company slow, inflexible and fragile, like every other bureaucratic public administration.

By focusing people on 'serving their clients' — striving to offer the city's residents the world's best public transportation system — it unlocked the energy of its talent. This led to an entrepreneurially-driven organization that was no longer weighed down by the negative effects of detailed targets.

Organizations with enabling-based systems are able to release their productive energies through a broad sense of purpose, cooperation and high connectivity. These are the features of highly resilient businesses.

DESIGN DECISIONS

Step 2: Act on Insights combines diagnostic insights with design decisions. These visual thinking aids present current capabilities and options to consider when discussing future capabilities. With this, further gaps and key issues can be identified.

Five design decisions come into play with Step 2:
1. Chapter 11 identifies the dominant management context.
2. Chapter 12 aligns leadership and systems with the anticipated future context.
3. Chapter 13 equips the Leadership Toolbox.
4. Chapter 14 aligns leadership with the needs of the business.
5. Chapter 15 prioritizes the development activities.

Two factors determine the ideal **management context**: the degree of the external challenges and the distribution of knowledge. At the same time, strategy and the business model need to match the dominant management context. Chapter 11 helps you decide on the future management context.

Four management levers frame the **management model**, and four context levers determine the dominant **decision-making style**. Both management and decision-making need to fit the expected context. Chapter 12 guides you in determining your preferred model and style.

The **Leadership Toolbox** in Chapter 13 offers 20 elements that are needed in every business operating system. The diagnostic offers an assessment of the toolbox and opens the discussion on the selection and development needs of all 20 rules, routines, interactions and tools.

Chapter 14 focuses on the design of the rules, routines, interactions and tools that make up the **operating system** of an organization. Our research has identified nine characteristic operating models that guide the design. The question then becomes how to scale the toolbox to make it support business growth.

Systems support leaders in their daily management job. But, not all **leadership** styles are effective in every context, given the challenges at hand. Chapter 14 offers a choice of styles to align leadership with the needs of the business.

Finally, with clarity on gaps and key issues, Diagnostic Mentoring then focuses on **prioritizing the development work** with initiatives and the creation of a road map.

ACT ON INSIGHTS

Act on Insights translates insights into action through design of management and the organization's operating system.

KEY CHAPTER IDEAS

- The team workshop and the expert briefing are the two interventions
- Visual thinking aids guide the steps
- The operating system needs alignment with the business model and the expected operating environment

ACTION AGENDA

Conduct the team workshop with all diagnostic participants to learn and distil the gaps and key issues.

Conduct the expert briefing to develop initiatives and create the road map.

Design your operating system following four action items: identify management context, align management with business, design the toolbox, decide on development priorities.

FURTHER READING

Michel, L (2017). *Management Design: Managing People and Organizations in Turbulent Times* (2nd ed.). London: LID Publishing.

CHAPTER 11

IDENTIFY THE MANAGEMENT CONTEXT

Management context is the anchor point for the steps that lead to a better design of management. Chapter 11 reviews the strategy, business model and business context to offer a choice of management modes.

So far, we have presented the four operating modes — control, engagement, change and enabling (Figure 95) — to describe the operating environment and the subsequent operating systems. For some businesses, that depth of analysis is more than sufficient to reach proficiency in better management. For complex organizations, Chapters 11-14 offer additional design insights. Eventually, we will all work toward the same goal and develop people-centric management, agile organization and a dynamic operating system.

The business model, distribution of knowledge, and degree of the external and internal challenges determine the choice of the dominant management mode. We will start with a look at the business model.

STRATEGY AND BUSINESS MODEL

The business model also determines the choice of management mode. As presented in Figure 87, strategy identifies the dominant business model. Nine generic strategies offer the choice of an *exploitation* or *exploration* type of business model. Exploitation aligns well with traditional, control- and rules-based management modes. Exploration requires a capabilities-based mode.

The strategy determines your business and operating models, which mark the starting point of every agile journey. MIT academics Arnoldo Hax and Nicolas Majluf (1996) suggest nine distinct strategies that cover most businesses, whether they're start-ups, traditional organizations, platforms or ecosystems of networked companies. The choices are presented in a table that aligns the positioning with a company's core processes. Figure 97 offers a choice of nine different business strategies to help you decide on your dominant strategy.

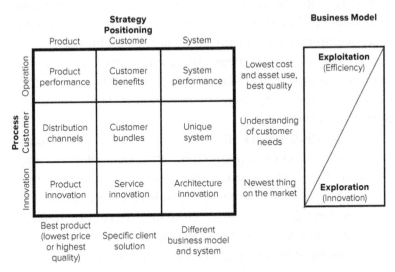

FIGURE 97: STRATEGY AND BUSINESS MODEL

The best product performance builds on traditional forms of competition. Customers are attracted by low cost or differentiation that introduces new features. Innovation is centred on internal product development. The 'total customer solution' strategy is the complete opposite of the 'best product' approach. Instead of commoditizing the customer, a deep understanding of the customer and the relationship is developed. An integrated supply chain links key suppliers and customers. Innovation is aimed at the joint development of distinctive products. The systems strategy includes the extended enterprise, with customers, suppliers and complementors (companies whose product adds value to your offering) as a network, a platform or an ecosystem. This relationship may span the entire value chain, from product to delivery. Distribution channels are a key consideration, as they involve ownership or restricting access.

Aligning the key activities with the three strategies follows three adaptive processes: operational effectiveness, customer targeting and innovation. Operations is about the manufacturing and delivery of products and services. It aims for the most effective use of assets, such as machines and infrastructure, to support the chosen strategic position of the company. Customer targeting is about the management of the customer interface. It should establish the best revenue infrastructure for the company. Innovation is about new product development. It should ensure a continuous stream of new products and services to maintain the future viability of the business.

With clarity on your strategy, you can now determine your dominant business model: exploitation business models concern choice, efficiency and selection, whereas exploration is about search, variation and innovation.

- **Exploitation model**: Exploitation includes such things as refinement, choice, production, efficiency, selection, implementation and execution. Exploitation involves the refinement of existing technology, requiring individual coordination. Exploitation as a business model requires traditional control-based approaches to management.
- **Exploration model**: Exploration includes things captured by search, variation, risk taking, experimentation, play, flexibility, discovery and innovation. Exploration is an adaptable and flexible process, which has to fit the new configuration the company pursues. It arises from individual deviation from the norm, as a source of innovation. Exploitation relies on innovation and requires a capabilities-based approach to management.

- **Hybrid/dual model**: Combining exploitation and exploration poses a dilemma, as they compete for the same scarce resources. The challenge is to combine both in a way that guarantees the survival of the company — a trade-off between variation and selection, between change and stability. The combination delivers learning as a concurrent development and diffusion of knowledge throughout the organization.

Operational effectiveness is all about exploitation, whereas innovation relates to exploration. The hybrid model combines both exploitation and exploration.

With this introduction to strategy and business models in Figure 86, give some thought to the following:

- What is your strategy and the corresponding business model? What does this mean for your management mode?

THE DISTRIBUTION
OF KNOWLEDGE

With distributed knowledge, innovation shifts to the client front. Business is about exploiting valuable opportunities and turning them into client benefits. This requires information and knowledge — the distribution of knowledge is the second trigger for the dominant management mode.

When knowledge is concentrated, control, command and central decision-making dominate. The speed of decisions and flexibility for action depends on the ability to search for information and the available knowledge.

When knowledge is widely distributed, managers engage people to collaborate and connect to build relationships, all with a deep sense of purpose. Complex structures are replaced by self-organized teams. They use inexpensive information and communications technologies in remote workplaces to detect opportunities early and act on weak market signals.

The distribution of knowledge distinguishes between traditional and people-centric management.

With this introduction, reflect on these questions:

- What is your current distribution of knowledge? What does it mean?
- What might your future distribution of knowledge look like?
- Where are the gaps and what are the key issues to resolve?

MANAGEMENT LEVERS

As with the people-centric levers, four management levers add more detail to the analysis and separate traditional from people-centric management. Traditional management corresponds to a context with concentrated knowledge; people-centric management relates to a context where distributed knowledge dominates. Figure 98 lists the levers that determine the management response part of the dominant management mode.

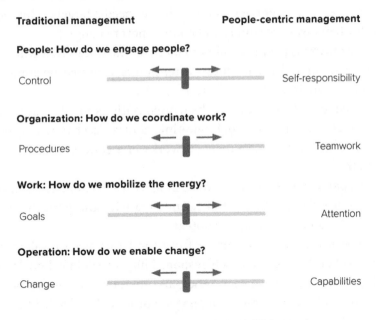

FIGURE 98: MANAGEMENT LEVERS

Each of the above principles warrants an entire book of relevant managerial content. Much has been written about them, and I've explained some of the principles in detail in my other books. I don't want to duplicate that here. It would not do justice to the wealth of insights. Instead, here is my short-version synopsis of what these principles mean:

Control assumes that only managers have the skills and knowledge to know what and how things need to get done. As such, they tell people what to do, and then come and check on whether it has been done.

Self-responsibility assumes that people can think, decide and act on their own. This allows managers to unlock their creativity, talent and potential.

Procedures are detailed routines that prescribe how a specific task needs to be performed. This increases predictability, efficiency and the ability to repeat tasks over and over, with little knowledge requirement.

Teamwork is the approach to getting work done that requires creativity and responsiveness in groups. It's needed when tasks require knowledge and flexibility.

Goals refer to stringent alignment through detailed performance objectives and incentives paid to achieve specific targets. This works well when tasks are simple and context never changes.

Attention is people's ability to focus on the things that truly matter for them and the business. Attention is a limited resource that requires care if it is to deliver full capacity.

Change is the process by which organizations adapt to alterations in the environment through one-time efforts. As change is a sort of replacement for management, it works in a context that is simple and that doesn't change.

Capabilities are the clues to dealing with a dynamic environment where people apply their full talent, creativity and performance to deal with an ever-changing context.

The principles that emerge from the levers need to align with each other. For example, self-responsibility and detailed goals don't align. They neutralize each other, and therefore require resolve. In Chapter 13 we will discuss management models. That will help us align the management levers.

With this introduction and the information in Figure 99, think through the following:

- What are your current management principles? What do they mean?
- How do your management levers enable people to apply their knowledge and perform?
- What are your desired future management principles?
- Where are the gaps and what are the key issues to resolve the gaps?

Metrics. The dominant management principle is calculated as follows:

The average of the people, organization, work and operation scores.
The scores are determined through four questions similar to those in Figure 87.

Evaluation. The answer is scored as follows:

0 = Traditional management, 100 = People-centric management, with stages in between the two opposites.

Meaning. The score indicates the following known symptoms:

- **Traditional management**. A low score indicates a traditional approach with knowledge concentrated at the top
- **People-centric management**. A high score means a people-centric approach with distributed knowledge

Interpretation. Linkages to other elements offer insights and root causes:

- **Operation modes:** leadership

Sources

- **Process**. *Management Design* (2nd Ed. 2017), pages 174-175

Facilitation. Use Post-it notes and the canvas for the answers:

What are the gaps? Use yellow Post-it notes.
What are the key issues? Use dark blue Post-its.

FIGURE 99: MANAGEMENT LEVER INSIGHTS

COSMETICS: WHEN TARGETS DISTORT FOCUS

The CEO of a traditional manufacturing-driven company asked for an introduction to agile for his leadership team, as part of a long-term initiative to become more innovative. The deal was that as part of that introduction, a pilot team would use the diagnostic to demonstrate Diagnostic Mentoring (Figure 100). The exercise yielded interesting results.

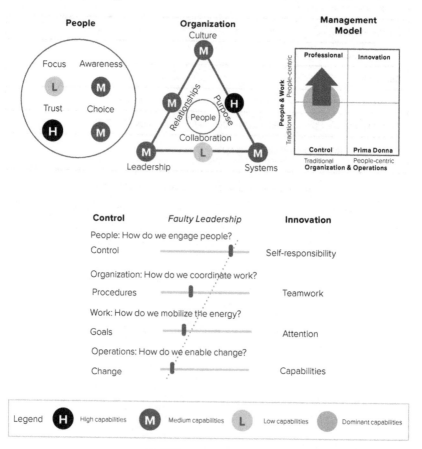

FIGURE 100: COSMETICS

People reported that they were unable to focus their attention. In addition, they failed to collaborate. Trust and purpose are the means to get work done. This is the combination where leaders try to do what is right, and help self-responsible people perform. However, the combination of self-responsibility and goal-setting points to faulty leadership. Self-responsibility and goals are opposites. One cannot explain to people that they should act on their own and then turn around and limit that freedom with detailed performance objectives. Goals limit self-responsibility.

Predetermined goals, purpose and interfering leaders combine to distort focus of attention. In addition, individual performance goals are the enemies of collaboration in teams. Both effects limit people's capacity to perform and to be creative. That was the story the CEO learned from the team workshop.

He reacted quickly. Corporate prerequisites for management-by-objectives were abolished and replaced with team goals and focus of attention, based on the pilot team's diagnostic results. Leaders were asked to help people focus their attention rather than strictly follow goals.

With these changes, the organization shifted to the professional mode that fitted with the CEO's aspiration for people-centricity. Since the business was part of a larger parent company, it stuck with traditional organization and operations. In combination, that shift helped the business become more innovative.

THE DEGREE OF CHALLENGES

People need systems that help them deal with external challenges. In a stable environment, control dominates. Leaders refine their decision-making and planning as a stable platform from which they decide, act and control as the situation requires. With increasing VUCA dissonance, agile approaches are necessary to quickly adapt to the new environment.

Complexity increases with size. In established businesses, detailed home-grown processes and bureaucratic structures increase complexity. But, as organizations grow and add complexity, the coordination of activities becomes increasingly important. Self-inflicted complexity is the result of *more of everything*, from the number of employees and operating locations to products on the shelf, segments served, functions performed and stakeholders with interests.

In a complex context, it is hard to understand — to hear weak signals, identify opportunities and be clear about what matters — and to find purpose. Yet, when we lack clarity, we ask for additional detail and more precise processes. We introduce additional bureaucracy, applying rules and coordinating procedures that work well in simple contexts. Complexity cannot be compacted. It cannot be addressed through methodologies. Self-organization through teams beats bureaucracy in complex contexts.

Ambiguity requires choice. Rules of the game change, markets evolve, certainties dissolve, industries merge and change, loyalty vanishes, taboos are broken and boundaries blur.

With increasing ambiguity, developing strategies and setting direction based on unpredictability and a variety of contextual settings requires information and knowledge. However, when ambiguity creeps up, we set new rules and limit the degrees of freedom. We reinforce stability because we know how to deal with that. In ambiguous contexts, it is hard to decide how to select valuable opportunities and move in one direction. Relationships with those who know are needed. Ambiguity cannot be ruled, and in that context, delegation beats power. As such, seeing through ambiguity requires natural, team-based approaches as opposed to rational steps and simple models.

Uncertainty challenges strategy. Challenges to stability include shorter life cycles, less stable results, greater dependencies, more transparency and higher reputation risks, particularly those that appear suddenly.

In an uncertain context, it's hard to act and collaborate — to ultimately turn opportunities into benefits. The risks of failure are high. But, when uncertainty rises, we second-guess ourselves, mistrust people and limit delegation. We give orders and prevent the use of knowledge. In a stable, certain context, power and authority work well to get things done. Uncertainty cannot be controlled. Still, self-responsibility beats command and order. Digitalization helps to decentralize decision-making without losing control. As such, uncertainty demands trusted management and non-linear approaches.

Higher volatility is the norm in this day and age. Globalization, speed, real-time processes, faster decisions, synchronization and immediate responses are required.

In a highly dynamic context, flexibility is needed. Efficiency and scale require rigid routines for consistency and quality that work well in a stable context. However, when control fails, we tend to implement more of it. We double down with the tools and reinforce alignment. In a volatile environment, it's hard to maintain focus on what truly matters, such as sticking with the opportunities. Narrow targets are always off. As such, attention beats detailed targets.

The degree of the external and internal challenges distinguishes between a stable and a dynamic environment.

With this introduction, ask yourself:

- What are your current levels of VUCA?
- What is your current environment? What does it mean?
- What are your likely future levels of VUCA?
- What do you expect your future environment to look like?
- Where are the gaps and what are the key issues to resolve?

CONTEXT LEVERS

Similar to the people-centric levers, four context levers add more depth to the analysis and separate a stable context from a dynamic one. Traditional tools, routines, interactions and standards work well in a stable management context. However, they fail to support management in a dynamic context. For a dynamic context, the entire toolbox requires a design with dynamic features. Figure 101 lists the levers that determine the context part of the dominant management mode.

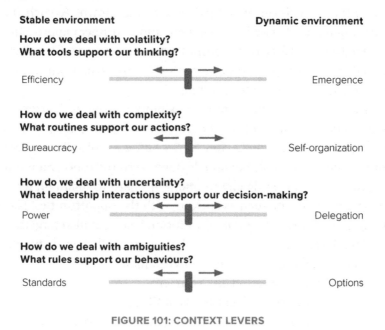

Stable environment   **Dynamic environment**

How do we deal with volatility?
What tools support our thinking?

Efficiency ——————————— Emergence

How do we deal with complexity?
What routines support our actions?

Bureaucracy ——————————— Self-organization

How do we deal with uncertainty?
What leadership interactions support our decision-making?

Power ——————————— Delegation

How do we deal with ambiguities?
What rules support our behaviours?

Standards ——————————— Options

FIGURE 101: CONTEXT LEVERS

Context levers offer options that vary depending on whether the environment is stable or dynamic:

Efficiency is the hallmark of traditional management. While no business succeeds without it, a pure focus on cost, productivity and risk prevention leaves no room for creativity and emergence. Efficiency with tight performance objectives hooks businesses into operating with the use of tools designed for a stable environment.

Emergence means flexibility and anticipation. The tools focus attention on the things that matter and trust in developing the capabilities that can handle a dynamic context.

Bureaucracy involves rigorous processes that work well in a stable context. But, they are not flexible enough to deal with complexity. While routines provide a stable platform, they need the dynamic design to support complexity.

Self-organization relies on teams with flexible routines to deal with increasing complexity. Teams with delegated authority outperform managers in a dynamic context.

Power works in a stable environment where outcomes are easily determined. Power relies on managers who know what they're doing and act accordingly.

Delegation and trust are the clues to managing in an uncertain context. In times of uncertainty, trust in one's self, and one's own capabilities, are helpful in dealing with it. Leaders who delegate and offer trust deserve respect.

Standards as 'standard operating procedure' work well in a stable and clear context. When outcomes can be predetermined, standards work well.

Options are needed in a time of ambiguous contexts. Using mental models that can deal with multiple outcomes can help you succeed in a dynamic environment.

The dominant principles that emerge from the levers need to align with each other. For example, emergence and centralized power for decisions don't align — they contradict each other. In Chapter 13 we will discuss decision-making. That will help us align the context levers.

With this introduction and the information in Figure 102, ask these questions:

- What is your current context? What are the principles by which you deal with that context? What does it mean?
- How do your principles enable people to deal with the prevailing context?
- What is your likely future context? What are your desired future principles?
- Where are the gaps and what are the key issues to resolve the gaps?

Metrics. The dominant context principle is calculated as follows:
The average of the VUCA scores. The scores are determined through four questions, with the following format: Is your toolbox ready to support people in a VUCA environment?
Evaluation. The answer is scored as follows:
0 = Capabilities for a stable environment, 100 = Capabilities for a dynamic environment, with stages in between the two opposites.
Meaning. The score indicates the following known symptoms:
• **Stable context**. A low score indicates toolbox (systems) capabilities sufficient to deal with a stable context • **Dynamic context**. A high score means toolbox (systems) capabilities suitable for dealing with a dynamic context
Interpretation. Linkages to other elements offer insights and root causes:
• **Operation modes:** systems
Sources
• **Process**. *Management Design* (2nd Ed. 2017), pages 174-175
Facilitation. Use Post-it notes and the canvas for the answers:
What are the gaps? Use yellow Post-it notes. What are the key issues? Use dark blue Post-its.

FIGURE 102: CONTEXT LEVER INSIGHTS

MANAGEMENT CONTEXT

Management context combines the decisions on the management and context levers into four bundles of managerial principles and capabilities. They are, as seen in Figure 103: rules, engagement, change and capabilities.

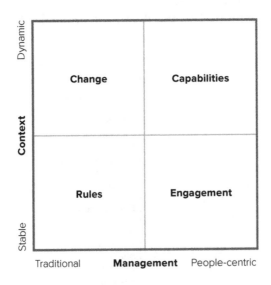

FIGURE 103: MANAGEMENT CONTEXT

Here is a summary of the four modes:

Rules-based management works well in a stable context where the knowledge is concentrated at the top. Bureaucratic procedures enable efficiency and help ensure the quality and reliability of products and services. People are here to follow orders. The rules-based mode is often combined with other modes in organizations that require a hybrid approach. A hospital emergency room is such an example. Teams normally follow standard procedures. When a special situation occurs, the staff's capabilities allow them to find creative solutions to the problem.

Engagement-based management works in knowledge-driven organizations that operate in a stable environment. Modern public administration of cities or states is a good example. People are encouraged to fully engage their talent.

Change-based management is favoured by companies that are highly regulated but need to frequently adapt their resource base to the changing environment. Financial services and the telecom sector are examples of industries that operate in this mode.

Capabilities-based management is preferred by businesses that favour a high degree of creativity and innovation. Start-up firms, research-based organizations and businesses in the exploration mode operate in this manner.

Figure 104 summarizes the dominant principles for each management mode.

Change	Capabilities
Command Procedures Targets Change Emergence Self-organization Delegation Options	Self-responsibility Teamwork Attention Capabilities Emergence Self-organization Delegation Options
Rules	**Engagement**
Command Procedures Targets Change Efficiency Bureaucracy Power Standards	Self-responsibility Teamwork Attention Capabilities Efficiency Bureaucracy Power Standards

FIGURE 104: MANAGEMENT MODE PRINCIPLES

In most organizations, these principles don't manifest in their purest form. You'll always find a mix of principles that make sense for the specific situation. The management and context levers (Figures 98 and 101) offer the tools to identify the principles that best fit the people and the business. However, it is important to ensure that principles are not in conflict with each other. Conflicts are frequent sources of interference, with lower scores on the Performance Triangle elements as a consequence. *People-Centric Management* (Michel 2020, pages 112-122) lists popular conflicting principles that are presented as faulty leadership, missing leadership, and out-of-control/erroneous systems.

Note that for purposes of this discussion, there is little difference between the operating modes in Figure 1 and the management modes in Figure 104. Figure 105 compares both concepts. Operating modes refer directly to the elements of the Performance Triangle. Management modes are based on a more detailed diagnostic assessment. This means we can always go back to previous chapters and use these discussions relative to various management modes.

	Operating Modes	Management Modes
Horizontal perspective	Leadership	Management
Vertical perspective	Systems	Context
Mode 1	Control	Rules
Mode 2	Engagement	Engagement
Mode 3	Change	Change
Mode 4	Enabling	Capabilities

FIGURE 105: COMPARING OPERATING AND MANAGEMENT MODES

For a more detailed discussion in Chapter 12, we continue with the management context concept.

Business models, the operating context and knowledge work determine the choice of management mode: rules-based, engagement-based, change-based or capabilities-based.

Exploitation business models operate in the rules-based or change-based modes. Exploration business models prefer the engagement and capabilities-based modes.

In a dynamic market environment where VUCA is the norm, change- or capabilities-based modes are preferred.

In organizations that are becoming increasingly oriented toward knowledge work, engagement- or capabilities-based modes dominate.

In every management mode, principles and capabilities must fit. That's why Diagnostic Mentoring reviews the elements of the Performance Triangle to ensure this alignment.

With clarity on the dominant management mode, the management model, how we lead people, and the decision-making styles, how systems support us can be determined in Chapter 12.

With this introduction, and the information in Figure 106, use the expert briefing to ask:

- What is your current management mode? What does it mean?
- What is your future management mode?
- What are the gaps and the key issues to close the gaps?

Metrics. The dominant management mode is determined as follows:
Use the scores of the dominant management and context levers/principles and identify the plot in the management context visual (Figure 103).
Evaluation. The answer is scored as follows:
Search for the box with the management mode that fits your plot.
Meaning. The score indicates the following known symptoms:
• **Rules**. Stable context and traditional management • **Engagement**. Stable context and people-centric management • **Change**: Dynamic context and traditional management • **Capabilities**: Dynamic context and people-centric management
Interpretation. Linkages to other elements offer insights and root causes:
• **Operation modes:** control, engagement, change, enabling
Sources
• **Process**. *Management Design* (2nd Ed. 2017), pages 174-175 • **Application**. *People-Centric Management*, pages 108-125
Facilitation. Use Post-it notes and the canvas for the answers:
What are the gaps? Use yellow Post-it notes. What are the key issues? Use dark blue Post-its.

FIGURE 106: MANAGEMENT CONTEXT INSIGHTS

IDENTIFY THE MANAGEMENT CONTEXT

Clarity on context is necessary to identify the dominant management mode.

KEY CHAPTER IDEAS

- The degree of the challenges and the distribution of knowledge determine the dominant management mode
- Strategy and business models need to fit each other
- The dominant management mode needs to align with the dominant business model
- Four management modes capture changes in context and managerial responses

ACTION AGENDA

Use the diagnostic results to determine the current context and management mode.
Identify the future strategy and business model.
Decide on the likely future context and management mode.
Use the team workshop to determine the gaps between current and future modes and the key issues to bridge the gap.

FURTHER READING

Michel, L (2017). *Management Design: Managing People and Organizations in Turbulent Times* (2nd ed.). London: LID Publishing.
Michel, L (2020). *People-Centric Management: How Managers Use Four Levers to Bring Out the Greatness of Others*. London: LID Publishing.

CHAPTER 12

ALIGN LEADERSHIP AND SYSTEMS WITH CONTEXT

Management context is the starting point for a refined analysis of management models and decision-making styles. Chapter 11 used context levers to define management models and management levers that describe decision-making styles. The purpose of Chapter 12 is to align management and decision-making with the context and the business model.

We are now reconnecting leadership and systems by aligning management models and decision-making styles with management context. To do that, Figure 107 offers four management models and four decision-making styles. Speed, agility and resilience require people-centric and dynamic capabilities to balance control, stability and renewal.

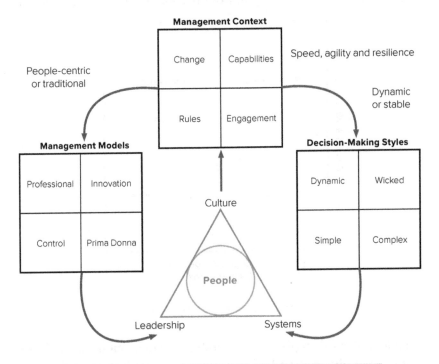

FIGURE 107: ALIGN LEADERSHIP AND SYSTEMS WITH CONTEXT

Let's first look at management models in detail and then examine the associated decision-making styles.

MANAGEMENT MODELS

Management models frame how we engage people and organize work through four distinct sets of managerial principles and capabilities, as seen in Figure 108: control, prima donna, professional and innovation.

FIGURE 108: MANAGEMENT MODELS

People and work represent the ends of management, as a choice between traditional and people-centric. Organization and operations combine to provide the means of management. As such, people remain at the centre of attention. Below (Figure 109) is a snapshot of what the four models are all about.

The control model favours traditional managerial approaches, with command, procedure, targets and change. 'Traditional' sees awards, celebrations and promotions playing a central role in how we lead people. Standard operating procedures, cost efficiency and quality control are part of how work gets done. This functions well when the work is simple, and knowledge resides with a few people at the top of the organization.

The prima donna model applies traditional ways of managing people, within a people-centric organizational setting where command, teamwork targets and capabilities are predominant. An internal market and rewards determine who the 'best' people are, with tight performance goals at this model's core. Prima donnas are stars who need an audience. The organization offers ample freedom for the few stars to unleash their full talent in return for bonuses.

The professional model favours a people-centric work context in traditional organizations. Self-responsibility, clear procedures, focus of attention and change are the features of this model. This approach works well when knowledge is standardized, and applied with a strict process, to ensure a consistent client experience. Within this frame, people find an inspiring place to work and are expected to serve their clients by engaging their full talent.

The innovation model offers a people-centric setting based on self-responsibility, teamwork, focus of attention and capabilities. The rigorous selection of people ensures that informal structures with lateral mechanisms and broad direction create a workplace that's fun, sometimes messy and often complex and demanding.

Professional	Innovation
Self-responsibility Procedures Attention Change	Self-responsibility Teamwork Attention Capabilities
Control	**Prima Donna**
Command Procedures Targets Change	Command Teamwork Targets Capabilities

FIGURE 109: MANAGEMENT MODEL PRINCIPLES

Aligning the management model with the future business model and the expected context works by first aligning the management context with the business model. Next, the selection of the management context determines the people-centric levers of the management model. Practitioners use this as a circular process until the desired management model and levers are determined.

The four management levers (Figure 98) determine the choice of management model — traditional or people-centric. While these attributes hardly ever exist in their purest form, the above bundles of capabilities offer guidance for selecting and developing the model that best fits the context, business model and strategy. It is important to take special care when aligning the levers, to prevent contradictory combinations. For example, self-responsibility and targets, or attention and command, are in conflict with each other — they're mismatched combinations that will lead to faulty leadership.

Every management model demands leadership with capabilities that anchor the four attributes. It is important that leaders adjust their interaction style to promote the dominant management model.

Our research confirms that when organizations lead through a distinct management model, their scores on performance, innovation, growth and success are significantly higher when compared with organizations with an undefined and flexible management model. Moreover, organizations with a management model that fits the context, business model and strategy clearly outperform other organizations.

With this introduction, and the information in Figure 110, use the expert briefing to discuss:

- What is your current management model? What does it mean?
- What is your future management model?
- What are the gaps and the key issues to close the gaps?

Metrics. The dominant management mode is determined as follows:
Use the scores of the dominant management lever/principle and identify the plot in the management model visual (Figure 108).
Evaluation. The answer is scored as follows:
Search for the box with the management mode that fits your plot.
Meaning. The score indicates the following known symptoms:
<ul><li>**Control:** Traditional management</li><li>**Prima Donna:** Traditional management in people-centric organizations</li><li>**Professional:** People-centric management in traditional organizations</li><li>**Innovation:** People-centric management</li></ul>
Interpretation. Linkages to other elements offer insights and root causes:
<ul><li>**Operation modes:** control, prima donna, professional, innovation</li></ul>
Sources
<ul><li>**Process**. *Management Design* (2nd Ed. 2017), pages 178-189</li></ul>
Facilitation. Use Post-it notes and the canvas for the answers:
What are the gaps? Use yellow Post-it notes. What are the key issues? Use dark blue Post-its.

FIGURE 110: MANAGEMENT MODEL INSIGHTS

FAST-FOOD:
AGILE CAPABILITIES

Traditional fast-food restaurants are driven by operational excellence, with a business model that delivers efficiency and reliable, uniform quality. In this particular instance, changing consumer preferences indicated the need for higher agility in adapting to changing needs.

The question was what it would take to become more agile and, perhaps, more innovative. The results from the diagnostic (Figure 111), with 40 executives participating, offered the insights.

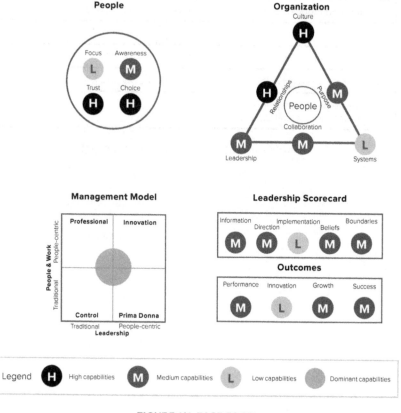

FIGURE 111: FAST FOOD

Agile needs a vibrant culture, interactive leadership and supportive systems. A high score on culture and a medium score on leadership offered a promising starting point. However, systems had a design for a stable, rather than a dynamic, context. The Leadership Scorecard reflected medium scores with limited implementation capabilities.

What was the way forward? With remotely conducted three-hour team workshops, participants were guided through their results and worked toward a list of key issues they felt had to be addressed. For instance, to upgrade for higher agility, managerial systems needed to support leaders operating in a more dynamic environment. The task was to first fix implementation systems, which would help people better focus their attention. After that, the entire toolbox needed an upgrade in support of greater agility.

With these changes, the company shifted to a professional model that allowed local adaptation, while overall corporate standards ensured no deviation from the operational excellence goals.

DECISION-MAKING STYLES

Decision-making styles determine how we think and get things done, with a choice of four ways. These are illustrated in Figure 112: simple, complex, dynamic, wicked. Four context levers (Figure 101) determine the decision-making style and the principles.

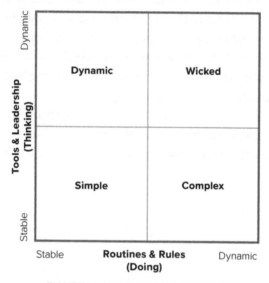

FIGURE 112: DECISION-MAKING STYLES

Tools and leadership interactions determine the thinking, with a stable or dynamic context in mind. Dynamic tools can handle volatility, while dynamic interactions deal with high uncertainty. Rules and routines determine how things get done (the doing), with either a stable or dynamic context in mind. Dynamic rules have a design that deals with ambiguity. Dynamic routines are the means to cope with complexity (Figure 113).

Simple decision-making works well in a stable context, with classic management tools that favour efficiency, power to exercise control and command, bureaucratic operating procedures and standardized rules. This works well when the same situations arise for people who require strong guidance on how to address the issues reliably, with high quality and timeliness.

Complex decision-making occurs in complex contexts that are clouded with ambiguity. Classic management tools and accountability in hierarchies apply flexible routines and guidance through models to address the situation. This works well in contexts that occasionally require technical expertise to clear confusion.

Dynamic decision-making is favoured in situations that require leadership action, with tools that help focus attention on what truly matters. Leaders use known processes and standardized rules to address the situation. This works well when uncertainty and volatility require experienced leadership intervention and action.

Wicked decision-making represents the ultimate art, science and practice of making decisions in an ultra-dynamic context with a high VUCA factor. The only way to resolve wicked problems is to rely on emergence, self-organize, delegate parts of the decision and keep options open. Wicked decision-making relies on tools that can handle emergence, routines for self-organization, leadership that delegates and rules that offer options.

Dynamic	Wicked
Emergence Bureaucracy Delegation Standards	Emergence Self-organization Delegation Options
Simple	**Complex**
Efficiency Bureaucracy Power Standards	Efficiency Self-organization Power Options

FIGURE 113: DECISION-MAKING PRINCIPLES

The alignment of the decision-making style follows the future business model and the expected context. The selection of the desired management context determines the dynamic levers and the dominant decision-making mode. Again, going back and forth from the context levers to the decision-making principles will determine the desired decision-making style.

Pure decision-making styles hardly exist in practice. Despite that, the four styles serve as a guide to identify what works in a specific context and management reality. Again, it's important to rule out combinations of principles that contradict each other.

Every decision-making style requires specific systems, with rules, routines, interactions and tools that support executives as they ponder decisions. It is important that leaders design their systems to precisely fit their decision-making needs.

Our research confirms that organizations that are clear about their specific decision-making style will deliver superior results. Organizations where the decision-making style fits the context, business model and strategy clearly outperform those that lack the appropriate design and alignment.

With this introduction and the information in Figure 114, use the expert briefing to discuss:

- What is your current decision-making style? What does it mean?
- What is your future decision-making style?
- What are the gaps and the key issues to close the gaps?

Metrics. The dominant management mode is determined as follows:
Use the scores of the dominant dynamic lever/principle and identify the plot in the decision-making visual (Figure 112).
Evaluation. The answer is scored as follows:
Search for the box with the management mode that fits your plot.
Meaning. The score indicates the following known symptoms:
• **Simple**. Stable context with a classic management toolbox • **Complex**. Complex, ambiguous context with flexible routines and systemic guidance • **Dynamic**. Leadership action in a context of uncertainty and volatility, through trust and guided attention • **Wicked**. Dynamic context that requires interactive leadership and a dynamic toolbox
Interpretation. Linkages to other elements offer insights and root causes:
• **Management models**: simple, complex, dynamic, wicked
Sources
• **Exercise**. *Agile by Choice*, pages 168-183
Facilitation. Use Post-it notes and the canvas for the answers:
What are the gaps? Use yellow Post-it notes. What are the key issues? Use dark blue Post-its.

FIGURE 114: DECISION-MAKING STYLE INSIGHTS

ALIGN LEADERSHIP AND SYSTEMS WITH CONTEXT

The dominant management mode aligns the management model and decision-making.

KEY CHAPTER IDEAS

- Management models and decision-making styles offer choices on the design of systems and the nature of leadership
- Four people-centric levers determine the management model and leadership capabilities
- Four dynamic levers determine the operating system with the systems capabilities to deal with the challenges of the environment
- Both the management model and the decision-making style must fit the management context

ACTION AGENDA

Use the diagnostic results to identify your current management model and decision-making style.

Decide on your future model and style.

Align the people-centric and dynamic levers. Decide on your future capabilities.

Use the team workshop to determine the gaps between current and future models and styles, and decide on the key issues to bridge the gap.

FURTHER READING

Michel, L (2017). *Management Design: Managing People and Organizations in Turbulent Times* (2nd ed.). London: LID Publishing.

EQUIP THE TOOLBOX

The Leadership Toolbox combines leadership and systems to offer the generic operating system equipment, providing rules, routines, interactions and tools that every organization needs. Chapter 13 introduces the toolbox, reviews the people-centric gaps, offers the principles that determine its purpose and defines the features of the various elements. A toolbox that fits the operating model and demographics enables management to scale their business.

THE LEADERSHIP TOOLBOX

The Leadership Toolbox (Figure 115) pulls together 20 tools that can help people understand, think, deliver, engage and adhere.

FIGURE 115: LEADERSHIP AND SYSTEMS TOOLS

The toolbox identifies 20 systems (Figure 116). Systems are made up of routines, rules and tools (the lower right corner of the Performance Triangle). Their role is to facilitate leadership interactions (lower left corner). They are the 'big' managerial systems every organization requires.

The Leadership Scorecard offers a horizontal view and a vertical view. The horizontal view follows the Performance Triangle elements. The vertical view aligns with the levers of people-centric management.

The shift from traditional to people-centric calls for a new set of tools that support people performing and getting work done in a dynamic environment.

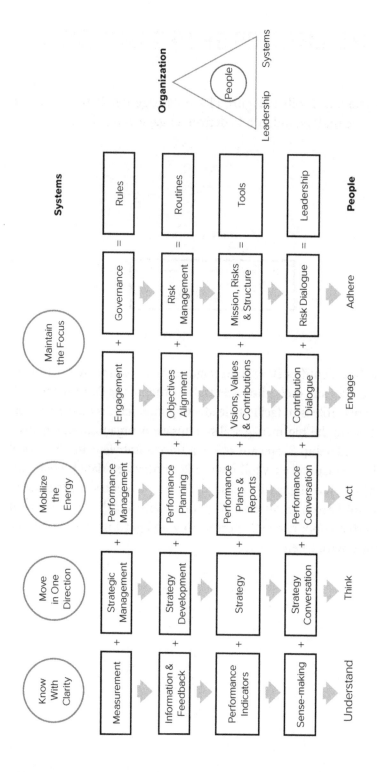

FIGURE 116: LEADERSHIP TOOLBOX

THE TOOLBOX FOR A DEEP UNDERSTANDING

The purpose shift calls for clarity and the means to find purpose in support of self-responsible behaviours and actions. Figure 117 outlines the requisite rules, routines, tools and skills, with a focus on information and feedback that enables people to find purpose.

	From Command	To Self-responsibility
Measurement	Budget review	Self-control through fast and frequent feedback
Information & feedback	Restrictive, limited to the top	Accessibility and transparency
Performance indicators	Many detailed metrics	Few relevant metrics
Sense-making	Directives and control	Interaction; enables people to find purpose

FIGURE 117: THE TOOLBOX TO UNDERSTAND

Measurement: how do we know? Measurement defines the model of how organizations think about performance. Dynamic measurement engages metrics beyond traditional financials, with a model that reflects the value creation of the entire business. Engage key people in your organization to define and apply your measurement system.

Information & feedback: how to create meaning? Information & feedback is the process by which people gain a deep understanding of what's going on. Access to relevant information and feedback, directed to where the work is being done, creates meaning.

Performance indicators: what metrics? Key performance indicators (KPIs) steer attention to what truly matters. Limiting performance indicators to seven, so people can easily memorize them, helps with selecting those metrics that must be kept in mind.

Sense-making: what's happening? Sense-making turns data into information and meaning, for a better understanding of what's happening. It is the interaction mechanism that enables people to find purpose.

The purpose shift requires a new, dynamic toolbox that helps people understand what matters most.

THE TOOLBOX THAT ENABLES THE THINKING

The relationship shift calls for direction, and the means to relate and connect, in support of delegated authority. Figure 118 outlines the necessary rules, routines, tools and skills, with a focus on detailed analysis that helps people shift to thinking and searching for opportunities.

	From Power	To Delegation
Strategic management	Analysis	Modeling for super decision-making
Strategy development	Competitive analysis and advantage	Search for opportunities
Strategy	A three- to five-year plan	Value proposition, shared intent
Strategy conversation	Top-down messaging	Encouragement to take risks

FIGURE 118: THE TOOLBOX TO THINK

Strategic management: what direction? Strategic management refers to the approach organizations use to select their opportunities and challenges. Dynamic strategic management follows a model that enables delegated structured thinking. It establishes a shared language for how people think about their business, and enables them to define and articulate strategy.

Strategy development: how to create the strategy? Strategy development guides the thinking. Dynamic strategy development is about innovation and new opportunities. Make it a continuous process that engages key people, not simply the topic of a once-a-year offsite executive meeting. Rather than cascading strategy downward, enable delegated decision-making in teams, allowing them to create their strategies.

Strategy: what direction? In simplest terms, strategy defines the value that the business promises to its stakeholders — clients, employees, suppliers, the public and shareholders. The brand of the business attaches specific values to its promises. This is why a dynamic strategy establishes a strong relationship with people and a shared intent to move in one direction.

Strategy conversation: why are we going there? Strategy conversation helps leaders establish direction. It's part of the daily routine to create shared intent. It is effective when it enables people to think, rather than providing them with a posted message.

The relationship shift requires a new, dynamic toolbox that enables people to make decisions in line with the intent. The toolbox works when the collective thinking results in opportunities as true innovations.

THE TOOLBOX THAT FOCUSES ON DELIVERY

The collaboration shift calls for delivery and the means to collaborate in support of self-organization. Figure 119 outlines the relevant rules, routines, tools and skills, with a focus on budgets and shifting to engagement as a means to create value.

	From Bureaucracy	**To Self-organization**
Performance management	Fixed budgets	Planning as a continuous and engaging process
Performance planning	Annual top-down budgeting	Just-in-time resource availability, rigorous (peer) performance reviews
Performance plans and reports	Fixed annual budgets	Relative goals
Performance conversation	Business planning	Interactive, dynamic coordination

FIGURE 119: THE TOOLBOX TO DELIVER

Performance management: what is our model? The main purpose of performance management is to implement the strategy. Self-organization demands a model that enables teams to manage their own performance. In a dynamic context, continuous planning and review based on relative goals beats traditional top-down budgeting.

Performance planning and business reviews: how to implement? In a dynamic context, strategy (the thinking) and implementation (the doing) are not separated. They are one continuous process that links hierarchical levels and seamlessly coordinates with related departments. Dynamic planning and review are by no means out of control. On the contrary, they enable peer-control through rigorous business reviews.

Performance plans and reports: what goals and steps? Dynamic plans and reports focus on action, not on financial projections. Rather than detailed targets, relative goals and actions are documented and reviewed regularly, based on two-page documents.

Performance conversation: are we on track, and what can we do? People-centric demands more interaction and less paper. As such, performance conversations facilitate resource allocation, action planning and performance reviews. These conversations have one goal: how to mobilize the right (and sufficient) resources to implement strategy collaboratively, as a team.

In simplest terms, planning is a mature conversation between the leader who demands the value and the leader who delivers it. It's a commitment and a contract between the two. This is accompanied by a process for how to get there. More important than the actual content of that contract is the conversation about any concerns with the plan. Knowing about the concerns takes the fear out of the alignment with your leader.

A business review is an after-action debrief. It is good practice to have that review facilitated by someone who's not part of the delivery and performance dynamic. A good business review is one where you can come in as the leader at the end and share your reflections — what have we learned from this? Be sure to capture and document these reviews, to feed and inform the next cycle or situation.

The collaboration shift requires a new, dynamic toolbox that uses the motivation of people to deliver performance in teams. The toolbox works well when teams apply their knowledge and energy to things they care about.

THE TOOLBOX THAT FRAMES ENGAGEMENT AND ADHERENCE

The learning shift calls for engagement and adherence, and the means to learn in support of broad direction. Figure 120 outlines the pertinent rules, routines, tools and skills — with a focus on targets and incentives — in the shift to enabling people to learn and act as entrepreneurs.

	From Targets	To Focus of Attention
Engagement, governance	Performance targets, rules and incentives	Shared values, social control, entrepreneurship
Objectives alignment, risk management	Incentives for plan achievement	Trust teams on self-control
Vision, values, contributions, mission, risks, structures	Narrow hierarchies with wordy directives	Base accountability on holistic factors and broad direction
Contribution and risk dialogues	Control	Learning

FIGURE 120: THE TOOLBOX TO ENGAGE AND ADHERE

Engagement: how to get the mileage? Traditional engagement models focus on performance targets and incentive plans. Dynamic engagement systems are based on motivated people who want to deliver performance. Performance targets and rewards are applied at team or unit levels, rather than given to individuals.

Governance: how to set the rules? In a dynamic environment, governance rules are defined as principles rather than strict operating procedures. This allows for entrepreneurial action rather than adherence to edicts. Social control replaces management action.

Objectives alignment: how to coordinate? In a hierarchical setting with performance targets and incentives, the downward cascading of objectives takes up considerable management time. People-centric demands the alignment of goals among departments that need to work together. In that way, objectives become the means to coordinate and align with the firm's goals.

Risk management: how to avoid the undesired? Risk management is often seen as a once-a-year executive assessment of the company's overall risks. In a dynamic context, risks are assessed continuously. It's a learning process that attempts to see the invisible and raise awareness of the organization's boundaries.

Vision, values and contributions: what expectations? Ambitions work like magnets; they create effortless pull. Vision and values are important sources of energy. They help people focus their attention on what truly matters: their contributions.

Mission, risks and structures: what rules? Dynamic boundaries frame what is inside and what is outside the confines of the business. They help people limit their activities to the set boundaries without limiting entrepreneurship.

Contribution dialogue: what do you need? The contribution dialogue is an ongoing interaction with leaders on what's needed to succeed and how we can still achieve our goals. Leaders help employees maintain their focus on the overall goals of the business.

Risk dialogue: where are the boundaries? The risk dialogue sets the boundaries for entrepreneurial action. Leaders are in a conversation with people regarding what decisions and actions are within and outside the boundaries of the business.

The learning shift requires a new, dynamic toolbox that focuses attention and limits distractions. The toolbox works well when people are encouraged to balance efficiency and entrepreneurship. It supports continuous learning rather than control.

Is your toolbox well equipped? With this introduction, and the information in Figure 121, use the expert briefing to discuss:

- What is your current leadership toolbox? What does it mean?
- What is your desired future toolbox? Use the people-centric attributes to help frame your answer.
- What are the gaps and the key issues to close the gaps?

Metrics. The Leadership Toolbox elements are determined …	
… through 20 individual questions that evaluate people-centric features.	
Evaluation. The answer is scored as follows:	
0 = Strongly disagree, 25 Disagree, 50 Neutral, 75 Agree, 100 Strongly agree.	
Meaning. The score indicates the following known symptoms:	
Use The Performance Triangle to review your scores, with detailed descriptions of all toolbox elements.	
Interpretation. Linkages to other elements offer insights and root causes:	
• **The Performance Triangle:** systems and leadership • **People-Centric Management:** four levers	
Sources	
• **Model**. *The Performance Triangle*, pages 229-251 • **Process**. *Management Design* (2nd Ed. 2017), pages 182-183, 198-199 • **Application**. *People-Centric Management*, pages 166-175	
Facilitation. Use Post-it notes and the canvas for the answers:	
Where is the potential? Use green Post-its. What are the instances of interference? Use red Post-its. What are the assumptions and principles? Use green Post-its. What are the gaps? Use yellow Post-its. What are the key issues? Use dark blue Post-its.	

FIGURE 121: LEADERSHIP TOOLBOX INSIGHTS

THE DYNAMIC FEATURES OF THE TOOLBOX

Figure 122 bridges people, organization and context at work to show the challenges of the outer game that people and organizations accept. "The greater the external challenges accepted by a company, team or individual, the more important it is that there is minimum interference occurring from within" (Gallwey, 2000). In this light, the job of the leader is to create a work environment that limits the negative effects of interference so that people can accept greater challenges. But, "resistance to change within the corporation is rooted in the prevailing command and control corporate culture" (Gallwey, 2000).

FIGURE 122: THE TOOLBOX BRIDGE

There are four ways to bridge people, organization and context with a toolbox:

1. **To cope with growing complexity, routines need to create awareness more than control**. Complexity is like water, in that it cannot be compacted. Greater awareness is the only way to deal with increased complexity. Traditional ways to address complexity include decomposing it, setting goals and delegating decision-making. Greater complexity is a frequent cause of bureaucratic routines and managerial processes being ineffective. The fix is appropriate design that addresses the lack of rigour. Prevention is the design of routines that enable higher levels of awareness. The task is to decide on a learning policy with the appropriate balance between enabling learning and the need for control.

2. **In ambiguous environments, rules need to enable choice while they regulate the game**. When the future is unclear, choice in decision-making performs better than standard operating procedures. Greater ambiguity is a frequent cause of infected rules and the lack of discipline to follow them. Agility and speed in dealing with ambiguities requires a design for choice. Decide your people policy and set your rules in a way that supports the right balance between self-determination and motivation by leaders.

3. **To cope with greater uncertainty, leadership needs to trust rather than command**. The only way to deal with uncertainties is to trust your own capabilities. With increasing uncertainty, it is important to define a leadership policy that balances responsibility and outside control. The fix for flawed leadership is an appropriate design of interactions for better relationships and collaboration. To prevent creeping uncertainty from hampering performance, interactions need a design with features to enable trust.

4. **To address changing dynamics, tools need to focus attention rather than aim**. When things change fast, people need something they can hold on to. Use tools that focus attention on what is important. With increasing volatility and changing market dynamics, it is important to get the control policy right, as a balance between enabling self-initiative and fostering goal-achievement. The fix for erroneous tools is their appropriate design for purpose and collaboration. Prevention is the use of tools that helps people focus their attention rather than just enabling control.

A toolbox that aligns with people's needs enables organizations to address a challenging environment. To close the people-centric gaps, organizations must equip their toolbox with people-centric features — the features that enact the inner game. The management model and its levers offer the choice between traditional and people-centric principles. To enable people to address the challenges of the outer game, the toolbox requires dynamic features. The decision-making style levers offer the choice between stable and dynamic systems features.

To close the people-centric gaps of the current Leadership Toolbox, and enable dynamic features, the above four principles guide the design of all routines, rules, interactions and tools.

With this introduction and the information in Figure 123, use the expert briefing to discuss:

- What are your current challenges? What does it mean?
- What are the anticipated future challenges? What implications do they have for your toolbox?
- What are the gaps and the key issues to close the gaps?

Metrics. The features of the toolbox are determined as follows:
Current and future degrees of VUCA determine the features of the toolbox. Current routines, rules, interactions and tools determine the ability to address current VUCA challenges. The future features of the toolbox are determined by the expected degree of challenges.
Evaluation. The answers translate as follows into toolbox features:
Greater complexity requires awareness more than control. Significant ambiguity requires rules that enable choice. Increasing uncertainty requires leadership that trusts. Greater volatility requires tools that focus attention.
Meaning. The principles determine the features of the toolbox.
Use the principles to determine the features of all toolbox elements.
Interpretation. Linkages to other elements offer insights and root causes:
• **Leadership Scorecard:** leadership elements.
Sources
• **Process**. *Management Design* (2nd Ed. 2017), pages 180-181, 196-197 • **Model**. *The Performance Triangle* (2013), pages 262-303
Facilitation. Use Post-it notes and the canvas for the answers:
What are the gaps? Use yellow Post-its. What are the key issues? Use dark blue Post-its.

FIGURE 123: DYNAMIC TOOLBOX FEATURES INSIGHTS

OPERATING MODELS

So far, we have identified the design for the parts of the Leadership Toolbox as a choice between traditional, people-centric and dynamic features. Principles and attributes offer guidance for all 20 toolbox elements.

There is a more generic choice to make for the Leadership Toolbox as a whole. It concerns the purpose of the toolbox. In *Strategy Safari*, the academics Henry Mintzberg, Bruce Ahlstrand and Joseph Lampel (1989) offered a map for what they call 'the strategy space.' They plotted 10 distinct strategies around how leaders see the external world (comprehensible and controllable, versus unpredictable and confusing) and how internal processes are proposed (natural or rational).

In alignment with this concept, our research has identified operating models that distinguish between how leaders think about the future (clear or unpredictable) and how work gets done (formal or informal). As a result, the clustering offered nine characteristic operating models (Figure 124). Every model comes with a distinct toolbox and the specifics of all 20 systems elements.

	Formal	Routines	Informal
Unpredictable	Institutional	Conglomerate	Innovation
Future	Clients	Mission	Political
Clear	Position	Service	Vision

FIGURE 124: OPERATING MODELS

The way people think about the future and how we get things done determines the dominant operating model, and with it the purpose of the Leadership Toolbox, with the attributes of all 20 systems.

The task is to fit the toolbox to the purpose of the dominant operating model. Nine models characterize distinct capabilities and systems features:

Innovation toolbox: Systems for an evolving, entrepreneurial and flexible organization designed for innovation in a complex, dynamic and venturing context.

> Rules: metaphors — innovation, guiding concepts, options
> Routines: framing — models (adaptations, interventions, bounded reality, models)
> Interactions: mental perspective (perception, interpretation, bounded reality, models)
> Tools: frames, models, innovation

Conglomerate toolbox: Systems for a conceptually-driven portfolio of businesses built around a common corporate core.

> Rules: frameworks — thought leadership and models
> Routines: learning — patterns (creative solutions)
> Interactions: unique patterns — entrepreneurship, venturing, championing, portfolio
> Tools: emergent themes and development

Institutional toolbox: Systems for research and development to explore responses for specific societal, economic, cultural and environmental challenges.

> Rules: policies — rigorous standard operating procedures, professional standards
> Routines: coping — programmes (structured interventions, creative solutions)
> Interactions: position (themes, complexity, insights, research)
> Tools: research, development, insights

Political toolbox: Systems to control challenges in conflictive and political contexts based on a collective, consensus-seeking or purely power-based approach.

Rules: doctrine — strategic and operation directives
Routines: defending — cooperation (adaptive interventions)
Interactions: political and cooperative pattern and position (stakeholders, politics, collective strategy)
Tools: conflict resolution, coalitions, tensions

Mission toolbox: Systems based on purpose, values, myths, culture or ideology, often in support of a dominant leader's ideals.
Rules: mission — scope, values, contributions, expectations
Routines: uniting — content (balanced)
Interactions: collective, unique perspective (culture, ideology, mission)
Tools: beliefs, boundaries, delivery

Client toolbox: Systems for high responsiveness and support of change to transform and re-focus on value for customers.
Rules: benefits — standards and feedback on value created
Routines: integrating — relationships (structured programmes)
Interactions: context (transformation, revolution, turnaround, client need)
Tools: focus of attention, targeting, client strategy, marketing

Vision toolbox: Systems in support of intensive interactions with a dominant and visionary leader.
Rules: ideas — images of the future
Routines: envisioning — ideas (adaptive interventions, framed content)
Interactions: personal perspective (imagination, vision, ideas)
Tools: business ideas and model

Service toolbox: Systems to establish well-aligned, distinct capabilities to serve clients with solutions that demonstrate unique value.
Rules: core competencies — service advantages
Routines: aligning — capabilities (organization, people, content)
Interactions: unique perspective (data, brand, quality, coordination)
Tools: alignment, coordination, advantage

Position toolbox: Systems to enable scale of commodity-like product manufacturers based on least asset usage, least cost and best quality.

Rules: performance — efficiency, quality, standards, programmes, results

Routines: analysing/optimizing — position (programme, frames, forms)

Interactions: generic position (experience, scale, value)

Tools: cost, assets, value chain, performance

These nine operating models explain the general purpose of the operating system and guide the design of systems. Diagnostic Mentoring uses this guidance to design and equip the Leadership Toolbox.

The dominant operating model follows the decision-making styles with thinking about the future, which is determined by tools and leadership, and by how things are being done, which comes from the rules and routines.

With this introduction and the information in Figure 125, use the expert briefing to discuss:

- What is your current operating model? What does it mean?
- What is your future operating model?
- What are the gaps and the key issues to close the gaps?

Metrics. The dominant operating model is determined as follows:
One question reviews how people think about and deal with the future. Another question reviews how people do things. The dominant operating model determines the purpose of the toolbox.
Evaluation. The answer is scored as follows:
Score of 0 = clear and formal; a score of 100 = unpredictable and informal. Search for the box with the management mode that fits your plot.
Meaning. The scores indicate one of nine operating models.
• **Operating Model:** A dominant pattern that reflects current organizational behaviours determines the purpose of the toolbox.
Interpretation. Linkages to other elements offer insights and root causes:
• **Leadership Toolbox:** the purpose of 20 elements.
Sources
• **Process**. *Management Design* (2nd Ed. 2017), pages 202-203
Facilitation. Use Post-it notes and the canvas for the answers:
What are the gaps? Use yellow Post-its. What are the key issues? Use dark blue Post-its.

FIGURE 125: OPERATING MODEL INSIGHTS

TOOLBOX FITTING

Systems elements with rules, routines, leadership interactions and tools equip the Leadership Toolbox. Context, the management model, the decision-making style, the operating model, and gaps from the diagnostic and demographics determine the features, purpose, gaps and purpose of the toolbox. Three action steps offer what I call *toolbox fitting* (Figure 126).

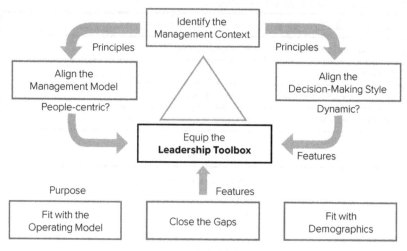

FIGURE 126: TOOLBOX FITTING

Fitting principles:
- The life cycle stage determines the choice of tools
- Structure determines the choice of routines
- Decentralization determines the choice of interactions
- Type of organization determines the choice of rules

The life cycle stage of an organization determines the choice of tools. In *Levers of Control* (1994), Harvard business school professor Robert Simons identified the evolution of management control systems over the life cycle of a firm. With this, and the Greiner (1997) life cycle model, Figure 127 suggests the following choices for an overlay of tools.

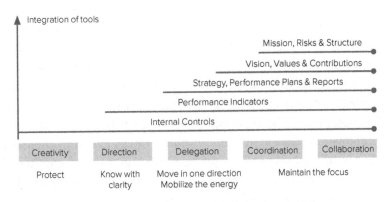

FIGURE 127: THE CHOICE OF TOOLS

Internal controls to free up creativity. In the creativity phase of start-up operations, there is little need for formal control systems. Because employees are in constant face-to-face contact and communicate with each other, there's no need for formal controls. Key assets of the business are protected through internal control systems. They ensure that assets are secure, and that accounting information is reliable and reflects the business operations.

Performance indicators to clarify direction. In the direction phase, when a business grows and direct, daily interaction with all employees is no longer possible, information systems with key performance indicators are needed to create shared observation points. This helps to focus attention on the things that matter, to compensate for less personal interaction. Feedback mechanisms ensure sufficient managerial control.

Performance Indicators

FIGURE 128: PERFORMANCE INDICATORS

Performance indicators (Figure 128) support self-responsible people with knowledge that's distributed throughout the organization, allowing them to know with clarity. Information works diagnostically. Few metrics offer feedback to where the work is being done. Leaders focus on interactions and offer sense-making. Collective awareness creates a culture with a shared understanding and purpose at its roots.

Delegation through strategy, performance plans & reports. In the delegation phase, with increasing size, decision authority is delegated to employees at the client front. Formal strategy and implementation tools become increasingly important. Strategy tools strengthen the alignment throughout the organization and implementation systems ensure that plans are regularly reviewed.

Strategy tools (Figure 129) enable the thinking in ambiguous contexts. Plans and reports get things going. Strategy and implementation are part of a continuous learning process. Leaders interact and offer strategic insights. In combination, this creates a culture based on a shared intent, for a delegated way of connected thinking.

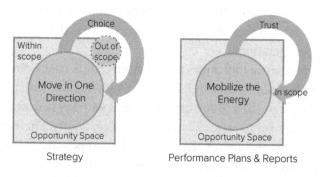

FIGURE 129: STRATEGY, PERFORMANCE PLANS & REPORTS

Dynamic performance plans and reports (Figure 129) to manage organizational performance enable action in self-organized teams when uncertainty is high. Resources are allocated on demand, with flexible plans and decentralized business reviews to support implementation. Leaders interactively challenge teams. Together, this leads to a culture with a shared agenda that facilitates the collaboration.

Coordination through vision, values, contributions. Businesses in the coordination phase operate in multiple markets and locations, which makes coordination across boundaries more difficult. Formal 'beliefs' tools are implemented, with mission and vision statements created and communicated to align business units, engage people and maintain the focus.

Collaboration through mission, risks and structure. In large, mature companies, managers rely on collaboration and opportunity-seeking behaviours of employees for innovation and new business ventures. At this stage, interaction complements management tools. Information, direction, implementation, beliefs and boundary tools combine to balance entrepreneurial action with clear boundaries that limit the risks.

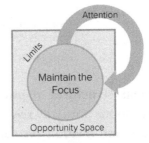

Vision, Values & Contributions   Mission, Risks & Structures

FIGURE 130: BELIEFS AND BOUNDARY TOOLS

Dynamic beliefs (vision, values and contributions) and boundary tools (mission, risks and structures, Figure 130) enable employee engagement and adherence to aspirations and norms in a context where knowledge and decision-making is distributed throughout the organization. Leaders interact and engage in dialogue on contribution and risks. Shared aspirations and norms create a strong culture, at scale.

Diagnostic Mentoring ensures that the choice of tool corresponds to the incumbent's current and future life cycle stage. With this introduction, use the expert briefing to discuss:

- What is your current choice of tools? What does it mean?
- What is your anticipated future choice of tools?
- What are the gaps and the key issues to close the gaps?

Organizational structure determines the choice of routines. Organizations vary greatly in how they structure accountability for decisions and actions. The portfolio of managerial routines gets bigger as more routines are integrated to address the greater organizational complexity. Figure 131 lists the portfolio of routines for four different organizations.

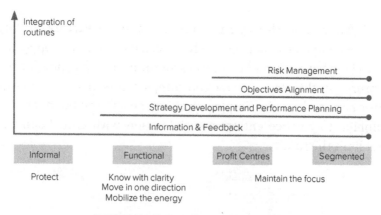

FIGURE 131: THE CHOICE OF ROUTINES

Informal structures require control routines. Small, informal organizations primarily rely on accounting cycles to review income and cost information. Managers know their people and therefore are able to directly influence their decisions, actions and behaviours. Annual control routines ensure that owners know how the organization is doing.

Information, feedback, strategy development, performance planning, routines, support functional structures. It's a big step from a small, informal business to a large, multi-function organization with distributed accountability. When managers separate work along functional lines and engage an executive team that represents them, they coordinate and align work across these organizational segments with routines that bring clarity, unity and engagement (Figure 132). Information and feedback create awareness, direction limits the choices and performance planning aligns the energy.

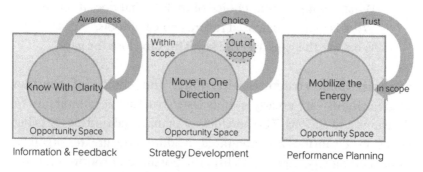

FIGURE 132: INFORMATION, STRATEGY AND IMPLEMENTATION ROUTINES

Objectives alignment supports profit centre structures. When companies are organized by quasi-independent business units, managers adopt routines that tie the leaders and employees of these units to the expected outcomes. By linking personal performance to organizational outcomes, they ensure that members of these units remain entrepreneurial while maintaining their focus on what delivers value. That's what objectives alignment does (Figure 133).

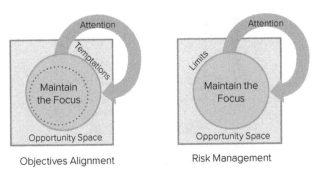

FIGURE 133: BELIEFS AND BOUNDARY ROUTINES

Risk management safeguards segmented structures. When products and markets cross lines of accountability, with multiple units taking the lead, managers introduce risk management to better balance the search for opportunities without stretching the limits of the company's mission. Risk management helps participants maintain focus on the core while stretching the limits. Risk management focuses attention on the overall outcome, rather than optimizing subunits.

Diagnostic Mentoring helps to choose routines that fit current and future organizational structures. With this introduction, use the expert briefing to discuss:
- What is your current choice of routines? What does it mean?
- What is your anticipated future choice of routines?
- What are the gaps and the key issues to close the gaps?

The degree of decentralization determines the choice of interactions. How organizations structure their decision-making varies from centralized to decentralized. In centralized organizations, decisions are made at the top. In decentralized organizations, decisions are made with employees at the client front.

Interdependencies and knowledge asymmetries determine the degree of decentralization (Figure 134). With greater interdependencies among organizational units or people, the decision-making migrates to a higher level that connects separate parts. With this, employees and managers need less time and energy to interact.

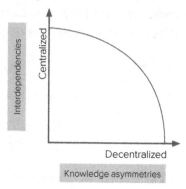

FIGURE 134: INTERDEPENDENCIES AND KNOWLEDGE ASYMMETRIES

With more knowledgeable employees at the client front, decision-making migrates to the periphery. Managers and employees need more time and energy to interact, share, align and coordinate work.

With this, the choice of interactions needs to take into account interdependencies and the distribution of knowledge. With increasing decentralization, the variety and integration of interaction mechanisms increases (Figure 135).

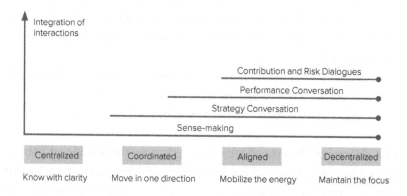

FIGURE 135: THE CHOICE OF INTERACTIONS

Sense-making compensates for centralized decision-making. With interdependencies among units, and when the knowledge is at the top of organizations, decisions migrate to the top. There is less need for interaction during the decision-making process. However, centralized decision-making needs to compensate for not involving employees by helping them make sense of the decisions they're confronted with. Sense-making strengthens the understanding of decisions and increases the likelihood that they are implemented as intended.

Strategy conversations coordinate decision-making. When the decision-making is distributed within a team that has the expert knowledge, a strategy conversation is needed to coordinate separate decisions. With conversations around the overall strategy, everyone can move in one direction. As such, decisions are coordinated without daily interaction with the team leader. Strategy conversations are the important interaction mechanism in self-organized teams.

Performance conversations align decision-making. With decisions being made at multiple hierarchical levels and in units beyond the control of the CEO, performance conversations align actions with the overall direction and goals. Performance conversations guide people to focus their attention on those things that are in line with strategy and goals. As such, knowledge is applied where it resides, and decisions are aligned to mobilize the energy throughout the entire organization.

Contribution and risk dialogues enable decentralized decision-making. When decisions are fully decentralized to quasi-independent teams and individuals across an organization, it's important to see that the overall focus is maintained and decisions are made within set limits. Contribution and risk dialogues are the interaction mechanisms for leaders to ensure control. Interaction means direct influence. And so, a conversation with employees about their contribution increases the influence. Conversations around risks ensure the necessary control over decentralized decision-making.

Diagnostic Mentoring guides leaders in their selection of interaction mechanisms that support their decision-making responsibility. With this introduction, use the expert briefing to discuss:

- What is your current choice of interactions? What does it mean?
- What is your future choice of interactions?
- What are the gaps and the key issues to close the gaps?

THE UNIT OF ANALYSIS DETERMINES
THE CHOICE OF RULES

Not every organizational unit requires the same set of rules. The choice of rules varies from teams to departments, divisions, businesses and conglomerates. Figure 136 shows the increasing integration of rules as units increase in size and complexity.

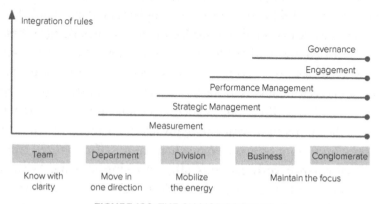

FIGURE 136: THE CHOICE OF RULES

A measurement system for every unit. In teams, people know each other, and team leaders are present. In this construct, interactive controls are dominant — with one exception. Teams determine their own measurement systems to monitor performance. That may be simple for a small team, and get bigger and more comprehensive in larger organizations. Businesses and conglomerates determine their own unique way of monitoring performance, to know how they're doing.

Strategic management for departments and bigger organizations. Departments that consist of multiple teams and perform specific functions, or are part of a large business, determine their own strategy to identify the key capabilities they need to perform. All of these units have their own way of defining, articulating and sharing strategy throughout their organizations. It helps all employees move in one direction.

Performance management to implement strategy. Divisions, businesses and conglomerates determine their own ways of managing performance within their units, and of controlling multiple units.

They establish their own, distinct performance management model to help them plan and review their reporting units' performance.

Engagement to encourage entrepreneurial behaviours. Companies' HR departments establish engagement policies and activities. Too often, engagement is limited to employee wellbeing, creating a good workplace or some other attempt to squeeze more performance out of people. The real value comes from policies that encourage entrepreneurial behaviours, within clear limits and practices that help people better focus attention, rather than edicts to follow outdated performance goals.

Governance to adhere to corporate standards and limit risks. The protection of company assets and limitations on entrepreneurial behaviour are required in business organizations that span multiple units. Often, legal policies determine the nature of the governance system, which may include reporting requirements.

Diagnostic Mentoring guides the selection of a governance system that meets the needs of organizational units. With this introduction and the information in Figure 137, use the expert briefing to discuss:

- What is your current choice of rules? What does it mean?
- What is your anticipated future choice of rules?
- What are the gaps and the key issues to close the gaps?

Metrics. The choice of toolbox is determined as follows:
Current and future demographics determine the choice of toolbox.
Evaluation. The answers translate as follows into the choice of toolbox:
Life cycle stage determines the choice of tools. Organizational structure determines the choice of routines. The degree of decentralization determines the choice of interactions. The unit of analysis determines the choice of rules.
Meaning. The scores indicate one of nine operating models.
• **Operating Model:** A dominant pattern that reflects current organizational behaviours.
Interpretation. Linkages to other elements offer insights and root causes:
• **Leadership Toolbox:** the purpose of 20 elements.
Sources
• **Process**. *Management Design* (2nd Ed. 2017), pages 202-203
Facilitation. Use Post-it notes and the canvas for the answers:
What are the gaps? Use yellow Post-its. What are the key issues? Use dark blue Post-its.

FIGURE 137: TOOLBOX FITTING INSIGHTS

SCALING MANAGEMENT

When businesses move through their life cycle stages, alter their structures, modify their decision-making approach and grow in size, their operating system needs to facilitate those changes. With a Leadership Toolbox that fits the purpose, dynamics and demographics, organizations can scale management in support of their business.

Scaling requires a toolbox with the dynamic features based on emergence, self-organization, delegation and options. It works best with a toolbox that fits its purpose, has dynamic capabilities and offers tools that align with demographics. This gives managers a set of tools that maximize the potential and minimize interference.

Scaling demands a toolbox that fits the:

Operating model: the purpose of the toolbox

Decision-making style: the dynamic features of the toolbox

Demographics: the choice of the toolbox elements

A toolbox that fits the purpose, favours dynamic features and is equipped with the right elements is reflective of good management, and the capacity to scale management as the business grows.

SUGAR MANUFACTURING: THE TOOLBOX FOR SCALING

This is the case of a start-up on a path to growth. It marked the first time the management team discussed what was needed to enable that growth. The team used Diagnostic Mentoring primarily for its design capacity, and less for the diagnostic results (Figure 138).

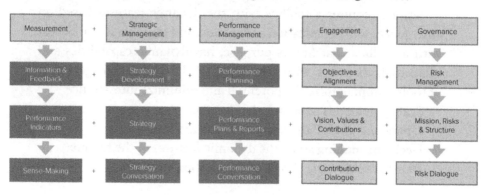

FIGURE 138: SUGAR.INC – TOOLBOX FOR SCALING

To support growth for another year, a set of performance indicators, strategy and performance plan were put in place. For the first time, mentors supported the executive team in facilitating key processes — information sharing, feedback, strategy development and performance planning. The set of routines culminated in a quarterly business review. All managers were then trained on sense-making, strategy and performance conversations. That package supported the growth process until the business was established, after which the toolbox was augmented with additional rules, routines, tools and interactions.

EQUIP THE TOOLBOX

The Leadership Toolbox combines leadership and systems to provide 20 rules, routines, interactions and tools. Principles, the operating model and demographics determine what's in every leader's toolbox.

KEY CHAPTER IDEAS

- The toolbox must fulfil its purpose, have dynamic features and fit aspects of the organization's demography
- The Leadership Toolbox represents 20 'big' systems — the system-relevant tools of the operating system
- A toolbox that fits enables the scaling of systems as organizations grow

ACTION AGENDA

Identify your Leadership Toolbox and its features.
Align the toolbox with the purpose of the dominant operating model.
Fit the toolbox to your organization's demographics.

FURTHER READING

Michel, L (2017). *Management Design: Managing People and Organizations in Turbulent Times* (2nd ed.). London: LID Publishing.

CHAPTER 14
ALIGN LEADERSHIP

Leadership represents the lower left corner of the Performance Triangle. Chapter 14 identifies four leadership styles, with their respective interaction mechanisms and capabilities. Leaders do not operate in isolation. Their style needs to fit the current operating model.

LEADERSHIP STYLES

Leadership is a contact sport. It is direct interaction with people. And, interaction is the most effective control mechanism — much more so than systems. Interactive leadership means direct influence over the thinking, decisions, actions and behaviours of people. That's why we need to care about finding a leadership style that meets the needs of people and fits the dominant operating model.

Four interaction levers (Figure 139) determine the dominant leadership style, along the involvement and structuring dimensions. Involvement means that leaders engage their teams in the understanding, thinking and doing. Structuring means that leaders create the conditions for teams to perform.

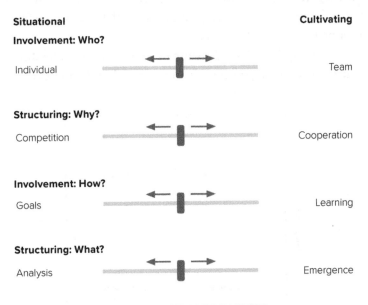

FIGURE 139: INTERACTION LEVERS

Individual leaders are self-involved. They assume that they have complete understanding, and communicate their insights from the top down.

Team leaders help people raise their awareness and make sense. They engage the team in decision-making, so they know with clarity.

Competing leaders distrust people and question their employees' ability to get things done. As such, they communicate performance outcomes and decide on corrective actions.

Cooperative leaders trust people to get things done. They conduct helpful performance conversations that mobilize everyone's energy.

Goal-oriented leaders own all the information and use detailed targets to control people's engagement and adherence to rules in setting standards.

Learning-oriented leaders engage in a dialogue about contributions and risks to ensure that teams maintain the right focus.

Analytical leaders have the unique ability to think and the authority to make critical decisions. And so, they communicate strategy from the top down.

Emergent leaders conduct productive strategy conversations, involve the team in the strategy and essential decisions, encouraging everyone to move in one direction.

Combining these levers results in four distinct leadership styles: situational, systemic, outbound and cultivating (Figure 140).

FIGURE 140: LEADERSHIP STYLES

Situational leadership is for heroic 'doers' who effectively get things done. Situational leaders use power for speed, flexibility and to make things possible. Their interaction is limited to communicating their decisions and ordering their implementation.

Systemic leadership is for 'corporate architects' with the power to shape work, organizations and management. Systemic leaders cooperate to cultivate processes and structures for efficiency and innovation. They communicate clear goals and involve teams to evolve their domains.

Outbound leadership resembles the style of successful sales people. They offer ideas, nudges and encouragement for people to decide and act. Outbound leaders are great motivators who get their teams to deal with the detail and compete. Their involvement focuses on teams with the capacity to structure the context.

Cultivating leadership is for people-centric leaders who work with their teams to create the future. Cultivating leaders encourage cooperation and learning with an emergent approach. They trust their teams to do the same.

Figure 141 compares the four leadership styles.

Cultivating	Outbound
Team Cooperation Learning Emergence	Team Competition Learning Analysis
Systemic	**Situational**
Individual Cooperation Goals Emergence	Individual Competition Goals Analysis

FIGURE 141: LEADERSHIP STYLE PRINCIPLES

In 'Be Like Me: The Effects of Manager-Supervisor Alignment,' Professor Johanna Anzengruber (Anzengruber et al., 2020) and her research team demonstrated that the fit of managerial capabilities between manager and supervisor predicts the effectiveness of the manager. "The most effective managers," she wrote, "show particularly high managerial capabilities that are in line with predominantly high managerial capabilities of their supervisors." One leader's leadership style gets adopted by other leaders around him or her. The style becomes dominant in organizations. That's why managers need to care about the effectiveness of their style. Effectiveness requires a fit between the leadership style and the dominant operating model.

We have identified five interaction mechanisms: sense-making, strategy conversation, performance conversation, contribution dialogue and risk dialogue (Figure 142).

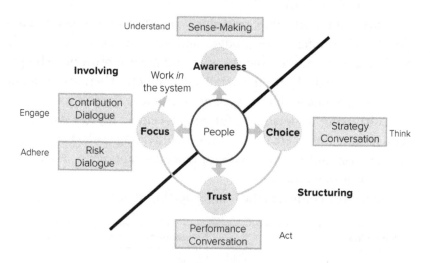

FIGURE 142: LEADERSHIP INTERACTIONS

Both *involving* and *structuring* are at work in the system. Leaders use both to interact with employees. Sense-making, contribution and risk dialogues help people understand, engage and adhere. Strategy and performance conversations support people in thinking and acting. The Leadership Scorecard expands on the rules, routines and tools leaders use for involving and structuring.

Each of the four interaction styles — situational, systemic, outbound and cultivating — are equally effective. But, their effectiveness depends on the prevailing operating context. Diagnostic Mentoring identifies the current leadership style and ensures that the appropriate style prevails, in line with the dominant operating model.

With this introduction and the information in Figure 143, use the expert briefing to discuss:

- What is your current leadership style? What does it mean?
- What is your anticipated future leadership style?
- What are the gaps and the key issues to close the gaps?

Metrics. The dominant leadership style is determined as follows:
Two questions identify leadership preferences between high and low, involving and structuring. The dominant leadership style determines how leaders interact with employees.
Evaluation. The answer is scored as follows:
Score of 0 = low involvement or structuring; score of 100 = high involvement and structuring. Search for the box with the leadership style that fits your plot.
Meaning. The scores indicate one of four leadership styles.
• **Leadership styles**: Dominant behavioural patterns that reflect leadership interaction mechanisms between involving and structuring.
Interpretation. Linkages to other elements offer insights and root causes:
• **Performance Triangle**: leadership • **Leadership Toolbox**: five interaction types
Sources
• **Process**. *Management Design* (2nd Ed. 2017), pages 206-209
Facilitation. Use Post-it notes and the canvas for the answers:
What are the gaps? Use yellow Post-its. What are the key issues? Use dark blue Post-its.

FIGURE 143: LEADERSHIP STYLE INSIGHTS

LEADERSHIP FITTING

The purpose of leadership fitting is to align the leadership style in use with the intended operating environment. The dominant operating model represents the prevailing way people think, act and behave in an organization. The dominant leadership style explains how leaders interact with employees. Both the institutional model and the individual style are invisible, and one can only sense them when they *do not* work as expected. This is why Diagnostic Mentoring makes the fit between leadership and the operating model visible, to help facilitate a deliberate decision (Figure 144).

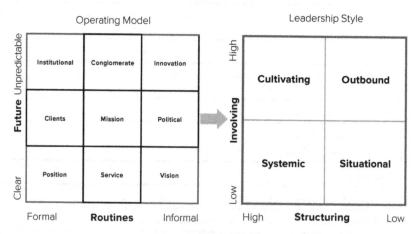

FIGURE 144: LEADERSHIP FITTING

While in theory there's no magic to the process of fitting, changing leadership styles is hard. The research that led to Diagnostic Mentoring has clearly identified four alignment paths.

In the **position** operating model, the **systemic** leadership style dominates. When there is clarity to make decisions and formal routines dominate, leaders need to structure the decision-making process. With this, they can rely on employees to deal with decisions without frequent involvement of the leader.

In the **vision** operating model, the **situational** leadership style dominates. Informal procedures fit a loose structuring style. When clarity on the future prevails, there is little need for extensive interactions.

In the **institutional** operating model, the **cultivating** leadership style dominates. In an uncertain environment that cannot be predetermined, high levels of involvement are needed to find best solutions. Proven formal routines and a tight structuring leadership style tend to be most successful.

In the **innovation** operating model, the **outbound** leadership style dominates. The information/entrepreneurial approach, with little structuring, meets an unpredictable context where high involvement with people is required.

This means that the expectations are that leaders eventually adapt their style to fit the dominant operating model. This does not come without doubts. Can leaders change their dominant style?

What happens if they don't? If the leadership style is more formal than routines demand, there's bound to be tension. Employees see over-structuring as unnecessary interference in an information environment. If the leadership style is less formal than routines demand, there will be stress. Little structuring causes a vacuum in a formal environment, which leaves employees uncertain about their actions and behaviours. Likewise, a high degree of involvement in a central environment creates tensions. People perceive leaders as intruding on their domain. In a decentralized environment, little involvement leads to a loss of control. Employees are ignored, and therefore act on their own. Tensions, stress and the loss of control reduce performance, and should obviously be prevented.

Diagnostic Mentoring guides the selection of a leadership style that meets the needs of the dominant operating mode. With this introduction and the information in Figure 145, use the expert briefing to discuss:

- What is your current leadership style? What does it mean?
- What is your anticipated future leadership style?
- What are the gaps and the key issues to close the gaps?

Metrics. The dominant leadership style is determined as follows:
Two questions determine the leadership style: the degrees of structuring and involving.
Evaluation. The answer is scored as follows:
Involving and structuring determine the leadership style. Leadership style and the operating model need to fit.
Meaning. The scores indicate one of nine operating models.
• **Leadership styles**: A dominant pattern that reflects leadership behaviour.
Interpretation. Linkages to other elements offer insights and root causes:
• **Leadership Scorecard:** the five interaction styles
Sources
• **Process**. *Management Design* (2nd Ed. 2017), pages 206-209
Facilitation. Use Post-it notes and the canvas for the answers:
What are the gaps? Use yellow Post-its. What are the key issues? Use dark blue Post-its.

FIGURE 145: LEADERSHIP FITTING INSIGHTS

INDIVIDUALIZING LEADERSHIP

As businesses evolve and change their operating model and demographics, become more formal or deal with an unpredictable future, leaders need to adapt their style. With a style that fits the dominant operating model, leaders can apply people-centric principles to make every relationship individual and special.

Individualizing requires people-centric features of leadership that support self-responsibility, teamwork, attention and dynamic capabilities. It works best with a leadership style that fits the dominant operating model, where managers can rely on practices that maximize the potential and minimize interference.

A people-centric leadership style that fits is the prerequisite for individualizing management. With a leadership style that fits, employees rely on the right amount of structuring and support from leaders.

FOOD – ESCAPING
THE EFFICIENCY LOCK-IN

This is the kind of industry where total control is necessary, to the extent that a single-degree temperature difference in poultry production facilities causes company-wide alarms to go off. No joke. Precision and quality control are essential in a processing environment where the thermostat is kept at 30 degrees Celsius.

The CEO maintained the same rigour in managing the executive team. While that was essential in the production area, more room to breathe was necessary in areas such as development, marketing and sales.

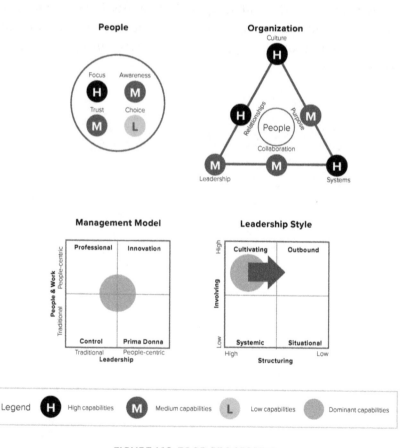

FIGURE 146: FOOD PROCESSING

With the diagnostic results (Figure 146), there was no doubt about the controlling management model. The only area where the company was able to explore innovative ways of marketing its products was the CEO's leadership style. The cultivating style was effective in work with the production team. However, less structuring was necessary with most other departments. It therefore made sense to structure the CEO's meetings and individual interactions such that he could play the cultivating role with the production side of the house, but switch to the outbound model when dealing with issues across all other parts of the company.

It was the sort of dual leadership style that helped the company achieve strictly managed operating excellence in manufacturing and distribution, and pursue innovation in product development and marketing. Mentoring helped maintain two parallel but different leadership and conversation styles.

ALIGN LEADERSHIP

Leadership is at the lower left corner of the Performance Triangle, so it is part of the operating system. Different levels of interaction and structuring combine to reflect four leadership styles.

KEY CHAPTER IDEAS

- The degree of structuring and involving frames four leadership styles
- The dominant leadership style needs to fit the prevailing operating model
- Five interaction mechanisms align with people-centric management
- Leadership styles help individualize management

ACTION AGENDA

Use the diagnostic results to identify your current leadership style. Decide on the features of your desired future leadership style. Determine the gaps between current and future leadership approaches, and decide on the key issues to bridge that gap.

FURTHER READING

Michel, L (2017). *Management Design: Managing People and Organizations in Turbulent Times* (2nd ed.). London: LID Publishing.

PRIORITIZE THE DEVELOPMENT

Chapter 15 translates insights into action. It dives into cause and effect and helps determine the development priorities and paths forward. Whether you zero in on Chapter 10 (the introduction to *Act on Insights*), or have gone through the detail of systems and leadership in Chapters 11-14, the task is the same. Namely, the gaps between current and future systems and leadership determine the key issues that must be addressed to close a gap. Key issues are addressed through initiatives. The road map puts them into action. Diagnostic Mentoring uses the expert briefing to distii initiatives and create the road map.

CAUSE AND EFFECT

With clarity on gaps and key issues to close the gaps, it's now time to review the portfolio of key issues and intervention points. The question becomes where to intervene in the system.

So far, we have looked at the details of an agile organization and the dynamic operating system. We've reviewed over 50 elements that offer feedback and an opportunity for design. To move to a new set of capabilities and change the operating system, we need to separate the triggers from symptoms, root causes from effects, and identify the outcomes. I often see that organizations address symptoms or effects with change programmes, and then find themselves back in the same mess within a few months. Changing leaders, cutting costs or restructuring are such examples.

A bold move is needed to address the underlying causes of interference or levers to unlock the potential. The cause-and-effect table (Figure 147) is a helpful tool to evaluate the list of key issues with respect to their role in systems: the symptoms, triggers, causes, effects, levers and outcomes.

Roles	Features
Symptoms	People with the inner game, resources, capabilities
Triggers	Volatility, uncertainty, complexity, ambiguity
Causes	Culture, leadership and systems (toolbox)
Effects	Collaboration, relationships and purpose
Levers	Agile, people-centric and dynamic capabilities
Outcomes	Performance, innovation, growth, success

FIGURE 147: CAUSE AND EFFECT

It's a common phenomenon that culture is only really noticed and thought about when something goes wrong. When everything is fine, there's no discussion about culture. As with people's personal taste, we only seem to notice when it deviates from our sense of propriety. The problem with this is that things can go wrong in small ways, and for quite a while, before they're detected. Just as the proverbial frog does not jump out of the pot as the water gets gradually hotter, these factors build slowly and never hit as a *big bang*. This is why Diagnostic Mentoring detects small changes in all people-centric, agile and dynamic capability elements.

People first sense a virus-infected culture, faulty leadership and erroneous systems when these elements interfere with their performance, when they cannot access their resources or when their potential is limited. For example, when their attention is diverted by leaders, when there's so much work that focus is impossible or when systems distort attention through conflicting goals. We have learned through Diagnostic Mentoring to carefully listen to these symptoms. The Performance Triangle helps us separate these symptoms from the causes and effects.

In most cases, problems with culture, leadership and systems are caused by changes in internal and external VUCA challenges. Again, these triggers are first detected when people have a distorted focus, when awareness is numbed, when trust fails or when there is no choice to decide and act. The causes come from leadership that has not adapted to the changes or a toolbox that's unable to deal with greater complexity.

The causes are always found with culture, leadership and systems (the toolbox). That is why I dedicated a large part of this book to the design of leadership and systems. Culture reacts slowly and changes are noticed only with a time delay. As such, culture is an outcome of systems and leadership. But, it is the element that shows the negative effects of missing collaboration, limited relationships and lack of purpose. But there is no culture screw to turn — culture can only be altered through changes in leadership and systems. The harmful effects of an infected culture can be seen through the lens of collaboration, relationships and systems. They are the collectively observed effect of the symptoms.

Our research has proven that most problems with culture, leadership and systems can be addressed through three levers: the agile features of organizations, the people-centric features of management and the dynamic features of the operating system.

Performance, innovation, growth and success are the results of the choices on these levers. They represent bundles of capabilities and principles that must be developed and aligned to lead to the expected outcomes. To prioritize the list of key issues, first think through cause and effect. This offers a first cut of initiatives that address the causes rather than symptoms.

With this introduction and the information in Figure 148, use the expert briefing to discuss:

- What are current gaps and key issues? What is their role?
- What are the initiatives that best address the key issues?

Metrics. Cause and effect is determined as follows:
Use the summary scores of all 50 elements and arrange the elements according to the cause-and-effect list.
Evaluation. The answers translate as follows into the ranking:
Separate symptoms, triggers, causes, effects, levers and outcomes.
Meaning. The ranking offers the priorities on initiatives.
• **Cause and effect:** Ranking key issues in line with their roles
Interpretation. Linkages to other elements offer insights and root causes:
• **Performance Triangle:** Use the cause-and-effect list to review the elements and their roles in the model
Sources
• **Model:** *The Performance Triangle*, pages 303-304 • **Process.** *Management Design* (2nd Ed. 2017), pages 216-217
Facilitation. Use Post-it notes and the canvas for the answers:
What are the initiatives? Use grey Post-its.

FIGURE 148: CAUSE-AND-EFFECT INSIGHTS

INITIATIVES

Cause and effect offers a first cut through initiatives. Intervention levers serve as our model to determine the development priorities.

The environmental scientist Donella Meadows (Meadows, 2001), co-author of a 1972 Club of Rome report, 'Limits to Growth,' defines what she called 'Leverage Points: Places to Intervene in Systems.' Leverage points are where a small shift in one thing can produce big changes in everything. Meadows suggests distinct places to intervene in systems, as summarized here, in eight levers arrayed in order of increasing effectiveness:

1. **Constants, parameters, numbers, resources** (subsidies, taxes, standards). It's like rearranging deckchairs on the Titanic. A lot of attention goes into these factors, but there's not a lot of leverage in them.

2. **Regulating negative feedback loops.** It's about buffers and stabilizing stocks. A buffer is like money in the bank rather than living off the flow of change through your pocket. These loops have a self-correcting, stabilizing effect. But, changing them is still low on the effectiveness scale.

3. **Driving positive feedback loops.** These loops are self-reinforcing. They're the sources of the growth and the ultimate collapse of a system. A system with positive feedback loops will eventually destroy itself. However, they're quite rare. Look for interest rates, infection rates and more. Carefully observe them.

4. **Information flows.** Who does and does not have access to information? Missing feedback is one of the most common causes of systems malfunction. It's a leverage point that counteracts people's tendency to avoid accountability for decisions.

5. **The rules of the system.** The rules — incentives, punishments, constraints — define the scope, boundaries and degrees of freedom of a system. Changing rules is powerful. Power over rules is *really* powerful.

6. **The distribution of power over the rules of the system.** It's the power to add, change, evolve or self-organize system structure. Self-organization means changing any aspect of a system

lower on this list. But, self-organization is the strongest form of resilience in a system. The intervention point is obvious, but changing it means losing control.

7. **The goals of the system**. It's the push for control, to bring more and more under central planning. Changing people in a system is a low-effectiveness lever. But, there's an exception: changing a single player at the top may generate power to change the system's goal.

8. **The mindset or paradigm**. It's the shared idea, the assumptions, the deepest beliefs about how things work. Paradigms are the sources of systems out of which their goals, power structure, rules and culture arise. Paradigms can be changed by modelling systems, which takes you outside the system and forces you to see the whole. It's hard, but not impossible.

For the purpose of prioritizing initiatives with the executive briefing, Diagnostic Mentoring translates Meadows' leverage points into a model of intervention levers (Figure 149).

High impact

Hard to change	10	**CEO**	The power to change paradigms
	9	**Culture**	The mindset and deeply rooted ideas and shared beliefs
	8	**Business model**	The agile capabilities that determine success
+/- change	7	**Management**	The people-centric principles
	6	**Rules**	The dynamic capabilities of rules
	5	**Routines**	The dynamic capabilities of routines
	4	**Leadership**	The interactive capabilities of leadership
Easy to change	3	**Tools**	The dynamic capabilities of tools
	2	**Cycle**	The management cycle
	1	**Operations**	The resources

Small impact

FIGURE 149: INTERVENTION LEVERS

Intervention levers range from 1 (small impact but easy to change) to 10 (high impact but hard to change). The challenge is to find the right balance between impact and ease of change.

High impact levers include the CEO's or top managers' power to fundamentally change paradigms. The complete transformation — starting from a traditional approach and moving to an agile organization, to people-centric management and to a dynamic operating system — is such a paradigm change. It's a distinct decision that is hard to change and, therefore, requires a Diagnostic Mentoring approach.

Culture is another high-impact lever. We've already noted that culture is more an outcome than an intervention point. Much of what we call culture is invisible, and is therefore hard to precisely address. Interventions into leadership and systems are the best way to change culture over time.

Agile core capabilities that lead to success represent the business model. Changes in capabilities require investments in development that take time. Another high-impact lever is the management model with a change from traditional to people-centric.

Rules, routines, leadership interactions and tools are the most promising and doable levers to achieve better management. We have discussed in depth how to adapt the toolbox to context, the management model and demographics.

Initiatives answer the following in five dimensions, in line with the canvas:

People: What initiatives unlock the potential for more creativity and performance?

Organization: What initiatives remove the barriers to more agility and innovation?

Work: What initiatives leverage our resources for more resilience and growth?

Operations: What initiatives allow us to effectively take on greater challenges?

Management: What initiatives support the decision-making in a dynamic context?

Initiatives combine key issues into actions that require the same development approach. From our work on many projects, we've learned that crafting initiatives is more of an art than a science. It requires experience and expertise in analysis and implementation. The executive briefing offers the opportunity to use a Diagnostic Mentor and benefit from that experience. This step requires utmost care.

Intervention levers offer a helpful tool to prioritize the initiatives. With this introduction, and the information in Figure 150, use the expert briefing to discuss:

- What are current gaps and key issues? What is their role?
- What are the initiatives that best address the key issues?

Metrics. Initiatives are determined as follows:
Use the scores of the 10 intervention levers.
Evaluation. The answers translate as follows into the ranking:
List the key issues in line with the intervention priorities. Then, decide on the priorities of the initiatives to develop the key issues.
Meaning. The list offers the priorities for initiatives.
• **Initiatives**: Prioritizing in line with impact and ease of change
Interpretation. Linkages to other elements offer insights and root causes:
• **Performance Triangle**: all elements • **Leadership Toolbox**: all elements
Sources
• **Model:** *The Performance Triangle*, pages 305-307 • **Process**. *Management Design* (2nd Ed. 2017), pages 218-219 • **Application**. *People-Centric Management*, pages 226-227
Facilitation. Use Post-it notes and the canvas for the answers:
What are the initiatives? Use grey Post-its.

FIGURE 150: INITIATIVES

THE ROAD MAP

With clarity on the development priorities, we now turn to the road map, the programme that puts initiatives to work. The road map answers what we will do in the five canvas dimensions:

People: How can we better leverage people's potential, skills and knowledge?

Organization: How can we develop agile capabilities throughout our organization?

Work: How do we enable meaningful work where people connect and collaborate?

Operations: How do we replace change with dynamic capabilities?

Management: How do we manage in the people-centric way?

There are four development paths to a road map that fit the preferred implementation method. The road map follows one of four distinct paths: Analysing, systematizing, learning or experimenting (Figure 151).

FIGURE 151: DEVELOPMENT PATHS

Here is what the four development paths mean.

Analysing follows a path through data, fact-finding, analysis, conclusions and an action plan. This works well in a stable and clear context. The analytical road map follows a plan of distinct projects, with predetermined and measurable outcomes. A project steering committee oversees progress and intervenes as needed.

Systematizing follows a path that fits a specific thought model, leaves options open or is guided by a specific development approach. It is favoured in a stable context with an opaque outcome. The systematic approach is clear about how to get to the desired situation, but leaves the outcome vague. A fluid team approach works best to manage the entire initiative.

Learning follows a path where the destination is clear but the way to get there may need adaptation as the context changes. It requires finding patterns and themes that are worthwhile to follow. The learning approach is iterative and requires frequent feedback for intermediate checks on progress. A programme committee supervises the overall effort.

Experimenting follows a path with an uncertain destination and a context that keeps changing. A trial and error approach is needed to find ways to tackle serious problems. Experiments start small in an area that is isolated and where the risks are acceptable. When experiments succeed, they can then be applied in other areas. Management teams oversee experiments to secure the necessary investment.

The road map combines initiatives into a comprehensive development programme that follows one of the paths. The diagnostic identifies your current path. With the expert briefing, discuss what works best for your organization, and then start developing your road map.

The road map may include managerial interventions such as coaching, training, development, design, projects, workshops, experiments, events and more. There is no limit, but it's an art to combine initiatives into a comprehensive programme that works. That's where experience is needed.

With this introduction and the information in Figure 152, use the expert briefing to discuss:

- What is your current and future development path?
- What is your road map programme that implements your initiatives?

Metrics. The dominant development path is determined as follows:
The environment is determined with the operating context. A diagnostic question assesses current clarity of direction.
Evaluation. The answers translate as follows into the framework:
Identify the development path that fits your scores.
Meaning. Development paths guide your road map plan.
• **Road map**: Combining initiatives into a plan that follows the desired development path.
Interpretation. Linkages to other elements offer insights and root causes:
• **Performance Triangle**: all elements • **Leadership Toolbox**: all elements
Sources
• **Process**. *Management Design* (2nd Ed. 2017), pages 192-193
Facilitation. Use Post-it notes and the canvas for the answers:
What is the road map? Use bright blue Post-its.

FIGURE 152: ROAD MAP

EXECUTIVE SEARCH – CRACKING THE POWER OF PRIMA DONNAS

The diagnostic results revealed what one would expect from an executive search firm that promoted world-class standards in everything they did and their product: mounting the best possible search for the best client positions.

This company had a classic structure, with country-level local offices led by well-known executives who knew their market and people. Nobody would dare interfere with their business. It's hard to influence such executives, as they claim to be very successful. They are classic 'prima donnas.' As such, the dominant management model favoured prima donnas.

The only challenge with this kind of structure and management model is that it lacks any cooperation between country operations. Since the market for best CEOs and other top executives is increasingly global, the local units missed out on valuable business opportunities. They only searched for the best candidate in their own space.

The recruitment firm's EMEA head decided to introduce a horizontal structure, with centres of excellence that would specialize in searches for CEOs and other senior executives. It was a sort of support function for the local units, which would then conduct the business. Each of the 10 centres of excellence had its home base and was managed by the local prima donna. Most prima donnas got their share. The challenge for the EMEA leader was how to introduce that kind of structure.

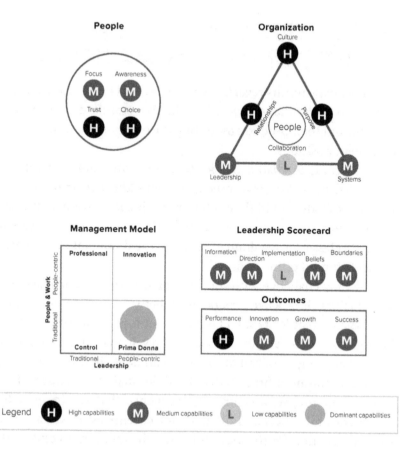

FIGURE 153: EXECUTIVE SEARCH

The idea was to engage all executives in the diagnostic and then conduct a workshop where they would work toward their own solution, to make the new structure work. The EMEA head had to conduct a one-on-one conversation with every country manager prima donna to ensure participation in the workshop. With one exception — who feared losing his turf and immediately called the US corporate headquarters, wanting to talk to the global CEO — all others agreed on the process.

The diagnostic results (Figure 153) revealed the kind of quality results one would expect. The combination of high trust and low collaboration was the clue to a conversation these executives likely never had before. Why would one not collaborate in a context where there is high trust? Yes, the conversations behind closed doors on trust were different from those in the team workshops. The EMEA head was able to point to those who challenged trust and tell them to be honest or leave the room. Period.

During the workshop, the executives agreed on a programme to introduce the new structure. Knowing about the low score on implementation, the EMEA head spent most of the remaining year and beyond going from one local manager to another, to ensure that what they said was what they now would do. It took about two years until the structure was visible and offered its first benefits to local prima donnas.

PRIORITIZE THE DEVELOPMENT

Initiatives and the road map translate insights into development action.

KEY CHAPTER IDEAS

- Intervention levers offer the model to prioritize initiatives
- Four development paths offer options on the road map that fits

ACTION AGENDA

Use the expert briefing to identify the initiatives and develop the road map with the team.

Prioritize the development with the help of cause and effect and intervention levers.

Decide on your road map in line with your preferred development path.

FURTHER READING

Michel, L (2017). *Management Design: Managing People and Organizations in Turbulent Times* (2nd ed.). London: LID Publishing.

STEP 2: ACT ON INSIGHTS

Part III in this book introduces Step 2: Act on Insights. Figure 154 summarizes Step 2.

Purpose: Step 2 uses the insights from the diagnostic and develops the road map action plan to develop future capabilities.	
Action: Use the team workshop and the expert briefing to move from ideas to action. The team workshop distils the gaps and key issues between current and future capabilities. The expert briefing develops the initiatives and creates the road map that translates key issues into an action plan.	
Mentor: Conducts the team workshop and the expert briefing.	**Organization:** Participates in the team workshop and expert briefing to develop their road map plan.
Focus: Operating systems, management context, management model, decision-making style, Leadership Toolbox, operating system, leadership styles, prioritizing initiatives.	
Tools: Diagnostic results, team workshop, expert briefing, canvas.	

FIGURE 154: ACT ON INSIGHTS

Use Figures 155 and 156 to summarize your action items from the canvas.

	Current	Future
Strategy		
Business model		
Management model		
Decision-making mode		
Operating model		
Leadership style		
Development path		

FIGURE 155: ACT ON INSIGHTS - DECISIONS

	Gaps, key issues	Initiatives
Strategy		
Business model		
Management model		
Decision-making mode		
Operating model		
Leadership style		
Development path		

FIGURE 156: ACT ON INSIGHTS - SUMMARY

PART IV

PEOPLE-CENTRIC MANAGEMENT

Part IV outlines Step 3: Learn Fast, to make people-centric management work. With the insights from the diagnostic and a road map plan, Part IV explores how to enable peak performance with the transformation to people-centric management as a competitive advantage.

CHAPTER 16

LEARN FAST

How do we develop the new capabilities? Chapter 16 introduces Diagnostic Mentoring Step 3: Learn Fast. The idea is to implement the road map through specific interventions. The step engages executives in experiential learning to work *on* the system.

POTENTIAL AND INTERFERENCE

The clues to performance are potential and interference. Interference limits the potential. With this, the question is what learning and development needs to focus on: the potential or sources of interference. Purpose, inner game techniques, resources and capabilities must be part of every road map development programme.

The overall goal of Diagnostic Mentoring is to help leaders create an operating environment where people can unlock their full talent. Agile organization, people-centric management and dynamic capabilities are features that do both: unlock the potential and limit interference. Figure 157 introduces the concept, with a focus on what people need in order to perform at their peak.

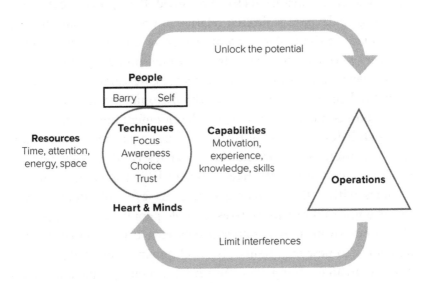

FIGURE 157: POTENTIAL AND INTERFERENCE

People come with potential, their heart, inner-game techniques, resources and capabilities. In addition, Barry (the imaginary Self 1) introduces self-interference. Operations offer the playing field. With this comes the commitment to support the development. And, they offer the ability to find purpose — the condition that allows people to be part of the organization, from their hearts to their heads.

The operating system with strategy, vision, values and a workplace where employees connect and build relationships helps to engage people's **hearts and minds**. Purpose is not a given. It needs to be developed and constantly nurtured. As such, it must be part of every road map and at the heart of any development initiative.

Inner-game **techniques** with awareness, choice, trust and focus offer a route to purpose, which helps people learn and perform at their peak. The purpose is to limit the interfering effects of Barry — the doubts, stress, fear, bias, limiting concepts and assumptions. With this, people are able to access their capabilities and resources. The ideal is leadership and systems with a design that fits and limits interference. Better management is not a given. It needs to be constantly reinforced as part of an ongoing process of training and development.

Resources are limited. Time that has passed cannot be recovered. Focus that is lost needs to be regained. Energy needs constant refuelling. And, space is limited relative to time — one can only be at one place in time. Managing one's own resources is demanding. Managers who care about a healthy work environment pay attention to how people manage their own resources. Research is quite clear about the benefits of a healthy work environment. Management's own resources must be part of every development initiative.

Capabilities such as motivation, experience, knowledge and skills are often taken for granted — 'That's what we hire people for.' Some call it talent. We have extensively discussed motivation: it comes with self-responsibility. Leaders can only demotivate. Any attempt to motivate self-responsible people has the opposite effect: demotivation. Experience comes with its use. Hence, exposing people to new experiences is development. Knowledge grows with use. In an enabling operating environment, people apply and grow their knowledge for the benefit of the organization. Most skills are context-specific. Applying them in other contexts may require additional training. It is important to note that most capabilities must be constantly applied to keep them at the expected level. Development is one of the means to keep capabilities ready to be used.

There are different roles when it comes to development in organizations: individual employee responsibilities, shared accountability

and institutional responsibility. Figure 158 identifies the accountabilities as follows:

Readiness: Accountability lies with the individual. Responsibility
is the driving force for motivation: the intrinsic contract as a prerequisite for people getting things done. The extrinsic contract is
an external-control tool that institutions use to motivate people to
perform in the desired direction.

Capability: There is shared accountability for capability between
the individual and the institution. The organization's mechanisms
for competence management define the talent's needs and offer
development opportunities. But, for this to be effective, individuals
have to make choices about learning.

Opportunity: People need to be given scope and opportunity to
perform. This is the sole responsibility of institutions. Leaders represent the institution and are accountable for creating a productive
working environment, with adequate resources, rules and processes.
Creating such an environment saves considerable managerial time
and puts the focus on opportunities, rather than ineffective control.

Development	Individual Self-responsibility	Institution Outside control
Readiness: want to do ... Accountability lies with the individual	Responsibility, awareness, focus of attention, intrinsic contract	Purpose, extrinsic contract, awareness
Capability: able to do ... Shared responsibility	Choice, skills, learning	Development, competencies
Opportunity: can do ... Accountability lies with the institution	The institution offers the playing field, work, employment for the individual	Degrees of freedom (room to move), resources, processes, tools (the system)

FIGURE 158: ACCOUNTABILITY FOR DEVELOPMENT

Development means both limiting interference and unlocking the
potential. As such, when it comes to development, getting accountability and responsibility right is of utmost importance.

EXPERIENTIAL LEARNING

For the purpose of Diagnostic Mentoring, I will argue that the transformation to better management starts with the leader, who personally makes the shift to agile, people-centric and dynamic. If leaders want their organizations to develop these capabilities, they first need to transform themselves, before they interfere in an attempt to change their organizations. The shift from traditional command-and-control to enabling people is a transformation that requires experience, which most leaders don't have. Just talking about agile, people-centric and dynamic capabilities is not the same as practising them. Without the initial personal shift and focus on people, the larger organizational shift is doomed to fail. As such, experiential learning guides your choice of agile, people-centric and dynamic, supports you to personally make the shift, and offers ideas and tools to help you achieve mastery in putting these capabilities to work in your organization.

How do we enable better management? With clarity on the design, Step 3 is about making people-centric a competitive advantage for operations in a dynamic environment. It follows the principles of inner-game learning.

Monitoring assumes that design is reversible and not frozen in place. While deeply embedded in organizational practices and rooted in the past, managerial design and capabilities can be changed through interventions.

The people-centric shift guides specific capability development projects in line with the decision on what needs to be changed. With this, the idea of permanent change is replaced by the notion of combined learning and doing. It's an iterative process.

People-centric principles stress that the way executives envisage the outcome and rally available resources defines a firm's destination. Moreover, learning processes have an integrative influence that leads to a creative use of resources in a dynamic environment. And so, development and learning processes are central to the application of people-centric and agile capabilities. The ecological and evolutionary theories of the firm assume that strong inertial forces severely constrain the organization's capacity to adapt to changes in the environment.

Many studies have noted that the capacity for learning and adaptation varies across organizations, and these differences appear to be caused by deeply-rooted management actions, policies and decisions.

Visual thinking heavily impacts the cognitive effectiveness of learning in a business context. Over the last two decades, visual thinking has become an integral part of knowledge sharing, collaborative learning, problem solving and developing competencies. Sketching, mapping, visual protocolling and graphical concepts have become part of everyday managerial practices. Today, visualization supports a variety of mental processes in learning, such as perception, memorization and development. Concept maps provide structures and mental models that support the learning. Strategy maps and scorecards have been in use in businesses for many years, combining performance measurement techniques and visual presentations.

In stable markets, the refinement of people-centric principles, agile capabilities and dynamic systems helps companies capture and defend competitive advantages. In highly dynamic markets, incremental change is not sufficient. Often, radical transformation is required.

Our mind is a product of the past — it has been shaped by our experience. The mind is present when our nervous system, which resides in our brain and body, is activated. The mind is the brain in action. It activates all our records of what we've learned and experienced in the past. These include habits, which are hardened and take a lot of energy to overcome.

Traditional minds assume that people need control to get things done. This is a negative assumption about people. As a consequence, they apply control, the dominant Anglo-Saxon management model. Agile minds rely on principles such as self-responsibility and delegation, which are based on positive assumptions about people.

Our thinking turns material thoughts into chemical information. When we activate thinking that we've activated before, patterns of the past are linked. The same thinking repeats, the same emotions continue. We call this 'conditioning.' Habits dominate, serving as our autopilot, with the same old thoughts, behaviours, actions and emotions. While this is very helpful in our daily life, it prevents us from digesting new things and learning. With the same routines, tomorrow is always the same. To change our condition, we need to change our thinking and feeling.

Traditional routines and habits have trained our minds in the traditional way. That is our experience. The choice of agile requires a different experience — the experience of the benefits of agile, which most leaders don't have. The switch from traditional to agile experience happens through learning.

Learning connects neurons and updates the brain. New patterns are created when we pay attention to knowledge and information that makes sense to us, and when we interact with the external world. Something new is 'printed' as a story in our brain that reinforces the connections. Learning creates these new connections. Now, we are at a new stage. And every time we remember something, we maintain our connections.

For most traditional leaders, new things, agile ways of doing things and delegating power to talented people feel like losing control. Overcoming that traditional state of mind and fear requires the individual to make the mind-shift to agile. The shift requires a state of mind and belief that agile and enabling people are superior to traditional control.

Changing energy requires clear intentions and strong emotions that create awareness, so as to attract new experience. The good news is that to attract new experience, we just need to pay attention and be aware.

It takes leadership with a clear intent (mind) and strong emotions (heart) to change our biology's orientation from the past to the future. Mind and body together impact matter and we can create reality. Feedback helps us understand whether we are doing things right. If we change the feelings and thoughts within us, we can see the change outside us. That's how we make agile, people-centric and dynamic a habit.

Diagnostic Mentoring is intended to raise your awareness, offer insights and provide learning opportunities to help you shift your mindset and embrace better management, thereby unlocking talent and developing leadership everywhere. The inner game (principles), the use of resources and superior decisions — how people can best manage and use their talents — are the means to get there.

WORK *ON* THE SYSTEM

Diagnostic Mentoring is work *on* the system, based on experiential learning and the inner-game technique. It applies the same principles as in working *in* the system: better management.

Work *on* the system follows five activities (Figure 159): understand context, apply the inner-game technique, follow people-centric principles, design the toolbox and make the shift to work *in* the system.

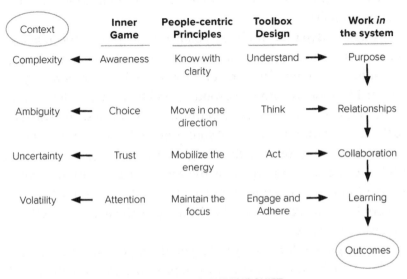

FIGURE 159: MAKE THE SHIFT

Every part requires your work *on* the system:

Understand context. With increasing VUCA challenges, agile, people-centric and dynamic capabilities help your organization quickly adapt to the new environment. They resolve the tensions between the challenges of the new context and the need for clarity, direction, energy and focus. Chapters 1-3 are about raising awareness in your team that the context has changed, which launches the quest for better management.

Play the inner game. People are best equipped to resolve the tensions the new context poses. They apply four inner-game principles — awareness, choice, trust and attention — to address the challenges of the outer game. Chapters 4-8 outline your choices for an agile organization based on these principles. Applying the inner game is a mindset question that has implications for the design of the four people-centric levers.

Follow people-centric principles. Know with clarity, move in one direction, mobilize the energy, maintain the focus, and offer a choice between traditional and people-centric management. Chapter 9 examines your decision for people-centric management with a choice of four principles: self-organization, delegation, self-responsibility and attention. It's a choice with implications for your leadership skills.

Design a dynamic toolbox. Following people-centric management calls for five managerial tasks: understand, think, act, engage and adhere. Chapters 10-15 require you to make a decision on your Leadership Toolbox with rules, routines and tools that leaders in your organization can use at scale to perform the four tasks. You will have to think about the right design of your systems, leadership and culture.

Work *in* the system. With the right design of your toolbox, your leaders can establish purpose as the source of motivation, connect people to nurture relationships, facilitate collaboration as a means to coordinate work, and expedite learning as the means to perform, innovate and grow.

Use Diagnostic Mentoring to get your team to design the dynamic toolbox that fits the people-centric approach, and apply the principles to help you deal with a dynamic environment and deliver superior business outcomes.

With your personal shift to better management, you are ready to engage your team in the same way you've made your journey through experiential learning. Assume that your talents are *motivated* and want to *learn* to gain that experience fast. This learning involves an investment in the skills required to play the inner game, use resources the agile way and make better decisions. Architects, translators and doers will support you in the shift.

Experiential learning is the cycle that establishes leadership everywhere, develops agile, offers client focus and drives performance. It applies the inner game (awareness, choice, trust and focus) to build experience among your team. At the same time, it uses the inner game to lead the agile way. Understanding the principles of the inner game is easy. Applying them requires skill and dedication.

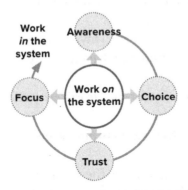

FIGURE 160: WORK *ON* THE SYSTEM

Experiential learning (Figure 160) simultaneously involves work *on* the system and work *in* the system (see Chapter 1). Start in one place in your organization and then expand the idea across all other units. Don't experiment — one does not experiment with people. Do it as a means to improve work, organization and management.

Better management is the goal. Awareness initiates the learning, to get you started. People-centric is your choice of leadership style. It replaces traditional change, which never worked anyway. Trust your team to care about clients. Focus your attention for superior performance, innovation and growth.

Experience is the opposite of education. It combines work *on* the system with work *in* the system. Don't try to educate your leaders through yet another executive development programme. Engage them in creating systems that support the transformation journey. To support your engagement, *Agile by Choice*, my previous book, offers 14 nudges to guide your team and wider organization with the following learning opportunities:

#1: Map your challenges: use your context to initiate better management

#2: Explore the dimensions: use individual and institutional dimensions of better management

#3: Engage your inner game: apply awareness, choice and trust to reach flow

#4: Turn on your lights: use awareness to reach clarity on agile

#5: It's your choice: rely on Self 2 to confirm better management

#6: Trust yourself and your team: mobilize all resources to make better management their way

#7: Return on management: invest in energy, attention and time

#8: Power up your energy: balance better management engagement and refuelling

#9: Focus your attention: learn to perform through better management

#10: Maintain the momentum: keep up the pace on better management

#11: Create your space: use the accountability template

#12: Establish leadership everywhere: develop better decision-making

#13: Unlock the talent: the better management mind-shift will make everyone a leader

#14: Learn from new experiences: engage everyone to work on better management

With this introduction to potential and interference, experiential learning and work *on* the system, use the expert briefing to discuss:

- What is your road map that implements your initiatives?
- How do you manage the development of capabilities?

LEARN FAST

Learn fast is the step that translates action into results. It's about the development activities that establish people-centric, agile and dynamic capabilities.

KEY CHAPTER IDEAS

- Potential and interference offer two development options
- Experiential learning applies the inner game techniques to capability development
- The design task is to work *on* the system
- 14 nudges get your team ready for the transformation

ACTION AGENDA

Start initiating your road map plan.

Get your team ready by having them work through *Agile by Choice*.

FURTHER READING

Michel, L (2020). *People-Centric Management: How Managers Use Four Levers to Bring Out the Greatness of Others.* London: LID Publishing.
Michel, L (2021). *Agile by Choice: A Workbook for Leaders.* London: LID Publishing.

CHAPTER 17

DEVELOPING CAPABILITIES

Diagnostic Mentoring promotes agile, people-centric and dynamic capabilities for today's knowledge work in a hyper-dynamic context. Chapter 17 summarizes the new capabilities and offers ideas and guidance on how to develop the capabilities. With this, the road map evolves from a programme to a development manual.

THE MANUAL

The development manual adds ideas and guidance to the road map programme. Agile, people-centric and dynamic capabilities require different interventions. Figure 161 summarizes capabilities, development interventions, resources and interventions. My previous books and other resources support the development in various ways.

Executive development engages managers in the inner game techniques for individual agility. Organizational development is the approach to develop agile at scale in organizations. People-centric management requires management development. Through systems development, managers design their toolbox. Leadership development then trains leaders in the use of systems.

The road map is a transformation programme with initiatives that address specific key issues and gaps. These initiatives range from self-study, organizational, managerial, design and operating initiatives to education, training and mentoring. The right combination of measures makes a transformation succeed.

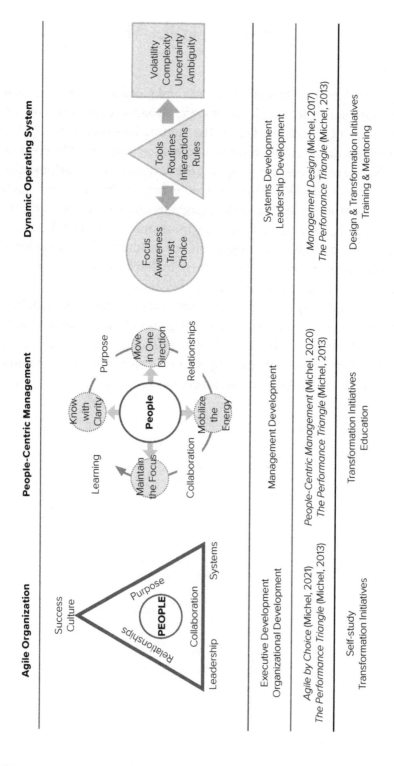

FIGURE 161: THE DEVELOPMENT MANUAL

AGILE

The Performance Triangle frames the capabilities of an agile organization. Figure 162 represents the essential capabilities of an organization's operating system. It summarizes the people, organization and work elements.

Elements	Learning Opportunities
People: The inner game with focus, awareness, choice and trust	Practise the exercises with Nudges 3-6 from *Agile by Choice* (Michel, 2021)
Resources: time, attention, energy, space	Be aware of your return on management Practise the exercises with Nudges 7-11 from *Agile by Choice* (Michel, 2021
Capabilities: motivation, experience, knowledge, skills	Practise the exercises with Nudge 12 from A*gile by Choice* (Michel, 2021)
Organization: systems, leadership and culture	Practise the exercises with Nudge 2 from *Agile by Choice* (Michel, 2021) Use the definitions, practices, insights and literature cited in *The Performance Triangle* (Michel, 2013) Retrieve sources and resources from the PRIORITY HUB[6]
Work: purpose, relationships and collaboration	Practise the exercises with Nudge 2 from *Agile by Choice* (Michel, 2021) Use the definitions, practices, insights and literature cited in *The Performance Triangle* (Michel, 2013) Retrieve sources and resources from the PRIORITY HUB[6].

FIGURE 162: AGILE DEVELOPMENT

The inner-game technique comes naturally to people. But, few are aware of their capabilities because they've lost the natural proficiency they had as a child. Moreover, executives who've been accustomed to the control mode cannot imagine what the inner game can do for them and their teams. That's why I created the exercises in *Agile by Choice* (Michel, 2021) — to help leaders gain that personal experience of the inner game. The master class offers Diagnostic Mentors the opportunity to experience the inner game. With our ShapeToFlow[7] courses, we offer inner-game experiences on skis or with the game of golf. These experiences have a high transfer value into daily business practice.

Return on management is a conceptual formula to measure how effectively we use our resources. Similar to the inner game, the practice of time, attention, energy and space requires experience and grows with its use. To get started, *Agile by Choice* offers another set of exercises.

In *The Performance Triangle*, I extensively documented the purpose, definitions, practices, insights and literature on the agile features of systems, leadership, culture, purpose, relationships and collaboration. With this, engaging executives in the diagnostic and the team workshop is the best development opportunity. Their own insights are the best motivation for successful change.

Agile comes from adding agile features to all elements of the Performance Triangle. With these initial ideas, use the expert briefing to discuss:

- What is needed to turn the road map into a transformation manual?
- What are the development opportunities?

PEOPLE-CENTRIC

Four principles, the Leadership Scorecard and the dominant leadership style determine people-centric management. Figure 163 presents learning and development opportunities for management.

Elements	Learning Opportunities
Principles: Self-responsibility, delegation, self-organization, focus of attention	Practise the exercises with Nudges 1-6 from *Agile by Choice* (Michel, 2021) Define and implement transformation initiatives in line with four shifts based on *People-Centric Management* (Michel, 2020)
Leadership Scorecard: 20 culture, leadership and systems elements	Use the definitions, practices, insights and literature cited in *The Performance Triangle* (Michel, 2013) Educate leaders on the people-centric scorecard
Leadership style	Train leaders on the dominant leadership style

FIGURE 163: PEOPLE-CENTRIC DEVELOPMENT

Altering managerial principles is a deep intervention. As such, it requires a carefully selected set of development and education initiatives. Moreover, better management isn't a quick fix to add to your existing way of running a business. It's a fundamental change in every principle, process and practice. And, while early successes will quickly materialize, it takes years of hard work to complete the transformation.

The Leadership Scorecard spells out the key capabilities needed for that transformation. *The Performance Triangle* offers the details of these capabilities in 20 elements. Embedding these capabilities into the organization takes education. Changing behaviour and the decision-making approach is hard, as old patterns dominate everything we do. And so, it takes training and persistence for a new leadership style to evolve.

Success comes from adding people-centric features to the Leadership Scorecard. With these initial ideas, use the expert briefing to discuss:

- How do we turn the road map into a transformation manual?
- What are the development opportunities?

DYNAMIC

The Leadership Toolbox adds dynamic features to the operating system. Figure 164 introduces learning and development opportunities for management.

Elements	Learning Opportunities
Leadership Toolbox: 20 elements as rules, routines, interactions and tools	Learn about Diagnostic Mentoring to decide on your dominant management context, the operating model and the principles to determine the design of your Leadership Toolbox. Use the definitions, practices, insights and literature from *The Performance Triangle* (Michel, 2013). Purpose: Identify the toolbox that fits the operating model. Features: Close the gaps in your existing toolbox. Choice: Select the elements that meet the needs of your organization's demographics. Develop and implement systems through specific transformation initiatives. Train and counsel leaders in the use of systems through dedicated leadership development programmes.

FIGURE 164: DYNAMIC DEVELOPMENT

Systems are the primary intervention point for change in people's behaviours, decision-making and actions in organizations. The Leadership Toolbox is the most effective lever to address a dynamic context. The design of a toolbox with dynamic features is the most important intervention in any organization. This is why the development and implementation of a new toolbox requires special care.

A large part of Diagnostic Mentoring is dedicated to the design of the toolbox with dynamic features. While design is an expert task, leaders need to understand how to use the toolbox to their own benefit. The design, development and implementation of a new Leadership Toolbox follows specific transformation initiatives. While change in the toolbox is a comparably easy intervention, it does not just happen by itself.

The toolbox is the means to scale management across an entire organization. A poorly stocked toolbox has long legs. It infiltrates all parts of an organization. This is why the design of the toolbox is expert work and requires the CEO's attention. With a dynamic toolbox, businesses have the capabilities to scale management.

Equally important is the training and mentoring of leaders in the use of the new Leadership Toolbox. This is important, because a dynamic toolbox is fundamentally different from a traditional tool-box. Such training must be part of the road map.

Success in a dynamic era comes from changing the Leadership Scorecard features from traditional to dynamic. With these initial ideas, use the expert briefing to discuss:

- How do we add the development of dynamic features to the transformation manual?
- What are the development opportunities?

DEVELOPING CAPABILITIES

The road map provides a set of initiatives to develop agile, people-centric and dynamic capabilities. Developing capabilities offers guidance and ideas that turn the programme into a development manual.

KEY CHAPTER IDEAS

- Developing agile, people-centric and dynamic capabilities combines dedicated initiatives, education, design, training and mentoring

ACTION AGENDA

Complement your road map plan with the development details and turn it into a transformation manual.

FURTHER READING

Michel, L (2017). *Management Design: Managing People and Organizations in Turbulent Times* (2nd ed.). London: LID Publishing.

CHAPTER 18
DECISION-MAKING

The transformation to better management is not just one big thing. To increase the chances for success, we need to introduce decision-making to develop a more granular approach and assign accountability for the parts. Chapter 18 introduces 'the babushka,' a tool that helps us map organizational structure. Then, we assign managerial roles and accountabilities to parts of the organization. This will help us plot delegated decision-making and align the toolbox with accountabilities.

ACCOUNTABILITY

Structure and accountability go hand-in-hand. Rather than redesign work, leaders should rethink their approach to delegation. Delegation means being responsible for the whole of a thing, so there is no disconnect between thinking and doing. Whoever is committed and responsible in keeping promises is accountable and makes decisions.

Accountability means responsibility for someone or something, with the duty to report to someone and the agreement of shared criteria for evaluation. Self-responsibility is accountability for one's own motivation. It means choice of autonomous action, the desire to take the initiative and responding by taking creative action.

Responsibility is the number one source of motivation. You get what you put in. People accept responsibility and are accountable for results. Responsibility requires choice. It is a moral position.

Accountability	Responsibility
Accountability is the liability created for the right and power to achieve results	Responsibility is the obligation to perform a duty
Making, keeping and managing agreements and expectations	Feeling of ownership
Cannot be delegated	Can be delegated
Cannot be shared	Can be shared
Outcome, solution, fulfillment	Task, project

FIGURE 165: ACCOUNTABILITY VS. RESPONSIBILITY

Figure 165 presents the differences between accountability and responsibility. In short, managing accountability is the systemic stuff of management (systems). Creating a culture of responsibility is the stuff of leadership. Accountability cannot be given; it is assumed. It cannot be delegated. Accountability originates with the tasks that are delegated. 'Not accountable' is the mentality of clearly-defined jobs, earned positions and given targets. Agile requires both accountability and responsibility.

Accountability is personal space. Agile is based on self-responsibility, with the choice to focus on Self 2. Assuming responsibility creates accountability, within space and time. As such, accountability defines your space. It therefore makes sense to use a practical tool to help you define your accountability in an agile context. Rather than fixed rights and duties, agile looks at accountability as a space that you can shape, move in and maintain to meet your needs.

Harvard Business School economist Robert Simons (2005), in his seminal book, *Levers of Organization Design*, proposes an elegant way to create your space with four levers. He outlines span of control, span of accountability, span of influence and span of support. Figure 166 combines these levers into the management space. A small span means little space. A wide span means lots of space.

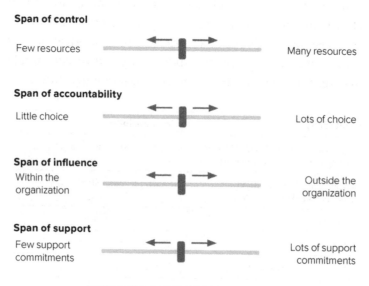

Span of control

Few resources   Many resources

Span of accountability

Little choice   Lots of choice

Span of influence

Within the
organization   Outside the
organization

Span of support

Few support
commitments   Lots of support
commitments

FIGURE 166: ACCOUNTABILITY LEVERS

Span of control defines the available resources under your control. It includes balance sheet assets as well as intangible resources and people. Span of accountability defines the critical performance measures you have available, which may be few or many. Few metrics allow for a wide span of accountability. Many metrics narrow your space of accountability. Span of influence defines the interactions you have within your organization and with others outside the organization. Span of support defines collaboration, with little or lots of support from others.

Span of control and span of support represent the supply of organizational resources. Span of control defines the formal resources directly controlled by individuals: decision rights, facilities, information, and other tangible and intangible resources. Soft resources, such as support, are important for the functioning of complex organizations. The important question here is: What resources can I rely on?

Span of accountability and span of influence represent individuals' demand for resources. The degree of accountability defines the trade-offs between critical performance measures and incentives. It creates demand among individuals for the resources they need to achieve their goals, such as access to people, knowledge, facilities, information, infrastructure and the like. Demand is also created by pressures associated with networks, outside resources or stretched goals. The important question here is: Whom do I need to interact with and influence to achieve my goals?

Executive space is defined by these spans:

- **Control**: What are the resources I can control to accomplish my tasks?
- **Accountability**: What measures can I use to evaluate my performance?
- **Influence**: Whom do I need to interact with and influence to achieve my goals?
- **Support**: How much support can I expect when I reach out to others for help?

Figure 167 combines the spans into a protocol that frames accountability as a space. It has been completed with an example relating to the accountability of a CEO. Tool #19 contains a blank version of the Accountability Profile for you to complete.

JOB: CEO	
POSITION	**ACCOUNTABILITY**
Responsibility: for the strategy and results of the organization **Reports** to: the board **Controls**: management team **Resources**: organization, balance sheet, business functions, support staff, joint ventures, partnerships	**Metrics and results**: growth, earnings, share price, corporate health **Tasks**: strategy, risks, reputation, talent, systems, coordination **Rights**: leads the management board; decides on strategy, reputation, talent, systems, governance, support
COLLABORATION	**PROFILE**
Influence: decisions of the management team **Duties**: informs the board, informs the organization **Support for**: management team **Supported by**: the board	**Span of control** Few resources — Many resources **Span of accountability** Little choice — Lots of choice **Span of influence** Within the organization — Outside the organization **Span of support** Few support commitments — Lots of support commitments

FIGURE 167: ACCOUNTABILITY PROFILE

Equilibrium is needed between costly, in-demand resources and the supply of resources. The presence of equilibrium is determined via 'the X test' (see the links between the spans in Figure 167). When the two lines cross, the resources are balanced in the space of the specific job.

Structure and accountability define organizational space and determine the demand for and use of organizational resources. By aligning the spans, executives design their accountability in line with the needs of greater agility. In this way, accountability can be designed for the benefit of teams, functions and departments — essentially every talent in the organization. As such, structure emerges based on people-centric principles. Individual space integrates accountability into the workplace. In this way, the design of the workplace takes on significant importance.

THE BABUSHKA

What we call 'the babushka' (originally, Russian or Polish for *grand-mother*) combines accountability and decisions into a map that helps us align functions and the toolbox for any organization. The babushka identifies generic business functions:

Firm infrastructure is responsible for overall results, oversight and governance. It wants economies of scale, flexibility and standardization. They are three conflicting goals that require balance.

Customer-facing units are responsible for top-line growth. They prefer wide span of control for flexibility and speed, with decentralized decision-making. However, they may duplicate functions, which impacts overall efficiency.

Production units are responsible for delivering products and services at the least cost, highest quality and lowest asset utilization. They want economies of scale through centralized and consolidated units for efficiency, bargaining power and best-practice exchange. But, resources may reside far from the market, which limits flexibility and speed.

Support / Service units are responsible for central services, support for others and governance. They want consolidated units for standardization and simplicity. But, people in these units may be administrators rather than entrepreneurs, which results in cumbersome norms, prescriptive standards and detailed processes.

Every business has elements of these roles. They may be called different things and manifest in great detail. Figure 154 shows a generic babushka. The visual limits the number of similar units to one. For example, if an organization has multiple production facilities that are similar, the babushka only shows one unit.

Next, we add key decisions to the babushka:

Economic payoffs: ROE, dividends

Corporate strategy: business model, value proposition, organization, alignment, coordination

Business strategy: product/market mix, target customer groups, channels

Customer demand: top-line growth, customer relationships

Budget: financing, capital allocation
Performance: business results
Innovation: new products and services
Efficiency: cost position and quality
Talents: supply, compensation and development
Risks: limits to entrepreneurial actions

Figure 169 shows a generic babushka with assigned accountability for key decisions. Both functions and decisions differ among organizations. This graphic represents a simplified example, but serves the purpose of explaining the use of the babushka tool.

Figure 168 aligns the toolbox with the babushka. Alignment links decisions with rules, routines, tools and interactions.

Economic payoffs	Corporate and business strategy	Budget, performance, customer demand, efficiency, innovation	Talents	Risks
Measurement	Strategic Management	Performance Management	Engagement	Governance
Information & Feedback	Strategy Development	Performance Planning	Objectives Alignment	Risk Management
Performance Indicators	Strategy	Performance Plans & Reports	Vision, Values, Contributions	Mission, Risks & Structure
Sense-Making	Strategy Conversation	Performance Conversation	Contribution Dialogue	Risk Dialogue

FIGURE 168: CORPORATE DECISION-MAKING

Going through the rigour of assigning accountability to decision-making specifies the Leadership Toolbox for any business and organization. With this introduction to accountability and decision-making, use the expert briefing to discuss:

* What is your babushka?
* What does it mean for the Leadership Toolbox?

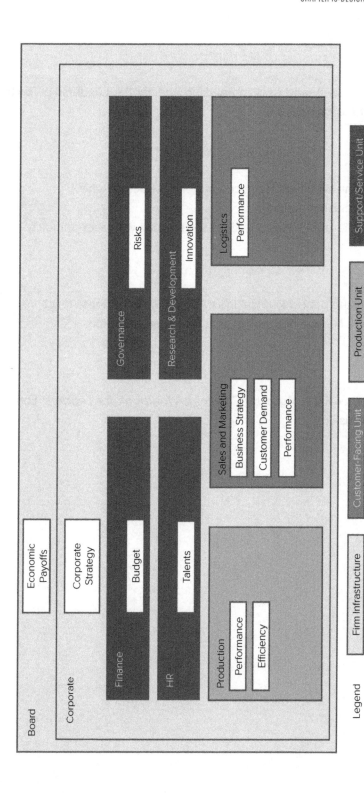

FIGURE 169: GENERIC BABUSHKA

DECISION-MAKING

Accountability and decision-making specify the Leadership Toolbox to fit the organization.

KEY CHAPTER IDEAS

- The distribution of accountability structures the decision-making
- The babushka tool aligns the toolbox with accountability

ACTION AGENDA

Identify the babushka. Assign key decisions to business functions. Create a Leadership Toolbox that fits the organization.

FURTHER READING

Michel, L (2021). *Agile by Choice: A Workbook for Leaders*. London: LID Publishing.

CHAPTER 19

TRANSFORMATION

Step 3: Learn Fast is all about developing capabilities through experiential learning. Agile, people-centric and dynamic capabilities require managers to work *on* their systems. We have identified the road map and the initiatives to develop these capabilities. The discussion around decision-making and accountability helps us to be very specific with respect to where work is needed. Sometimes, it's the entire organization — all systems — but at other times one can focus on just a single part. In most cases, that work on the system is a transformation: it fundamentally alters how people behave and how they get work done. Chapter 19 offers insights into transformative Diagnostic Mentoring.

THE QUEST FOR
A NEW PARADIGM

Most Diagnostic Mentoring projects are a transformation. They alter the dominant paradigms in organizations. The shift from control to enabling is a paradigm shift to agile, people-centric and dynamic capabilities (Figure 170). But, there can be no shift without a stable platform to start from.

FIGURE 170: THE PEOPLE-CENTRIC SHIFT

While control represents a stable platform with traditional managerial principles, enabling requires capabilities and tools with the ability to deal with a dynamic context. These new capabilities are in sharp contrast to traditional leadership and systems. It's a paradigm shift to a conscious new management mindset, set of skills and toolbox.

A mindset shift usually means changing corporate culture. The new skills require leaders to learn new behaviours and decision-making styles. A new toolbox requires an operating system that helps leaders enable good work rather than control. People-centric is here to stay. It is the adaptive manifestation of management in a dynamic era. The people-centric shift requires a holistic transformation of capabilities and the toolbox, not just a quick fix on tools.

The shift to better management reconfigures resources that make a company different — those that are valuable, rare and can't be substituted. In a dynamic environment, organizations need to constantly adapt their resource base. Agile capabilities offer the ability to select and use resources and competencies as processes that create, redefine, integrate, reconfigure and renew capabilities to achieve new outcomes, such as greater agility in a fast-changing environment.

But, better management is not limited to a dynamic environment. The paradigm shift is about better exploiting existing capabilities and the exploration of new capabilities. The shift balances stability with agility.

A stable platform with traditional principles in support of exploitation cannot simultaneously be agile and constantly change to enable exploration. A strong focus on stability reduces agile forces. Stabilizing and destabilizing require different processes; one process cannot perform both. Applying and selecting the right tools is about stabilizing. On the other hand, observation and reflection facilitate the learning for a dynamic context. They enable organizations to create a dynamic toolbox. In combination, stabilizing control and enabling require a design with agile capabilities.

As such, the people-centric shift not only develops and applies agile capabilities and dynamic tools, but it also deals with its inherent risks. It selects capabilities based on templates and patterns to solve the control problem, and it reduces the risks of dysfunctional viruses through early warning (self-reflection). With the people-centric shift, capabilities emerge through learning as a routine that frequently deals with change of capabilities and innovation. Design requires selection of the right systems and a learning process for the development of these capabilities. It offers rules for change, learning mechanisms to accumulate experience, and ways to articulate and codify knowledge.

For managers, the challenge of the shift is to build the new capabilities and tools without losing control. A shift always requires a stable foundation, so making the shift successfully will require clarity on the starting point.

In a report titled, 'How to Create an Agile Organization,' the global consulting powerhouse McKinsey (2017) argues that agile organizations excel at both stability and dynamism. Moreover, the report convincingly spotlights 18 dynamic practices that outperform stable practices in most aspects of strategy, process, structure, people and technology. Traditional organizations can improve performance by applying agile capabilities.

With a successful shift to people-centric principles, agile capabilities and a dynamic operating system, the new mindsets, skills and tools become an advantage. Such agile capabilities and dynamic systems are unique, and therefore difficult to copy. They are the foundations for a sustainable competitive advantage.

With this introduction to transformation, use the expert briefing to discuss:

- What is your stable platform? What can you rely on?
- What does this mean for your transformation?

SCALING AND INDIVIDUALIZING

Scaling and individualizing the operating system prepares management for hybrid modes, with dual enabling dynamic features, while offering stability and efficiency. Agile, people-centric and dynamic features combine scaling and individualizing.

In the previous section, on the quest for a new paradigm, we distinguished between a stable platform and a dynamic one. A hybrid context exists when organizations experience a stable and a dynamic context, or operate with parts that are stable and dynamic. A hybrid context also exists when events or parts of the organization require control and others demand agile responses at the same time. Managers have a choice. They can operate in two different modes with two operating systems, or they can operate in a dual mode, with a dual operating system that can handle both. Scaling and individualizing offer a solution for dual operating systems. It also helps to have the choice of maintaining two separate operating systems and the capabilities necessary to switch between the two.

Systems offer the rules, routines and tools that help us operate in our specific context. Leadership interaction is how we use systems to support individuals, teams and networks in applying their knowledge and getting work done.

Scaling adds people-centric features to efficiency where people need to deal with increasing VUCA conditions. Talented people are all different. They come with different ambitions, talents and skills. Individualizing leadership adds agile to efficiency in ways that help every individual unlock their talent and contribute to create value.

Figure 171 frames scaling as a vertical intervention that requires dual systems and individualizing as a horizontal intervention in how we use dual systems in support of leadership.

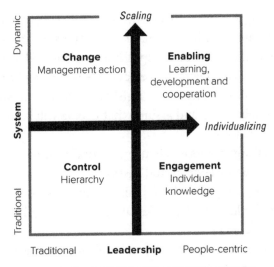

FIGURE 171: SCALING AND INDIVIDUALIZING

SCALING SYSTEMS

The challenge for organizations that operate in a hybrid mode is to scale management with an operating system that spans the entire organization. Hybrid modes demand the dual systems' features of traditional, people-centric or dynamic. People-centric and agile can also do traditional.

Control and change. If you are an organization with a stable platform, but need to speed up change to reduce costs, drive immediate profitability and strengthen competitive advantage, you need to mobilize resources and facilitate self-organization by showing trust in their implementation. That helps create a work environment that supports collaboration.

Engagement and enabling. If you're an entrepreneurial organization with highly engaged people, but need to respond to rapid changes in the environment, be people-centric and capture new technology-related opportunities, you need to delegate power to teams, tap into networks by providing direction, and facilitate everyone moving in one direction. That provides for a work environment that nurtures new relationships.

Stanford University management science expert Robert I. Sutton articulated this in a *Harvard Business Review* article, 'Eight Essentials for Scaling Up Without Screwing Up' (2014). He asserted that scaling management is all about the following:

- Spreading a mindset that instils the right beliefs and behaviours
- Scaling may require eliminating traditions, strategies, practices and roles that were once helpful but have outlived their usefulness
- You have two choices: make people believers, and then let them freely localize the rituals, or legislate the behaviour you've identified as being best, and assume that people will become believers and act that way
- Rational arguments for change are insufficient; use positive emotions to channel energy and passion
- Exposing people to leadership rhetoric is not enough; you should build or find excellence, and use it to guide and inspire more excellence
- Cut cognitive overload but embrace necessary organizational complexity
- Build organizations where people come to feel, 'I own the place, and the place owns me'
- Bad is stronger than good; clear away the things that stand in the way of excellence

INDIVIDUALIZING LEADERSHIP

People who operate in a hybrid mode have a greater need for individual leadership. This is leadership that supports and interacts with learning, while at the same time offering clarity and the means to focus attention. This can be achieved through:

- **Offering meaningful work.** Individualizing leaders focus on the *why* when they discuss work, goals and projects. The idea is that employees come up with their own solutions to problems they're asked to solve
- **Delegation and feedback.** Individualizing leaders have trust in people and teams, create an environment with degrees of freedom — along with a sense of safety — and offer feedback and support at eye level
- **Learning in networks.** Individualizing leaders favour networks over hierarchies, and they enable learning in peer-to-peer contexts
- **Balancing dual operating systems.** Individualizing leaders operate in ambidextrous ways that stretch between traditional

and agile. They adjust their leadership style to what people and the context require, without losing consistency

- **Leading virtually and enabling diversity**. Individualizing leaders interact face-to-face and digitally. They enable diversity by supporting heterogeneous teams

In short, we're talking about individuals who search for purpose, connect and build relationships, naturally collaborate and focus attention to learn. But, learning is a shared responsibility between individuals and the organization, represented by its leaders. To individualize leadership, we need a dual operating system that combines traditional and agile interactions.

Control and engagement. If you're a successful, well-positioned organization, but want to benefit from digitalization and tap into the knowledge of people, you need empowered employees who thrive on self-responsibility through information that raises awareness. They know with clarity, and that makes for a work environment where people find purpose.

Change and enabling. If you're a flexible organization that's always reacting to changes in the environment, but you want to speed up learning, proactively capture opportunities and align dispersed teams, you need to align the means and provide broad direction. This can be achieved through focus of attention, beliefs and boundaries, allowing people to maintain the focus. That makes for a work environment where they can learn.

Individualizing and scaling require ambidextrous capabilities from employees, leaders and the operating system. Stress, conflicts and role ambiguity limit the individual ability for ambidexterity. Diversity in leadership teams is a key factor in following an ambidextrous strategy. Leaders with a diverse background and teams with different experiences are more likely to explore new directions and capabilities while maintaining current operations. However, integrating individualizing and scaling functions in one responsibility tends not to work and, in fact, reduces overall ambidexterity. What works is individualizing leadership, and top management ensuring that managerial systems are designed to scale.

People-centric demands interactions with individuals. Interactions are an effective means of control. People-centric interactions are individual and specific to every person. The shift to people-centric demands that leaders be out at the client front, interact with stake-holders and 'interfere' as the means to exercise control. As interactions become more intense and take up a large part of senior executives' time, it makes sense to delegate (by a CEO) some of the organizing and planning work to a chief of staff, to an assistant (by senior leaders) or to junior managers (by other leaders). They can give you time to be with your people at the client front. Chiefs of staff can triage data and feed to leaders what they need in order to lead.

Scaling and individualizing are two complementary features of a dual operating system, for organizations wanting to make the shift, operate in a hybrid mode, and enable people-centric management. Scaling addresses the systems, to operate in a dynamic environment, and individualizing updates leadership in the context of distributed knowledge. Intervention in any operating system is a transformation, as it alters the behaviours, decisions and actions of people in organizations.

With this introduction to scaling and individualizing, use the expert briefing to discuss:

- What are your scaling and individualizing needs?
- What does this mean for your transformation?

HYBRID MODES AND DUAL OPERATING SYSTEMS

Throughout this book, I have argued for four dominant operating modes to establish a theory on operating systems. However, the diagnostic results of organizations reflect business reality. That reality hardly ever fits the pure theory. Hybrid modes are what we find in practice. The question is what this implies for operating systems.

Figure 172 shows an example of an organization with a dominant control/engagement operating mode. Leadership is divided between command and self-responsibility, and targets and focus. Either we find both control and engagement leadership modes, or they have merged into one.

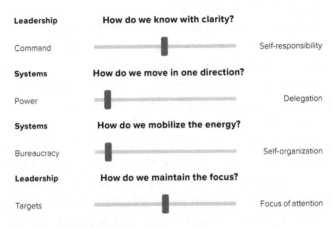

FIGURE 172: EXAMPLE OF A HYBRID MODE

Operating modes translate into operating systems through choices offered by nine operating models (see the Operating Models section) on the toolbox. The toolboxes for control and engagement differ widely. For example, leadership interaction with self-responsible people is supportive and encouraging. Alternatively, leadership interaction in the control mode leverages hierarchy, with the purpose of checking on people. Engagement is all about helping people focus their attention, whereas control works on setting and controlling performance targets. The differences could not be greater. It is obvious that this requires resolve in order to not create tension or stress, and eventually lead to the use of an erroneous system or promote faulty leadership.

I have extensively documented faulty leadership, missing leadership — as well as out-of-control and erroneous systems — in *People-Centric Management*. These modes are not viable options. But, they are not the same as dual operating systems.

This leaves us with the question of merging operating systems or maintaining two (what we call dual operating systems). It's a big question indeed, as it arises from the discussion about exploitation and exploration business systems and their demands on management models. The topic has received increasing attention in practice and in research. Following is my position on a diverse discourse.

Merging operating systems creates confusion. Target setting and focus of attention are opposites that don't align well. It takes sophisticated leadership and employees to do both. The experience is generally not very promising.

Selecting one operating system is a valuable option, and it must be the engagement toolbox. Engagement can also handle control. But, control cannot handle engagement. Therefore, the engagement toolbox is an honest choice. Experience shows that the engagement toolbox renders superior results in the control mode — beyond what the control toolbox can ever accomplish.

This leaves us with the last option: the dual operating system. That option is a deliberate choice to maintain both operating systems, acknowledging that some people operate in the control mode and others in the engagement mode. That is a condition for the dual mode. As such, there is a toolbox for leadership in the control mode and one for the engagement mode. This means that leaders need to be proficient at understanding and operating in both modes. It's obvious that collaboration, employee engagement, motivation and control require more energy for leadership and work than normal. People need to function in an ambidextrous operating environment. Experience shows that this works, although it's not easy.

I have made the case for the control/engagement mode. The same principles hold for any other combination of modes. Readers may follow the same analytical logic via levers, and their implications on operating systems, to find out whether their combination is feasible. Our diagnostic tool offers utmost clarity on your current mode and the options to consider. The experience of Diagnostic Mentors is valuable, as they have insights through practice cases on the specific choice of options. That limits the risks considerably on a key concept of Diagnostic Mentoring — the thought that business models, management models and operating systems need to match if peak performance is the goal.

Given the desirability of high efficiency and high innovation, hybrid contexts and dual operating modes, ambidextrous contexts are more common in business reality than we think. I need to add the following: in an ambidextrous, hybrid, dual mode it is more important than in any other mode to sense early signs of dysfunction, erroneous systems or faulty leadership. That's where Diagnostic Mentoring comes back into play, with its emphasis on raising awareness, acting on insights and learning fast.

With this brief introduction to hybrid modes and dual operating systems, use the expert briefing to discuss:

- How can you make your operating mode work for you and your team?
- What does this mean for your transformation?

TWO INTERVENTION PATHS

So far, we have explored scaling and individualizing as concurrent interventions to make the shift to people-centric and dynamic. However, there are two alternative paths that set different priorities for the intervention: disruption or evolution.

Figure 173 outlines both intervention paths. Disruption as an intervention first alters systems to scale agility, and then develops leadership to individualize people-centric management. Conversely, evolution first trains leaders on people-centric, and then scales people-centric throughout their organizations.

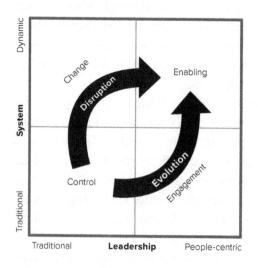

FIGURE 173: TWO INTERVENTION PATHS

It's a choice with different assumptions. Disruptions assume that behaviours change through altering the rules, routines and tools for people to get work done. And, they assume that once these systems are designed to address a dynamic environment, it's time to train leaders on the use of systems to enable people-centric management. On the contrary, evolution assumes that leaders with the right attitude and mindset can engage in people-centric management and *then* change systems for a dynamic context.

Philosopher and organizational behaviour author Charles Handy, in his seminal book, *The Second Curve*, introduced an S-shaped curve as a means to project the future. The S-shape indicates an initial period of investment, when input exceeds the output. As you begin to show results and progress is made, the line moves up. But, there is inevitably a time when the curve peaks and begins its descent. The good news is that there's always a second curve. Disruptive innovations (Christensen, 2015) create that second curve.

Traditional management (Figure 174) evolved along the first curve over the past 100 years. It was a success story during a period of relative stability. People-centric management is the second curve — one that disrupts the traditional and will continue to evolve. When speed is important, but systems and processes slow you down, you know that disruption has arrived. Management, organization and leadership are at an inflection point between traditional and people-centric.

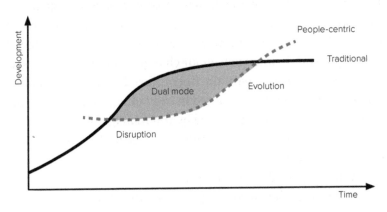

FIGURE 174: DISRUPTION AND EVOLUTION

Dynamic disrupts traditional management, but traditional will continue for a while. In fact, efficiency and reliability attributes will be needed more than ever to delight customers. Neither will go away altogether. The transformation means that both traditional and dynamic will coexist and perform as intended: traditional for exploitation and dynamic (agile) for exploration. This coexistence will require the hybrid mode of operations with a dual operating system.

Over time, evolution replaces disruption. The transformation mode shift will take you from adopting the operating system to training leaders and employees how to be effective in the agile mode. Training and education will do the job. But, Harvard Business School's Amy Edmondson (2018) suggests that organizations need 'fertile soil' in place before 'seeds' of training interventions can grow. And, she notes, people need a sense of 'psychological safety' at work for transformations to succeed.

Can you first evolve and then disrupt? While companies spend billions annually on training and education (Beer, Finnström and Schrader, 2016), the evidence of success is slim. Why do they continue what clearly doesn't work?

First, organizations are viewed as aggregations of individuals. By that logic, people must be selected and trained on the right skills, knowledge and attitudes. The expectation is that this then translates into changed organizational capabilities. But, organizations and systems consist of interconnected subsystems and processes that drive behaviour and performance. If systems don't change, they won't support individual behaviour change. Second, it's hard to confront senior executives with the uncomfortable truth that failure to change or implement isn't rooted in individuals' deficiencies, but in the policies and practices created by top management.

With this introduction to intervention paths, use the expert briefing to discuss:

- What is your dominant path?
- What does this mean for your transformation?

HOLISTIC AND COMPLEMENTARY

As we have seen, systems, leadership and culture frame the operating system of an organization. These elements complement and depend on each other. Diagnostic Mentoring is a holistic approach that addresses all elements. Quick fixes on one element miss the point. Systems and leadership are constraints on culture (Figure 175).

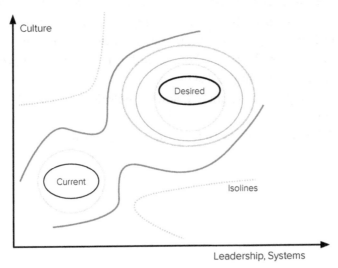

FIGURE 175: CONSTRAINTS ON CULTURE

I often hear, 'We need to change the culture to improve results.' But, culture is an outcome that depends on systems and leadership interventions. You can only intervene by altering your managerial system or updating the skills of leaders. When done in combination, this will improve the overall culture.

The people-centric shift from current capabilities to the desired capabilities requires getting rid of the old and developing the new. Think of it as a mountaineering tour, where you visualize climbing the next peak as you stand on your current peak. You first have to walk down your current mountain to then climb to the desired summit. If your current peak represents your current agile capabilities, and your desired mountain your desired agile capabilities, it becomes clear that the descent requires getting rid of some of the weight of your current capabilities in order to build the desired new ones.

In organizational theory, the descent is called 'unlearning.' It is often a necessary step to enable new systems, leadership, behaviours and culture.

But, it's often the case that optimizing the current is insufficient for success in a dynamic environment. Rather than asking, 'Can't we do better?' a true transformation asks, 'Can we not do it much better *differently?*' This opens up the unusual and undiscovered potential in organizations. Most transformations demand that leaders overcome the current system. They start by asking questions, sharing points of view and challenging the present, beyond the comfort zone.

With this introduction to holistic and complementary approaches, use the expert briefing to discuss:

- Does your road map follow a holistic and complementary approach?
- What does this mean for your transformation?

WHY TRADITIONAL FIXING DOES NOT WORK

Both efficiency and innovation are part of every organization. Efficiency without the growth of innovative new products is not sustainable. Similarly, just being innovative without consistently delivering value to clients is not an option. Most organizations want a hybrid: the benefits of both traditional and people-centric management, in their own specific mix. Traditional management adds stability to agile. Agile brings cooperation back into traditional management. The specific mix and the dual features come from a dynamic operating system with a design based on people-centric principles.

Traditional management is deeply embedded in the Anglo-American management mindset. This approach is practised as what Harvard Business School's Chris Argyris called 'theory-in-use.' It is not the philosophical views that are expressed when you speak to managers. This predominant 'Cartesian' view — derived from the teachings of philosopher René Descartes — sees management as an engineering-like applied science, where the conscious mind and the actor (manager) are detached. Their role is to rationally analyse, decide and give practical instructions.

Many of the traditional management 'innovations' of the past failed because of this predominant mindset. It assumes and transcends an impoverished and inadequate view of humankind. The scholar and educator Sumantra Ghoshal (2008) called it the negative assumption that underlies traditional management.

However, the Cartesian mindset does not work when it is applied to complex and dynamic systems where parameters are unstable, agents are interdependent, and cause and effect is non-linear. There is no manual for that. Dynamic contexts require an organic, ecological, adaptive approach. Things emerge, develop, and are nurtured and cultivated. It may be true that no two situations are the same, but history matters. And, experience is what puts things into habit.

People-centric has emerged from a different history, with a different mindset. It's a mentality that's closely related to the humanist view of the world. Ghoshal (2008) summarized this ethos as the set of positive assumptions that make up agile management.

People-centric needs to be experienced. Only then can the learning that the inner game promotes be translated into action. I truly believe that managers should research, learn more about and embrace elements of the Reformation and Humanism, to better understand the ways of thinking needed to grasp agility. Unfortunately, as mired as they are in the Cartesian mindset, it's unlikely that many will make that shift without a change in identity, and existential change in the way of looking at the self.

Today, competitive advantage is determined by interactions and relationships with customers, and based on motivated, talented and skilful people. The strategies of the traditional model, with its myopic focus on growth and profitability, are replaced by 'Why do customers buy from us?' and 'What else might they want?'

Traditional bureaucracy simply can't get this job done. Enabling, people-centric, agile and dynamic models are well suited to it. With the goal of delighting customers, managers don't need to motivate employees to do the job. With managers and employees sharing the same goal — creating and retaining a customer — the humanistic, agile practices of awareness, choice, trust and focus become not only possible but downright necessary.

People-centric, agile, and dynamic capabilities have the potential to return management to what it should have always been: the ends. The traditional Cartesian mindset is unsuited for a transformation to better management. It adds more of the same, traditional management to the existing approach. It simply does not work. This is why a successful, transformative leader needs to apply the same people-centric, agile and dynamic principles to the transformation as he or she does to achieving better management. That's exactly what Diagnostic Mentoring helps managers to do.

With this introduction to the people-centric and Cartesian mindset, discuss the following in the expert briefing:

- Does your road map follow the desired mindset?
- What does this imply for your transformation?

A SYSTEMIC INTERVENTION

Any transformation is an intrusion into a system. That's why it's worth borrowing from the leading systems thinkers.

The environmental scientist Donella Meadows, co-author of a 1972 Club of Rome report, 'Limits to Growth,' knows a great deal about sustainable transformations. Her manuscript for an unpublished book, *Dancing with Systems* (Meadows, 2001), suggests viewing management and organization as your system:

- **Get the beat.** Before any interference in a system, watch what it does. This keeps you from falling too quickly into your own beliefs, which are subject to natural bias. What does the system do? How did it get there?
- **Listen to the wisdom of the system.** Systems run themselves. Before you intervene to 'make things better,' pay attention to the value it already brings. Don't destroy a system's self-maintenance capacity.
- **Expose your mental model to the open air.** Hold your model up to the scrutiny of peers who challenge assumptions and add their own. Everything everybody knows is only a model. Flexibility to rethink the model is needed in a dynamic setting.
- **Stay humble. Remain a learner.** Trust your intuition more than your rationality. Use both, but be prepared for surprises. When learning, rely on small steps, constant monitoring and a willingness to change course as you find out more. Honour, facilitate and protect timely and accurate information.
- **Locate responsibility in the system.** Intrinsic responsibility means that the system is designed to send feedback directly and quickly to the decision-maker. Pay attention to triggering events, the outside influencers.
- **Adopt feedback policies for feedback systems.** In a dynamic environment, systems need effective control and governance that adapt to the systems state. This means not only feedback loops, but loops that modify and extend loops. These second-order policies design learning into management.

- **Pay attention to what's important, not to what is quantifiable.** The cult of measurement has taken over in organizations, but most of what makes up an organization are the intangibles. Quality, not quantity, is the outstanding characteristic in this world.
- **If something is ugly, say so.** If it's tacky, inappropriate, out of proportion, unsuitable, morally degrading, ecologically impoverishing, or humanly demeaning, don't let it happen. If you don't speak up on what systems are *not* designed for, they'll continue to exist and infect your broader system.
- **Go for the good of the whole.** Don't optimize parts of systems while ignoring the whole. Aim to enhance total systems capabilities, such as creativity, stability, diversity, resilience and sustainability. Parts of the system cannot survive without the whole system.
- **Expand time horizons.** Business schedules follow quarterly results, annual budgets and three-year strategies. Systems don't distinguish between short-term and long-term. Actions sometimes have immediate effects, and they sometimes span decades. You therefore need to watch, short-term and long-term.
- **Expand thought horizons.** Systems span traditional disciplinary lines. To understand systems, observe them and learn from economists, chemists, psychologists, theologians, philosophers and others. Interdisciplinary conversation beats particular lenses when it comes to solving real-life problems.
- **Expand the boundary of caring.** Life in a world of complex systems requires greater breadth of caring. There are moral reasons to do that. Systems thinking provides the practical reasons to back up the moral ones. They are not separate and distinct. People know the interconnections.
- **Celebrate complexity.** The fact is that the world is non-linear, turbulent, chaotic, and poses its share of wicked problems. It's dynamic. It self-organizes and evolves. It creates diversity, not uniformity. That's what makes the world interesting and what makes it work. Straight lines and simple structures are human constructs. Nature designs fractals, with detail in every scale.

- **Hold fast to the goal of goodness.** Examples of bad behaviour and action are held up, amplified and affirmed by culture. The far more numerous examples of human goodness are barely noticed. They're not news. We know what to do about eroding goals. Don't weigh the bad more than the good. Keep standards absolute.

As an experienced leader, you'll certainly note how Meadows' guidelines have been woven into the four principles, the people-centric shift and transformation. People-centric management foremost is an operating system transformation.

With this introduction to systemic interventions, discuss the following with your Diagnostic Mentor:

- What are your principles?
- What does this mean for your transformation?

WHERE TO START

The scale of an organization-wide transformation effort is huge. Successful transformations I've seen hardly ever start with a budget or from the top. But, as we've seen, people-centric is a capability that permeates an entire organization. As such, lower-level department or team efforts to transform to people-centric have little chance of survival.

So, where to start? What are the characteristics of successful transformations? The following is what we have learned from organizations we've accompanied on this journey:

- **It starts with the idea.** Often, the idea comes from an individual who sees the need for a positive approach and seeds the thought. That person can come from anywhere in the organization. Mostly, though, that champion is someone from middle management, positioned close to where the decision is made and connected to people on the ground.
- **It can be anywhere.** Do you need to start at the top, in the middle or with a department? Experience tells us that agile development must range across an organization, touching points where people need to collaborate. That can be a department, a geographic unit or an organization as a 'how.' And, it must have the right, and the ability, to change systems, leadership and culture.
- **Diagnosis establishes awareness.** Apart from providing the data for the transformation, diagnosis creates awareness of what is and what matters. This is an essential condition in order for people to contribute with their ideas.
- **Motivation comes from participation.** People-centric capabilities are context- and organization-specific. People-centric is individual to every leader. Hence, engaging leaders and employees in evaluating and developing agile is a must.
- **Design creates prototypes.** People-centric capabilities are specific and in need of tailoring. *Copy and paste* does not work. People-centric, for most, is untested ground. It requires a decision on mindsets, skills and tools. That decision is all

about design. Prototypes help keep options open and refinement loops going.

- **It's a development, not a project.** People-centric principles require design and development based on an organic and people-centric approach. Traditional project management is built on traditional management, with control and command in mind. It's the best way to kill the idea at square one. Having said that, agile development is focused and disciplined. Progress will be assessed, and feedback helps steer adjustments based on what's been learned.
- **Top management must support it.** The transformation changes management from traditional to people-centric. And, the accountability for managerial systems lies with management. It's a responsibility that cannot be delegated. Top management must establish the umbrella, the frame and the mindset for the transformation.
- **A mentor can help.** Because there is nothing new in this world, external experience can help accelerate the development. Reflection, diversity and interaction with people from different backgrounds stimulate the conversations and energize the development. I believe that most organizations possess the capabilities to make the transformation. Occasional mentoring keeps the development on track.

Keeping these characteristics in mind will help you figure out what the transformation might look like in your organization.

TRANSFORMATION

A transformation changes the way we understand, think and decide, act, engage and adhere. It touches all parts of an organization.

KEY CHAPTER IDEAS

- The transformation is a fundamental change from control-based to enabling-based management
- Development requires simultaneous scaling and individualizing
- Reality reflects hybrid modes; dual operating systems are the likely solution
- Two intervention paths guide the transformation
- It's a holistic and complementary intervention
- Traditional fixing does not work — the transformation follows agile, people-centric and dynamic principles
- It's a systemic intervention

ACTION AGENDA

Continuously refine the development road map while you implement. Apply experiential learning. Decide on where to start.

FURTHER READING

Michel, L (2020). *People-Centric Management: How Managers Use Four Levers to Bring Out the Greatness of Others*. London: LID Publishing.

CHAPTER 20

A COMPETITIVE ADVANTAGE

Chapter 20 is about better management as a competitive advantage. Research shows a strong linkage between capabilities and outcomes with comparative information on the operating models.

CAPABILITIES AND OUTCOMES

The people-centric and dynamic shifts matter. Figure 176 illustrates how capabilities deliver results in four different operating modes. Better management leads to superior outcomes.

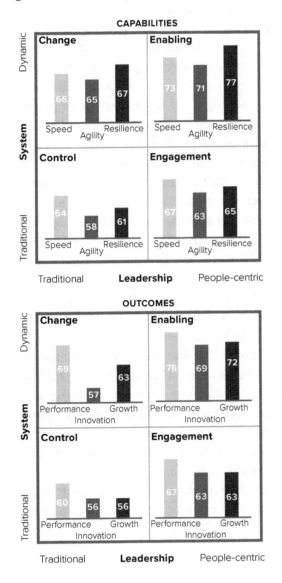

FIGURE 176: CAPABILITIES AND OUTCOMES

Our research results[8] with 250 organizations from around the world between 2010 and 2020 confirm that agile, people-centric and dynamic capabilities correlate with positive organizational outcomes, such as performance, innovation and growth. Investment in better management — the enabling mode — provides the capabilities for greater speed, agility and resilience. These capabilities lead to improved organizational outcomes.

However, not all shifts have the same return on investment.

The classic moves by financial services and telecom firms — from control mode to change mode every time the context changes — create greater agility and some resilience. This impacts employee performance (one might say it squeezes more performance out of people) but it has no effect on innovation and little on growth. As these companies keep repeating their change projects, there is little visible evidence of sustainable outcomes.

Another classic shift is when organizations embark on extensive employee engagement activities. Many technology firms and public services fall into this trap. By nature, the engagement mode yields better scores on the dynamic capabilities when compared to the control mode. However, the people-centric shift brings higher performance, more innovation and better growth. The investment does a lot of good for employees and the work environment in organizations. However, it does little to enable competing in a dynamic environment. It lacks the toolbox to do that.

One could argue that the above two shifts are an intermediate step to the enabling mode. Either shift requires building people-centric or dynamic capabilities — they are effectively half-shifts. Given either half, the payoff is better capabilities and better outcomes. As such, the shifts to better management lead to superior results.

With this introduction to capabilities and outcomes, discuss the following in the expert briefing:

- What are the expectations for your transformation?
- How does that impact your transformation path?

INDUSTRY BARRIERS

Creating advantage may require breaking industry barriers. I know from many client projects that there is natural resistance to changing anything that relates to management. In particular, I've learned that industries protect their natural barriers. These barriers preserve incumbent practices, such as management, due to the fact that many managers are appointed from within. This means that styles and models travel through time with little adaptation or change. This creates an amorphous mass of managers who furiously protect their turf. Industry barriers seem most dominant.

Figure 177 plots industry groups with respect to their dominant operating model, based on the research[8] that went into *Diagnostic Mentoring*. The chart shows that industries differ widely with respect to their dominant operating model. And, I have learned that the positioning of industries does not change much over time.

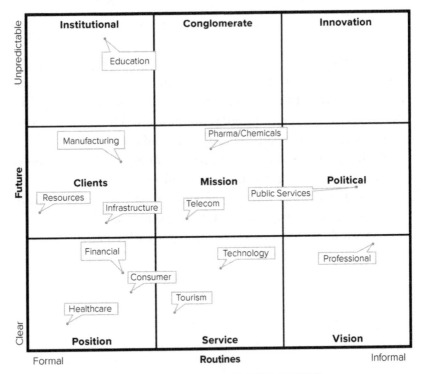

FIGURE 177: INDUSTRY OPERATING MODELS

Management as a true competitive advantage may require unlocking industry boundaries to find your own best approach. This will require developmental energy until it releases productive energies. The shift to people-centricity does not come for free. For most of us, traditional ways of doing things are known and deeply anchored in our habits. Overcoming our habits and leaving behind things that have worked in the past requires energy. However, from many successful transformations, my organization has observed that the investment in attention and time reaches a tipping point (Figure 178) where the energy becomes productive and the results become visible.

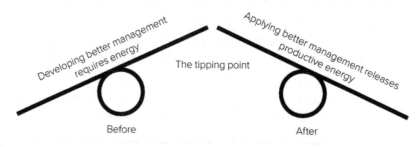

Developing better management requires energy

The tipping point

Applying better management productive energy releases

Before

After

FIGURE 178: THE TIPPING POINT

The tipping point is one of those defining moments when flow occurs and the return to traditional is no longer an option. Leaders who have 'crossed the Rubicon' to agile explain that energy flows, they've recovered time for important things, and their focus of attention enables them to continuously learn and adapt.

With this introduction to industry boundaries and tipping points, discuss thte following in the expert briefing:

- How does your operating model compare with your industry?
- What do you expect your tipping point will be?
- How does that impact your transformation path?

DYNAMIC OPERATING SYSTEMS

The Leadership Toolbox is the source of competitive advantage. We've learned that the operating model determines the toolbox, and with it the entire operating system. It influences how managers use systems, how they interact with people and how this shapes culture over time. As shown in Figure 179, distilled from of our research,[6] there is a unique Leadership Toolbox that organizations can use in line with their dominant operating model.

	Formal	Routines	Informal
Unpredictable	**Institutional** 68 Contribution Dialogue 67 Performance Indicators 67 Performance Plans & Reports 64 Risk Dialogue 63 Strategy Conversation 63 Strategy Development 62 Objectives Alignment	**Conglomerate** 81 Performance Feedback 81 Performance Indicators 80 Performance Planning & Review 78 Strategy Development 74 Objectives Alignment 73 Sense-making 73 Vision, Values, Contributions	**Innovation** 82 Performance Plans & Reports 80 Strategy 75 Sense-making 73 Objectives Alignment 71 Vision, Values, Contributions 70 Risk Dialogue 69 Performance Management
Future	**Clients** 78 Strategy Development 76 Sense-making 76 Performance Plans & Reports 74 Performance Management 74 Governance 74 Engagement 73 Performance Feedback	**Mission** 68 Objectives Alignment 67 Sense-making 67 Vision, Values, Contributions 65 Risk Dialogue 63 Strategy 63 Mission, Structure and Risks 62 Performance Management	**Political** 83 Governance 79 Vision, Values, Contributions 78 Sense-making 77 Engagement 77 Strategy Development 76 Performance Conversation 76 Performance Management
Clear	**Position** 68 Sense-making 67 Measurement 67 Vision, Values, Contributions 67 Performance Plans & Reports 66 Objectives Alignment 65 Performance Management 64 Performance Planning & Review	**Service** 73 Engagement 73 Vision, Values, Contributions 73 Objectives Alignment 71 Strategic Management 71 Strategy 71 Strategy Development 69 Performance Management	**Vision** 74 Contribution Dialogue 73 Risk Dialogue 69 Performance Indicators 68 Vision, Values, Contributions 67 Strategy 66 Risk Management 66 Performance Feedback

FIGURE 179: DYNAMIC OPERATING SYSTEMS

With our research, we have ranked all 20 elements of the Leadership Toolbox in line with their score. About 25 organizations employ the top seven tools in every one of the nine operating models. Looking at every operating model at a distance, for the specific composition of the toolbox, it seems that every toolbox very much reflects the dominant thinking and doing in organizations.

For example, conglomerates are groups of businesses that are managed by a corporate infrastructure. Their approach focuses on managing the performance of their units, with performance feedback, performance indicators, and performance planning and reporting as their top three elements. Business unit strategy development and the personal objectives of their leaders also get attention. In combination, corporate management uses performance and strategy as their means of controlling their units.

With this introduction to the toolbox in different operating models, discuss the following in the expert briefing:

- How does your toolbox compare with the toolbox of your dominant operating model?
- What are the implications for your transformation?

COMPETITIVE ADVANTAGE

Better management leads to superior outcomes. To be a true differentiator, better management needs to fulfil the criteria of a competitive advantage. In line with strategic management professor Jay B. Barney's resource-based view of the firm (1991) and the VRIN criteria for competitive advantage (valuable, rare, inimitable and non-substitutable), our research has identified a model with six components to signal whether management qualifies as a competitive advantage (Figure 180).

FIGURE 180: MANAGEMENT AS A COMPETITIVE ADVANTAGE

Management must fulfil all six criteria to qualify as a competitive advantage. The criteria and their components are as follows:

Does the work environment enable people to get work done? Does it unlock the potential of its people and limit interference? Our diagnostic uses culture, purpose, relationships and collaboration to size up the work environment, as the measure of whether management gets work done.

Does the organization enable people to create value? Does your organization deliver the expected results? Our diagnostic uses performance, innovation, growth and success to determine organizational outcomes and reveal whether management creates value.

Is management specific? Does it have a design that fits people and context? Our diagnostic uses ten questions to review whether management applies a control-based (traditional management) or an enabling-based (people-centric management) approach to leading people. This tells us whether management is specific.

Is the way people perform and learn hard to copy? Is the approach to mobilizing the energy throughout the organization distinct, effective and difficult to imitate? Our diagnostic uses awareness, trust, choice and focus of attention to clarify whether management is hard to copy.

Does the operating system prevent shortcuts? Does the toolbox keep managers from cutting corners on formal procedures? Our diagnostic reviews the rules, routines, interactions and tools to evaluate whether they have a design for a traditional or a dynamic environment. That shows whether management prevents shortcuts.

Is the use of the toolbox deeply embedded in the culture? Are routines, rules, interactions and tools part of the day-to-day culture? This tells us whether the management approach is rooted in the culture.

With our database, we have identified the thresholds for every component to answer the question of whether your management is a competitive advantage. In the next section, I use competitive advantage to identify levels of management fitness.

With this introduction to management as a competitive advantage, discuss the following with your Diagnostic Mentor:

- Is your management a competitive advantage?
- What does this mean for your transformation?

MANAGEMENT FITNESS

The previous section, Competitive Advantage, now serves as the foundation to evaluate the fitness of management. Management fitness is handy, as it allows managers to compare the capabilities of their organization with others in the same category. And, the fitness measurement tool helps managers spot areas that need attention on one page (Figure 181).

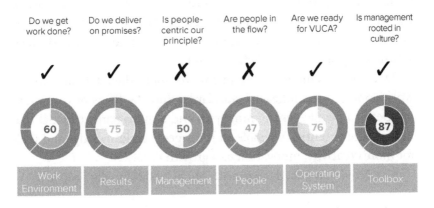

FIGURE 181: MANAGEMENT FITNESS

Six levels of fitness offer an actionable overview, with the option to dig deeper. Every level comes with a specific standard that we have identified: a tick means that the organization fulfils the criteria; a cross signals work ahead.

Level 1: Work Environment reviews the capabilities that make up an engaging work environment. The threshold signifies 'solid organizational practices 101,' related to culture, purpose, relationships and collaboration.

Can people fully engage their knowledge and skills? To reach Level 1 standards, remove the interference that keeps people from exploiting their potential in an increasingly dynamic era.

Use *The Performance Triangle* (Michel, 2013) to dig deeper.

Level 2: Results reviews the elements that represent outcomes. The threshold is an average organization that delivers in the green zone on people performance, innovation, growth and success factors.

Does the organization deliver results? To reach Level 2 standards, determine the elements of your results and identify the levers that will help you build the desired capabilities.

Use *Agile by Choice* (Michel, 2021) to dig deeper.

Level 3: Management reviews the principles of management, with traditional or people-centric capabilities. The threshold is a score of 75, which indicates strong people-centric principles. People-centric principles build self-responsibility and promote delegated decision-making among knowledge workers.

Does management enable people to apply their talents and get work done? To reach Level 3 standards, shift the focus of your management to people-centric principles and a management model that unlocks the potential of people and engages their knowledge and skills for more creativity, innovation and growth.

Use *People-Centric Management* (Michel, 2020) to dig deeper.

Level 4: People reviews employees' ability to perform and learn based on inner-game principles. The standard is set by top-tier organizations with a score of 75. High scores enable people to experience flow more often.

Can people unlock their potential and performance at the peak? To reach Level 4 standards, identify the principles of the inner game to focus your attention and release more energy in times of stress. Learn how to deal with adversity and master new challenges.

Use *Agile by Choice* (Michel, 2021) to dig deeper.

Level 5: Operating System reviews the range of capabilities between traditional and dynamic. The standard is set at 75 for dynamic capabilities. Dynamic capabilities enable organizations to better deal with internal and external challenges.

Can operations deal with disruptions, volatility and complexity? To reach Level 5 standards, align the systems principles with your challenges and refine your operating system accordingly.

Use *Management Design* (Michel, 2017, 2nd Ed.) to dig deeper.

Level 6: Toolbox reviews the fit with people. The standard is set by organizations in the top tier and a score of 75. High scores indicate a toolbox that enables people to deliver peak performance and take on greater challenges.

Does the toolbox support people in tackling tougher new challenges? To reach Level 6 standards, design your toolbox to perfectly fit your principles, the challenges and the demographics of your organization.

Return to previous chapters of this book to dig deeper.

In the example in Figure 181, management passes the first two levels, work environment and results. However, it misses management and people. Both levels are related, as they deal with the people side in organizations. The organization achieves both systems levels, the operating system and the toolbox.

The six levels of fitness offer a first-cut review of capabilities. The levels show increasing sophistication, with Level 1 being the easiest and Level 6 the most difficult to achieve. As with the example in Figure 181, it is possible to reach higher levels without passing lower levels, as they are all independent. Fixing missing levels starts with the low-hanging fruit; the easier levels only then align with the more challenging levels. In the example, the first fix would be management, then people.

With this introduction to management fitness, discuss the following with your Diagnostic Mentor:

- What is my management fitness? Do we pass all levels?
- What does this mean for your transformation?

A COMPETITIVE ADVANTAGE

Better management is a competitive advantage. Six fitness levels offer insights into management as a competitive advantage.

KEY CHAPTER IDEAS

- Capabilities and outcomes are strongly linked
- Creating advantage may require breaking industry barriers
- The Leadership Toolbox is the source of competitive advantage
- Six criteria determine whether management is a competitive advantage
- Six fitness levels offer the gauge for better management

ACTION AGENDA

Use the diagnostic to determine your fitness level.
Distil what you can do to enhance management as a competitive advantage.

FURTHER READING

Michel, L (2017). *Management Design: Managing People and Organizations in Turbulent Times* (2nd ed.). London: LID Publishing.

ENABLING PEAK PERFORMANCE

Chapter 21 demonstrates Diagnostic Mentoring as the means to support your management team and organization to establish better management as a sustainable competitive advantage and persistently deliver peak performance.

DIAGNOSTIC MENTORING

Diagnostic Mentoring creates the learning experience you need to successfully transform to better management. Awareness, insights and learning guide your journey, with the toolbox to engage your team (Figure 182).

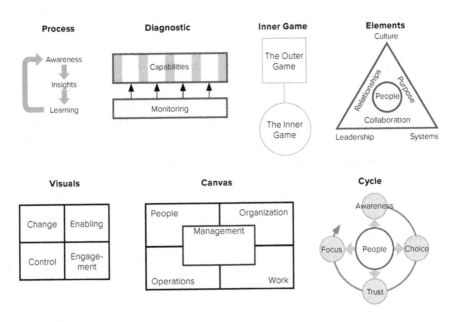

FIGURE 182: THE DIAGNOSTIC MENTORING TOOLBOX

Raise awareness of better management: The diagnostic establishes observation points. Monitoring is a discipline that can be used to observe and alter design. By observing (scanning) capabilities, potential faults and malfunctions can be spotted at an early stage. By becoming aware of critical signals, potential design requirements can be identified. In this way, leaders can decide whether or not to address issues. As such, monitoring initiates design changes relating to capabilities.

Act on your insights on better management: The Performance Triangle distils the elements of better management. The use of agile, people-centric and dynamic capabilities, and design, is selective. The decision to employ a specific design excludes other alternatives.

The design process is about the selection of managerial tools, routines and rules that make for better management. Design requires reflection and interactions. It is not free from politics. The setting of these conversations determines much about the design's quality.

Expedite the learning about better management: The inner game offers the techniques for learning. Monitoring assumes that the design is reversible and not frozen in place. While deeply embedded in organizational practices and rooted in the past, managerial design and capabilities can be changed through interventions. The shift to better management guides specific capability development projects in line with decisions on what needs to be changed. In this way, the idea of permanent change is replaced by the notion of combining learning and doing. It is an iterative process.

The agile, people-centric and dynamic capabilities transformation starts with the personal shift every leader needs to make. Self-responsibility, delegation, self-organization and focus of attention are principles that aren't part of the experience of most leaders. It takes experience to make the shift. This is why I suggest that leaders first work through *Agile by Choice*, the book that offers gentle nudges for the shift.

The traditional negative assumptions about people, and the dominant Cartesian mindset, are the main obstacles to any transformation. Success means applying the same people-centric, agile and dynamic principles to the transformation as it does to better management. It builds on the humanistic tradition in Europe. Readers can find the details in *People-Centric Management*, the book that serves as a guide to better management.

Every organization, executive and operating system is unique. That's why Diagnostic Mentoring uses a diagnostic to monitor capabilities, applies the inner-game techniques for expedited learning, uses visual thinking aids to offer options, facilitates conversations with the canvas, and guides management with the people-centric cycle. It's the process that uses experience, suggests principles and guides the transformation to better management. Better management means leadership everywhere. It's a team process that simultaneously works *on* the system while people work *in* the system.

WORK *IN* THE SYSTEM

Business is about identifying, selecting and transforming opportunities into value. With the people in mind, managers can now use four principles as their means to deliver value with their teams in a dynamic environment. People-centric managers apply the following principles with their teams (Figure 183):

1. **Know with Clarity: raise awareness. Help people find purpose**. They know that motivation stems from self-responsibility. Purpose replaces incentives. All leaders need to do for people is help them make sense of what truly matters. That's the best way to identify opportunities and deal with the complexity in your business.

2. **Move in One Direction: enable choice. Relate with people to enhance knowledge.** People-centric leaders delegate decisions and relate with people to enhance their skills and knowledge. Choice and direction are their means to bundle the energy, help them select the right opportunities and move in one direction as their way to deal with ambiguity.

3. **Mobilize the Energy: build trust. Facilitate collaboration.** People-centric leaders facilitate self-organization based on trust as the means to deal with uncertainty. They mobilize resources in ways that enable collaboration across organizational boundaries, which turns opportunities into value.

4. **Maintain the Focus: focus attention. Enable learning.** People-centric leaders use beliefs and boundaries to keep attention centred on what truly matters. They know that focus enables learning as the means to unlock creativity, and to stick with chosen opportunities, despite the turbulence of higher volatility.

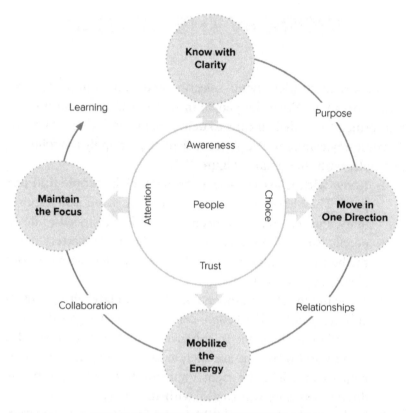

FIGURE 183: PEOPLE-CENTRIC MANAGEMENT

Applying people-centric management is work *in* the system. You should expect all your managers to follow these four principles and develop their enabling approach to management, which caters to the people as individuals.

THE BETTER WAY

Better management is needed to operate in the new dynamic business context. Diagnostic Mentoring is the better way to transform how we lead people, organize work and perform in that dynamic environment.

Diagnostic Mentoring combines mentoring, diagnostics, design thinking and experiential learning, with the goal being to develop agile organizations, people-centric management and dynamic operating systems with teams. The journey starts with the leader, who personally makes the shift to people-centricity. Agile establishes the necessary work environment for people to unlock their talents. The dynamic operating system enables businesses to operate in the context. With this, leaders can engage their teams in Diagnostic Mentoring to transform their organization to better management.

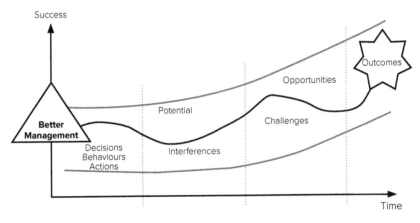

FIGURE 184: BETTER MANAGEMENT

Better management (Figure 184) is a dynamic capability. In the previous chapter, we demonstrated that capabilities strongly correlate with organizational outcomes. The investment in better capabilities leads to better decisions, behaviours and actions. With it, people unlock their potential, remove interference, capture valuable opportunities and surmount challenges as they arise.

Better management is every manager's primary job. Diagnostic Mentoring is the social technology that offers the observation points to create awareness, intervention points for the call to action, and leverage points for expedited learning. It comes with a process, a diagnostic, the inner-game mental technique, 50+ elements, 30 visuals, the canvas facilitation tool and a mentoring cycle. It's the better way for managers to remove outdated management practices by creating awareness, action on insights and expedited learning.

Early signs are promising as I see the new practice inform new theories used in business schools to train future leaders in better management. It's exciting to learn that the initial set of classes were deemed a success, conveying stuff that truly matters to managers, and that the first MBA schoolbook on Diagnostic Mentoring is about to be published.[9]

With this, now it's your turn to engage in Diagnostic Mentoring and transform to better management as a competitive advantage.

ENABLING PEAK PERFORMANCE

Diagnostic Mentoring enables individuals, teams and organizations to perform at their peak by transforming management into a sustainable competitive advantage.

KEY CHAPTER IDEAS

- Diagnostic Mentoring follows inner-game principles in three steps
- It enables managers to work *in* the system
- As such, the transformation is the better way to better management

ACTION AGENDA

Transform your management to better work *in* the system.

FURTHER READING

Michel, L (2020). *People-Centric Management: How Managers Use Four Levers to Bring Out the Greatness of Others*. London: LID Publishing.

STEP 3: LEARN FAST

Part IV in this book introduces Step 3: Learn Fast. Figure 185 summarizes this next step.

Purpose: Step 3 implements the road map plan through specific interventions to develop future capabilities.	
Action: Use additional expert briefings to translate ideas into action and management implementation. Implementation integrates a broad spectrum of development areas with a wide range of development tools.	
Mentor: Supervises the development of future capabilities through mentoring and expert briefings.	**Organization:** Engages everyone in developing future capabilities.
Focus: Executive development, organizational development, management development, systems development, leadership development.	
Tools: Coaching, training, development, design, projects, workshops, experiments, events and more.	

FIGURE 185: LEARN FAST

Use Figure 186 to summarize your implementation items from the canvas.

	Learning experiences	Refocus
People		
Organization		
Management		
Systems		
Leadership		

FIGURE 186: LEARN FAST - SUMMARY

APPENDIX 1:
BETTER MANAGEMENT

Foundations, elements and principles distinguish traditional and better management (Figure 187).

	Traditional Management	Better Management
Foundations		
Purpose	Extract value	Create value
Context	Stable context	Dynamic context
Core process	Operational excellence	Efficiency and innovation
Elements		
Culture	Pay per performance	Shared values and norms
Leadership	Control & command	Individual interaction
Systems	Standardization	Dynamic support and scaling
Purpose	Paid to do work	Apply knowledge and skills
Collaboration	Competition	Natural cooperation
Relationships	Hierarchy	Source of new knowledge
Principles		
Operations	Control	Enabling
Management	Traditional	People-centric
Organization	Traditional	Agile
Toolbox	Traditional	Dynamic

FIGURE 187: BETTER MANAGEMENT

APPENDIX 2:
AGILE SUPERVISOR

Agile supervisors support CEOs, their teams and executives throughout the organization on the transformation to shift management and organization from traditional to agile, people-centric and dynamic. Figure 188 outlines their generic job description.

JOB: Agile Supervisor

POSITION	ACCOUNTABILITY
Responsibility: supports the CEO, the executive team and leaders on transformation. **Reports to**: the CEO, head of corporate development or the like. **Control**: supervisors' transformation initiatives. **Resources**: none, or as required.	**Metrics and results**: transformation quality and success. **Tasks**: supervision, support, mentoring, training. **Rights**: leads the diagnostic process. Plans and reviews the diagnostic transformation initiative.

COLLABORATION	PROFILE
Influence: dynamic capabilities and transformation strategy. **Duties**: project proposal, supervision, status reporting. **Support for**: all leaders and experts. **Supported by**: AGILITYINSIGHTS.	**Span of control** Few resources — Many resources **Span of accountability** Little choice — Lots of choice **Span of influence** Within the organization — Outside the organization **Span of support** Few support commitments — Lots of support commitments

FIGURE 188: AGILE SUPERVISOR JOB DESCRIPTION

APPENDIX 3:
THE EXECUTIVE
BRIEFING AGENDA

The executive briefing is a 1- to 3-hour informational presentation for the executive in charge, outlining the diagnostic results.

Participant: Executive in charge, with no additional people, to maintain the privacy of conversations

Report: Executive Briefing report

Content: Follows the briefing report with key visuals in Figure 189

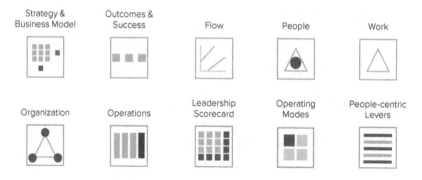

FIGURE 189: EXECUTIVE BRIEFING

Style: Conversational; walk the executive through the report

Material: One flip chart to document key issues

Slide pack: No extra slide pack

Agenda: 45-minute presentation, followed by a discussion on the key issues and next steps. The executive in charge needs to decide on what results will *not* be shared with diagnostic participants, based on disclosure considerations.

APPENDIX 4:
THE CANVAS

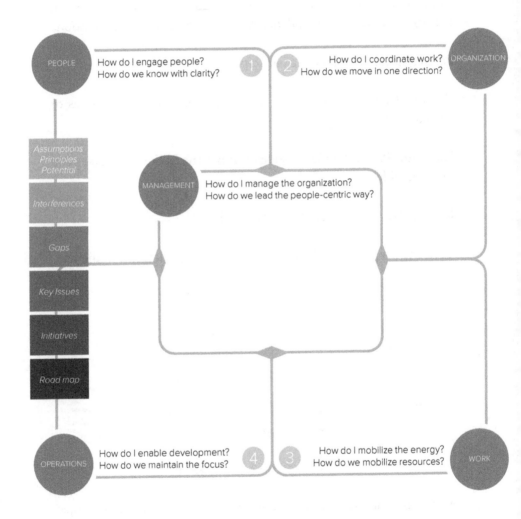

PEOPLE

How do I engage people?
How do we know with clarity?

1   2

How do I coordinate work?
How do we move in one direction?

ORGANIZATION

Assumptions
Principles
Potential

Interferences

Gaps

Key Issues

Initiatives

Road map

MANAGEMENT

How do I manage the organization?
How do we lead the people-centric way?

OPERATIONS

How do I enable development?
How do we maintain the focus?

4   3

How do I mobilize the energy?
How do we mobilize resources?

WORK

APPENDIX 5:
THE TEAM WORKSHOP AGENDA

The team workshop is a one-day session with all diagnostic participants, to learn about the results and identify the issues that require attention.

Participants: All diagnostic participants

Groups: Create groups of 6-8 diverse participants (roundtables or virtual spaces)

Handout: Provide copies of slides, but not the full report (makes you more flexible).

Report: *Team Workshop* (for leaders only)

Content: Depends on the participants; adapt pack to the audience

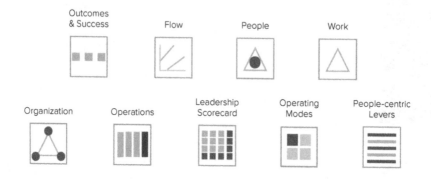

FIGURE 190: TEAM WORKSHOP

Material: One flipchart, pin walls (one per group), projector, projection wall

Canvas: Print Agile Canvas on A0 or A1 posters

Slide pack: Use template package to cut and paste visuals from the report into slide deck

THE PROGRAMME:

Introduction | 60' | presentation
Presentation: Why agile, people-centric and dynamic?
Question: What do you expect from agile? Collect voices

Diagnostic results: | 60' | presentation, discussion
Presentation: Diagnostic results
Task: Share your #1 insight with your neighbor; collect voices

Gaps | 120' | presentation, workshop
Presentation: Dynamic capabilities / introduce the canvas
Workshop: What are the gaps? What are the key issues?

Key Issues | 60' | group presentations
Group presentation: Canvas, poster with key issues (mentor: aggregate)

Summary, closing / next steps
Alternative to gaps and key issues: Three workshops, at 60 minutes each, on the three issues identified by the executive briefing

APPENDIX 6:
THE EXPERT BRIEFING AGENDA

The expert briefing is one workshop, or several, with the experts from the organization, intended to translate the key issues from the team workshops into a road map plan with initiatives.

The first session (Figure 191) is a decision-making meeting where participants determine the dominant management model, the operating model, the leadership style and the development path.

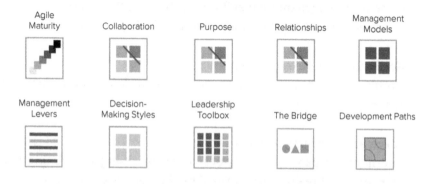

FIGURE 191: EXPERT BRIEFING KEY DECISIONS

Key decisions include the following:
- Desired agile maturity level
- Collaboration, purpose and relationship strategies
- The desired management model
- The desired management principles
- The desired decision-making styles
- The desired context principles
- The desired development path

The second session (Figure 192) is a design meeting for experts. They make the decisions to identify the capabilities needed to implement the desired models and principles. The second task is to translate the key issues into a road map and initiatives.

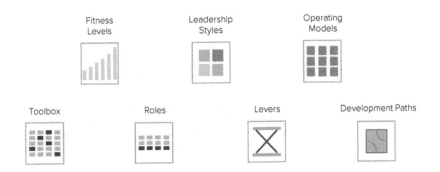

FIGURE 192: EXPERT BRIEFING DESIGN & DEVELOPMENT

Key design and development decisions include:
- The expected fitness level and what it means for capabilities
- The aligned leadership and systems with future context
- The equipped Leadership Toolbox
- The aligned leadership style
- The prioritized development activities
- The road map plan and initiatives

NOTES

1. Schwartz, Barry, TED Talk 2005, https://www.ted.com/talks/barry_schwartz_the_paradox_of_choice. Last retrieved on 15 January 2021.

2. **Context matters**: for a detailed discussion on the new context and its implications on management, read the scientific publication: Michel, L; Anzengruber, J; Wölfle, M; and Hixson, N (2018). Under What Conditions do Rules-Based and Capability-Based Management Modes Dominate? *Special Issue Risks in Financial and Real Estate Markets Journal*, 6(32).

3. **Management needs fixing**: See *People-Centric Management*, pages 25-28 and 48-56, for additional insights and the reasons why I am making this statement.

4. This section heavily draws on the work of Timothy Gallwey, whom I was fortunate to get to know and with whom I have shared my organization's work. I especially draw on Gallwey's *The Inner Game of Work* (2000).

5. **Levers separate things**: Many of the management, dynamic and people-centric levers have been explored by writers and scientists around the world. I acknowledge and support most of that insight and writing. Rather than duplicate that work, I offer brief summaries to make the case.

6. **PRIORITY HUB with resources**: The HUB is our online platform, providing access to webinars, events, research, books, publications, tools and our certification programmes. It connects the community to engage in our mission of changing the world through better management. To access the Hub, go to: https://agilityinsights.net/en/about-us/the-hub.

7. **ShapeToflow Inner Game training**: This is our groundbreaking two-day personal development programme for individuals who want to learn how to unlock their potential, perform at their best and experience flow more often. Go to: https://agilityinsights.net/en/training/shapetoflow.

8. **Research 2010-2020**: AGILITYINSIGHTS conducts research in collaboration with business schools in the US and Europe. Much of that work is published in journals. Go to: https://agilityinsights.net/en/resources/research.
   Every five years, we publish studies on agile, people-centric and dynamic capabilities on our website, to offer a timely perspective and an up-to-date series on capabilities for a dynamic era. For the 2018 study and all previous publications, go to: https://agilityinsights.net/en/resources/studies.

9. **Teaching**: Current teaching at the MBA level happens at business schools in the US, Austria, Switzerland and Thailand. For MBA classroom teaching and schoolbooks, contact the AGILITYINSIGHTS research director, Professor Herb Nold, of Polk State College in Lakeland, Florida. Go to: https://agilityinsights.net/en/about-us/our-team.

BIBLIOGRAPHY

Ansoff, H (1980). Strategic Issue Management. *Strategic Management Journal*, 1, 131-148.

Anzengruber, J; Bergner, S; Nold, H and Bumblauskas, D (2020). Be Like Me: The Effects of Manager-Supervisor Alignment. *Leadership & Organization Development Journal*.

Argyris, C (1990). *Overcoming Organizational Defenses*. Boston: Allyn and Bacon.

Barney, JB (1991) Firm Resources and Sustained Competitive Advantage. *Journal of Management*, 17(1): 99-120.

Beer, M; Finnström, M; and Schrader, D (2016). Why Leadership Training Fails – And What to Do About It. *Harvard Business Review, October*.

Christensen, CM (2015). *The Innovator's Dilemma: When New Technologies Cause Great Firms to Fail*. Boston: Harvard Business Review Press.

Csikszentmihalyi, M (1990). *Flow: The Psychology of the Optimal Experience*. New York: Harper & Row.

Dunning, D (2011). The Dunning–Kruger Effect: On Being Ignorant of One's Own Ignorance. *Advances in Experimental Social Psychology*: (44) 247–296.

Gallwey, WT (2000). *The Inner Game of Work*. New York: Random House.

Greiner, LE (1997). Evolution and Revolution as Organizations Grow: A Company's Past has Clues for Management that are Critical to Future Success. *Family Business Review*, 10(4), 397-409.

Habermas, J (1988). *Moralbewusstsein und kommunikatives Handeln*. 3. Aufl. Frankfurt a M.

Hax, AC and Majluf, NS (1996). *The Strategy Concept and Process: A Pragmatic Approach*. New York: Palgrave.

Luhmann, N (1995). *Social Systems*. Stanford: Stanford University Press.

McKinsey (2017). How to Create an Agile Organization. Survey report. Last modified 2 October 2017. https://www.mckinsey.com/business-functions/organization/our-insights/how-to-create-an-agile-organization

Martin, R L (2017). Use Design Thinking to Build Commitment to a New Idea. *Harvard Business Review*, January.

Meynhardt, T; and Gomez, P (2013). Organisationen schöpfen Wert für die Gesellschaft. In: Heuser, J et al. *DIE ZEIT erklärt die Wirtschaft* (199–207). Hamburg: Murmann.

Michel, L (2021). *Agile by Choice: A Workbook for Leaders*. London: LID Publishing.

Michel, L (2020). *People-Centric Management: How Managers Use Four Levers to Bring Out the Greatness of Others*. London: LID Publishing.

Michel, L; Anzengruber, J; Wölfle, M; and Hixson, N (2018). Under What Conditions do Rules-Based and Capability-Based Management Modes Dominate? *Special Issue Risks in Financial and Real Estate Markets Journal*, 6(32).

Michel, L (2017). *Management Design: Managing People and Organizations in Turbulent Times* (2nd ed.). London: LID Publishing.

Michel, L (2013). *The Performance Triangle: Diagnostic Mentoring to Manage Organizations and People for Superior Performance in Turbulent Times*. London: LID Publishing.

Mintzberg, H and Ahlstrand, B (1998). *Strategy Safari: A Guide through the Wilds of Strategic Management*. Prentice Hall Europe.

Nold, H (2012). Linking Knowledge Processes with Firm Performance: Organizational Culture, *Journal of Intellectual Capital*, 13(1), pp. 16-38.

Nold, H; Anzengruber, J; Michel, L; and Wölfle, M (2018). Organizational Agility: Testing Validity and Reliability of a Diagnostic Instrument. *Journal of Organizational Psychology*, 18(3).

Nold, H and Michel, L (2016). The Performance Triangle: A Model for Corporate Agility. *Leadership & Organizational Development Journal*, 37(3).

Petriglieri, G (2020). Are Our Management Theories Outdated? *Harvard Business Review*, June.

Schein, E (2010). *Organizational Culture and Leadership*. San Francisco: Wiley & Sons. 3rd Edition.

Scholtes, PR (1998). *The Leader's Handbook: Making Things Happen, Getting Things Done*. New York: McGraw-Hill.

Schwartz, B (2004). *The Paradox of Choice: Why More is Less*. New York: Harper Perennial.

Senge, PM (1990). *The Fifth Discipline*. New York: Doubleday.

Simons, R (1995). *Levers of Control: How Managers Use Innovative Control Systems to Drive Strategic Renewal*. Boston: Harvard Business School Press.

Sutton, RI (2014). Eight Essentials for Scaling Up Without Screwing Up. *Harvard Business Review*, February.

von Foerster, H (1984). *Observing Systems*. Seaside, CA: Intersystems Publication.

LIST OF FIGURES

ABOUT THE AUTHOR

Lukas Michel is the owner of Agility Insights AG, based in Switzerland, and CEO of AGILITYINSIGHTS.NET, a global network of experienced business mentors.

In addition to lecturing at universities, licensing his own agile mentoring methodology, writing on management issues and building his consulting network, Lukas is a business leader with a track record of balance sheet accountability in his work for global corporations in Europe and Asia.

Over the course of his 40-year career he has worked with executive teams around the world, focusing on management and agility for a diverse range of local, national and global organizations.

For the last 20 years, Lukas has been developing Diagnostic Mentoring, a methodology that offers diagnostics and a common framework and language for scaling capabilities across all organizational levels.

He holds a master's degree in management from North Carolina State University and bachelor's degrees in textile management and teaching.

Lukas is the author of *The Performance Triangle*, *Management Design*, *People-Centric Management* and *Agile by Choice*.